G00014644

Using the *Teach Yourself* in 24 Hours Series

Welcome to the *Teach Yourself in 24 Hours* series! You're probably thinking, "What, they want me to stay up all night and learn this stuff?" Well, no, not exactly. This series introduces a new way to teach you about exciting new products: 24 one-hour lessons designed to keep your interest and keep you learning. Because the learning process is broken into small units, you will not be overwhelmed by the complexity of some of the new technologies emerging in today's market. Each hourly lesson has a number of special items, some old, some new, to help you along.

Minutes

The first 10 minutes of each hour lists the topics and skills that you will learn about by the time you finish the hour. You will know exactly what the hour will bring with no surprises.

Minutes

Twenty minutes into the lesson, you will have been introduced to many of the newest features of the software application. In the constantly evolving computer arena, knowing everything a program can do will help you enormously now and in the future.

Minutes

Before 30 minutes have passed, you will have learned at least one useful task. Many of these tasks take advantage of the newest features of the application. These tasks use a hands-on approach, telling you exactly which menus and commands you need to use to accomplish the goal. This approach is found in each lesson of the *24 Hours* series.

Minutes

You will see after 40 minutes that many of the tools you have come to expect from the *Teach Yourself* series are found in the *24 Hours* series as well. Just a Minutes and Time Savers offer special tricks of the trade to make your work faster and more productive. Cautions help you avoid those nasty time-consuming errors.

Minutes

By the time you're 50 minutes in, you'll probably run across terms you haven't seen before. Never before has technology thrown so many new words and acronyms into the language, and the New Terms elements found in this series carefully explain each and every one of them.

Minutes

At the end of the hour, you might still have questions that need answered. You know the kind—questions on skills or tasks that come up every day for you, but that weren't directly addressed during the lesson. That's where the Q&A section can help. By answering the most frequently asked questions about the topics discussed in the hour, Q&A not only answers your specific question, it provides a succinct review of all that you have learned in the hour.

How to Use This Book

This book offers 24 separate hours devoted to specific topics. You should read them in order in the time frame you prefer—whether it's one hour a day, a few hours a week, or the whole shebang in one long caffeine-blasting, keyboard-tapping, type-A-personality day.

Special Highlighted Elements

TIME SAVER

When there's a shortcut or other way to do something more quickly and easily, you'll find it under this heading.

JUST A MINUTE

If something needs a little extra attention, the 24-hour clock stops for a bit and it's described here.

COFFEE BREAK

When there's some information that's worth noting despite its complete irrelevance to the task at hand, you can take a break from more serious matters and find out about it in these sections.

CAUTION

When there's something you need to watch out for, you'll be warned about it in these sections.

Q&A, Quiz, and Activities

Each hour ends with a brief Q&A section covering some questions you might want to ask. After that, there's a three-question quiz you can take, and one or more suggested activities for you to undertake related to the hour's subject matter.

This Book's Web Site

You're not the only one who can create a home page on the World Wide Web after using this book. Author Rogers Cadenhead created an official home page for *Teach Yourself to Create a Home Page in 24 Hours* at the following address:

http://www.prefect.com/home24

You can also contact the author at any time by sending e-mail to home24@prefect.com. Feel free to drop him a line with any questions, comments, criticisms, or error reports, and be sure to let him know if you share his opinion that the Dallas Stars should sign one of the Detroit Red Wings goaltenders if they let Andy Moog go.

Teach Yourself

TO CREATE A HOME PAGE

in 24 Hours

Teach Yourself
TO CREATE A HOME PAGE
in 24 Hours

Rogers Cadenhead

201 West 103rd Street
Indianapolis, Indiana 46290

To Dad. No matter how much stuff doctors take out of your brain, you'll still have enough left to be the smartest person I know.

—Rogers

Copyright © 1997 by Sams.net Publishing

FIRST EDITION

International Standard Book Number: 1-57521-325-7

Library of Congress Catalog Card Number: 97-66678

2000   99   98   97   4   3   2

Interpretation of the printing code: the rightmost double-digit number is the year of the book's printing; the rightmost single-digit, the number of the book's printing. For example, a printing code of 97-1 shows that the first printing of the book occurred in 1997.

Composed in AGaramond and MCPdigital by Macmillan Computer Publishing

Printed in the United States of America

Trademarks

Publisher and President   Richard K. Swadley
Publishing Manager   Mark Taber
Acquisitions Manager   Beverly M. Eppink
Director of Editorial Services   Cindy Morrow
Managing Editor   Brice P. Gosnell
Director of Marketing   Kelli S. Spencer
Product Marketing Managers   Wendy Gilbride
Kim Margolius
Associate Product Marketing Manager   Jennifer Pock
Marketing Coordinator   Linda Beckwith

Acquisitions Editor
David B. Mayhew

Development Editor
Scott D. Meyers

Software Development Specialist
Bob Correll

Production and Copy Editor
Lisa M. Lord

Indexing Manager
Johnna L. VanHoose

Indexer
Kelly Talbot

Technical Reviewer
Karly Vernon

Editorial Coordinators
Mandie Rowell
Katie Wise

Technical Edit Coordinator
Lorraine E. Schaffer

Resource Coordinator
Heather E. Butler

Editorial Assistants
Carol Ackerman
Andi Richter
Rhonda Tinch-Mize
Karen Williams

Cover Designer
Tim Amrhein

Book Designer
Gary Adair

Copy Writer
Peter Fuller

Production Team Supervisors
Brad Chinn
Charlotte Clapp

Production
Michael Dietsch
Polly Lavrick
Paula Lowell
Gene Redding

Overview

Contents

Acknowledgments

To the prime numbers at Sams.net—especially Mark Taber, Deborah Frisby, David Mayhew, Scott Meyers, Lisa M. Lord, and Karly Vernon—who all factored into the quality of the book. Now that all the editing's done, I've lifted the restraining order. Feel free to contact me via telephone, e-mail, fax, or beeper.

To my agent, Brian Gill, and his newly married spouse (married to him, that is). Congratulations! In answer to your question, yes, I am cheap enough to offer this acknowledgement in lieu of a wedding gift.

To my own married spouse, M.C., and my son, Max. He's beginning to get into letters and numbers for the first time, and I'm extremely proud of his work on L, Z, M, and the number 5.

About the Author

Rogers Cadenhead

(rogers@prefect.com) is a writer, computer programmer, and Web developer, but it all pales in comparison to the 10 minutes he was a guest host of the Gordon Keith Extravaganza on KTCK 1310 AM/The Ticket in Dallas, Texas. Cadenhead also wrote *Teach Yourself Java 1.1 Programming in 24 Hours* and co-authored three other books for Sams.net Publishing.

Tell Us What You Think!

As a reader, you are the most important critic and commentator of our books. We value your opinion and want to know what we're doing right, what we could do better, what areas you'd like to see us publish in, and any other words of wisdom you're willing to pass our way. You can help us make strong books that meet your needs and give you the computer guidance you require.

Do you have access to the World Wide Web? Then check out our site at http://www.mcp.com.

JUST A MINUTE

> If you have a technical question about this book, call the technical support line at 317-581-3833, or send e-mail to support@mcp.com.

As the publishing manager of the group that created this book, I welcome your comments. You can fax, e-mail, or write me directly to let me know what you did or didn't like about this book—as well as what we can do to make our books stronger. Here's the information:

Fax: 317-581-4669

E-mail: newtech_mgr@sams.mcp.com

Mail: Mark Taber
            Publishing Manager
            Sams.net Publishing
            201W. 103rd Street
            Indianapolis, IN 46290

Introduction

At the rate the World Wide Web is growing, there will be a home page for every man, woman, and child on Earth by next Tuesday.

Actually, in the time it took you to read the previous paragraph, we had to revise the estimate forward half a day to Monday afternoon.

You better hurry if you want to catch up! Fortunately, you can be an expert on the Web in less time than it takes to cook 1,441 one-minute eggs. *Teach Yourself to Create a Home Page in 24 Hours* makes it possible for you design World Wide Web pages without learning any complicated programming languages.

You'll learn quickly how to develop your own home page and other Web pages using a version of the popular Claris Home Page 2.0 software that's included on this book's CD-ROM.

The World Wide Web is the first mass medium to be born since television, and you can reach an international audience easily with your own Web pages. This book teaches home page creation in plain English instead of jargon, with step-by-step examples of working pages you can create.

If you can use a computer to balance your checkbook or create an attractive resume, you can *Teach Yourself to Create a Home Page in 24 Hours.*

PART
I

Your First Home Page

Hour

Hour 1

Getting Started

You're only one hour away from creating your first home page. Before you're ready to do so, you need to review some of the history and terminology involved in the World Wide Web, so you have a much better idea of what you're in store for during the coming hours. You will also need software on your system that can be used to create Web pages—fortunately, some is included in the CD-ROM that accompanies this book.

The following topics are covered during this hour:

- ☐ How home pages are created
- ☐ Why programming skills aren't needed
- ☐ The origins of the World Wide Web
- ☐ Why people are putting Web pages up
- ☐ How to set up your page creation software

Home Page Creation: No Experience Kneaded

Most people take bread for granted. Aside from the Amish and uber-homemaker Martha Stewart, we don't readily manufacture our own bread and many of us couldn't do so if we had to. Personally, I know breadmaking involves flour plus some kind of milling and baking process, and I'm pretty sure that grain is involved. Beyond that, though, I'm dependent on the fine folks of Wonder, Mrs. Bairds, and other bringers of bread.

As someone who uses the World Wide Web, you might feel about it the way I feel about bread: Web pages are created by some nebulous and probably difficult process before being offered for public consumption. You don't want the details even if you're crazy for the finished product.

You might have seen some books describing HTML, the programming language used to create home pages. That exposure could have been enough to scare you away from the subject. "If creating a Web page requires programming and the mastery of unusual acronyms," you declare, "there are numerous things I'd prefer to do first. I have expensive elective dental surgery scheduled. The bathroom tile needs regrouting. There's a Pauly Shore film festival. I need to spend quality time with my in-laws up in Love Canal. Golf's on TV."

However, save those excuses for a real emergency. You can create a home page without learning HTML or anything else resembling hard work.

JUST A MINUTE

> HTML stands for HyperText Markup Language, but you don't need to know that for any reason at all to use this book.

With the use of page-creation tools such as Claris Home Page, Microsoft FrontPage, or Netscape Navigator Gold, creating your own home page is as easy as using a word processor. If you can print a nice-looking resume or the directions to next weekend's ToughLove support group meeting, you can make your own home on the Web.

All it takes is a little bit of time—24 hours, say—and some kind of home page creation software. (Actually, a computer helps, too). The program you'll be using in this book is Claris Home Page 2.0 Lite, which you'll learn about later during this hour.

Before then, you ought to take a look at the place most pages call home: the World Wide Web.

Everything Is Connected

As someone with an interest in home pages, you have probably used the World Wide Web enough to be familiar with how it works. This brief review will cover some of the terminology because you'll be using it throughout the coming hours.

NEW TERM The World Wide Web is a collection of documents and other types of files that are stored on computers all around the world. These documents and files are called *pages*, and the things used to connect these pages are called *links*.

Links make use of URLs, which are the unique addresses that identify each page. The name *link* comes from the ability to connect all the pages on the Web together. *URL* is short for *uniform resource locator*, but that's an intimidating way of saying it's an address. A URL indicates where a Web page can be found on the Internet, in the same way your mailing address tells where Publisher's Clearing House can find you when you win a million dollars. Some people say *URL* like a word rhyming with *pearl*. Others call it by its letters, making it sound like some kind of government agency that wants to tax your Publisher's Clearing House winnings.

URLs can be complicated-looking things, with all kinds of punctuation, like slashes and tildes, and odd acronyms, such as HTTP and FTP. You'll learn more about them as you create some of your own pages during Hour 3, "Adding Links to Other Pages." For now, a brief introduction is enough. The following are all examples of URLs that can be used in links:

```
http://www.leary.com
http://www.mcp.com/sams
http://www.metaverse.com/empire.html
```

URLs can appear in several different ways:

- ☐ URLs that indicate a specific site on the World Wide Web. `www.leary.com` is the home page of the late Dr. Timothy Leary. It won several awards in 1996 and is still being actively updated.

- ☐ URLs that contain references to directories on a site. `www.mcp.com/sams` links to the main Sams.net directory on the Macmillan home page. Visit it for details on upcoming Sams.net books and to read the full text of many Sams.net publications.

- ☐ URLs that refer to a specific Web page on a site. `www.metaverse.com/empire.html` is a page on the Metaverse home page. That page shows a current picture of the Empire State Building in New York, and it's offered as a way for the Internet community to watch out for any oversized misanthropic gorillas.

If you know a World Wide Web page's URL, you can take a look at that page while you're using the Web. Figure 1.1 shows a Web page that presently has the URL `http://www.big-brains.com/ironkids/Pages/home.html`. It's part of the official IronKids Bread home page, which can be visited using the URL `http://www.ironkids.com`.

The IronKids page shown in Figure 1.1 was loaded with Netscape Navigator, a type of software called a *browser*.

Figure 1.1.

An example of a Web page.

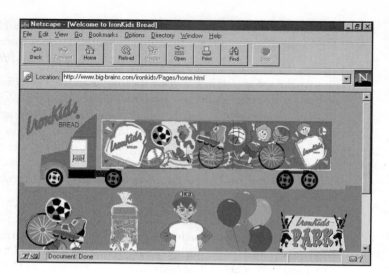

 NEW TERM A *Web browser* is software used to view Web pages and the types of information pages can contain: graphics, sound, video, and other forms as yet unimagined. Because *browsing* isn't a very cool gerund, using a browser to travel the World Wide Web is called *surfing.*

The majority of Web pages today are viewed with either the Netscape Navigator or Microsoft Internet Explorer Web browsers. Dozens of other browsers are used, too—some by people with special needs and others by people with bitter grudges against Netscape, Microsoft, and perhaps humankind in general. Many libraries use Lynx browsers because they display text and skip all the images on Web pages, which means the pages load faster, so even older computers can handle using the World Wide Web. The text-only limitation also prevents images that would startle passers-by from appearing onscreen.

The use of a text-only Web browser, such as Lynx, highlights an important point about the World Wide Web: You cannot create a Web page that will look the same to all the people who view it. This is one of the things that makes the Web much different from a medium such as the printed page. The appearance of your home page varies, depending on the Web browser being used to check it out.

Because Netscape and Microsoft browsers are so popular, most people creating Web pages try for the best possible appearance using those browsers. You'll get tips on how to do this during the coming hours, along with some advice on how to make your pages useful for others as well.

Pages become a part of the World Wide Web when they are stored on a computer that's permanently connected to the Web. As you'll see during Part VI of this book, "Home Page Publishing," there are many different ways to find a home for your home page. Many Internet service providers and online services, such as America Online, offer their subscribers a place for home pages, and there also are companies that offer inexpensive or even free Web page storage.

After you have put your own home page on the Web, it will have a permanent link that can be used by anyone who wants to view it. The home page for this book was recently put on the Web, and it has the following link:

```
http://www.prefect.com/home24
```

If you type that address into a Web browser's address or location field, you'll see the home page I created for the book using Claris Home Page 2.0 Lite.

Ensnared in the Web

A Web page can be made up of many different types of information: text, images, sound, programs, movies, and even 3-D worlds. There was a time when the Web was almost entirely text-based, and it was used primarily by scientists, computer programmers, universities, the military, and former MTV VJ Adam Curry.

COFFEE BREAK

Before the Internet and World Wide Web became so wildly popular, Adam Curry was a Net user who registered the Internet domain `mtv.com` and used it for some personal projects as well as MTV-related material. There was a minor skirmish between the cable channel and its former VJ when he wanted to keep `mtv.com` and they wanted to claim it, but the matter was eventually resolved and Curry gave up the rights to it. He moved his projects to `metaverse.com`.

Everyone else—even the media—started noticing the Web when it began featuring images and other types of visual information in 1993–1994. This revolution was sparked by the creation of the Mosaic Web browser at the National Center for Supercomputing Applications at the University of Illinois at Urbana-Champaign. Marc Andreesen, a student who was supposed to be doing something else, wrote the Mosaic Web browser to expand the kind of information that could be delivered through the World Wide Web, especially image files. There's no documented indication of what images Andreesen had in mind, but Pamela Anderson-Lee joined the cast of *Baywatch* in the same general time period. Draw your own conclusions.

Image was everything. In a year's time, the Web changed from an obscure Internet service into a mass medium.

Today, the World Wide Web offers so many different types of information that it's hard to figure out exactly what the Web is. In previous books of this kind, the Web was described as the world's largest encyclopedia. You could flip from one page to another by clicking a link, just as you could flip from Volume D's listing for **Dallas Cowboys football team** to Volume U's listing for **urinalysis drug testing**.

However, the Web now offers audio, video, and much more. It's not like a book, or any other type of mass medium, anymore. This versatility might be one of the reasons you'd like to create your own home page. There are things you can deliver through the Web that would be cumbersome to do by other means. Some things are possible only on a Web page.

Another feature that appeals to many Web page creators is the global audience the Web offers. Once you put a home page up, it can be reached throughout the world. Your prospective audience ranges from Burbank to Burkina Faso to Burma. This global aspect appeals to merchants, who take to the Web with visions of selling their products all over the planet. It also appeals to publishers and others with information that's worth calling up onscreen.

The Web makes it possible for anyone to get a message out to the world. Of course, there's no guarantee that the world will care. As you learn how to create a home page, you'll learn some tips that help you create a more interesting, visually appealing, and popular Web site.

Although it helps, you don't need a good reason to put your home page on the Web. Because you can put Web pages online at little or no cost, you're the editor, publisher, and chairman of the board of your home page. Media critic A.J. Liebling once said, "Freedom of the press belongs to those who own one."

Because you live during the age of the World Wide Web, you now own your own press.

Trying Out Claris Home Page

The software you'll be using throughout this book, Claris Home Page 2.0 Lite, is included on the book's CD-ROM. Claris, a subsidiary of Apple Computer, creates software for both Microsoft Windows and Apple Macintosh users. Version 2.0 of Claris Home Page has received accolades from the press because of its features, and the Lite version gives you a chance to try the software for free before buying the full version at $99 retail.

By using Home Page throughout this book, you can learn how to create your own home pages without learning HTML. Even if you decide afterwards to choose a different home page–publishing tool (or to learn HTML), the skills you're building won't go to waste. Learning how to use a Web page creator is like learning how to use a word processor. Once you learn one, you can usually pick up others in an afternoon.

1

Claris maintains a home page for this software at the following address:

http://www.claris.com/support/products/clarispage/

This site is primarily for people who have upgraded to the full version, but there's some information related to the software's Lite version.

JUST A MINUTE

Because Home Page 2.0 Lite is available for free evaluation, Claris doesn't offer any technical support or documentation for the product. Like many Apple products, Home Page Lite is relatively easy to use even without any manuals, although you'll miss out on a lot of the nuances of Web page creation and general Web publishing. All features of the Lite version are documented in this book. In the opinion of those whose economic livelihood depends on the sale of *Teach Yourself to Create a Home Page in 24 Hours*, you need the book like Howard Stern needs no-tangle shampoo.

Table 1.1 shows the minimum system requirements to use Home Page on Windows and Macintosh systems.

Table 1.1. Home Page 2.0 Lite requirements.

System component	Windows	Macintosh
Processor	Intel 486	68020, PowerPC, PowerMac
Operating system	Win 95/NT 3.51	System 7.1
Memory	8M (16M NT)	8M

Installing the Software

To set up Home Page on your system, follow the instructions for your computer system in Appendix C, "This Book's CD-ROM." It's a simple process to install the software directly from the CD-ROM, and within five minutes, you should have a directory on your system containing Home Page and its related files.

After Home Page is installed, run the program to make sure it has been set up correctly. Once you get past the title screen, it should resemble Figure 1.2.

Figure 1.2.

The startup screen for Claris Home Page 2.0 Lite.

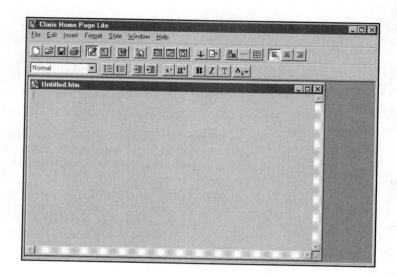

Summary

After you have a copy of Home Page 2.0 Lite installed, you're ready to stop talking about the World Wide Web and start making it a little wider. During the next hour, you'll create your first home page.

Before the big hand on the clock moves to Hour 2, you can review the material introduced during this hour. Each chapter will feature a question-and-answer section, a short quiz, and suggested activities.

Q&A

Q Most books about Web publishing teach HTML programming. How is it possible to create home pages without using HTML?

A It's possible to avoid HTML because software like Home Page does the HTML programming for you. You use it the same way you would use a word processor, but Home Page inserts the HTML commands behind the scenes. If you ever use a pull-down menu command on your browser to see a Web page's "source code," you'll see what HTML looks like.

Q I don't currently have an Internet provider, America Online, or any other place where I can put Web pages. Do I need to get a subscription before I can use this book?

A Not at all. You can view the Web pages that you create on your own computer without putting them on the World Wide Web. All you have to do is open the page with your Web browser and you can use it normally. You won't have to start thinking about finding a home for your home page until the last four hours of the book.

Q If most home pages call the World Wide Web home, what do the rest call home?

A Many companies are setting up their own private Webs, and the Web pages placed there can't be accessed by the general public. These private Webs are called *intranets*—as opposed to the Internet—and many companies are finding them an effective way to communicate. You might end up using skills developed from this book to create pages for a company Web site.

Q Do I need to be connected to the Internet while I'm working on the examples in this book?

A Not at all—the only time you need to be actively connected to the Internet is when you're actually putting your pages on the World Wide Web, as you'll see during Hour 22, "Publishing Your Site." You will, however, be using the Web during many hours to visit real Web sites and make use of resources that are available for Web page developers.

Quiz

Test your knowledge of this hour by taking this brief three-question test.

Questions

1. What do you call each document that can be found on the World Wide Web?
   - (a) A link
   - (b) A page
   - (c) A spider

2. Which of the following is not a reason to use a no-image Web browser, such as Lynx?
   - (a) Pages load more quickly.
   - (b) There's no possibility that objectionable images can be viewed.
   - (c) Pages created with Claris Home Page look better with Lynx.

3. Who created Mosaic, the Web browser that helped fuel the medium's popularity in 1993–1994?
   - (a) Bill Gates
   - (b) My aunt Pam
   - (c) Marc Andreesen

Answers

1. b. A link is used to connect one Web page to another, and a spider is a program that searches the World Wide Web collecting information.

2. c. Home Page can be used to create text-only Web pages, but it supports many features that aren't supported by Lynx browsers.

3. c. Today, Andreesen is a top executive at Netscape, where he continues to have a large role in the World Wide Web's future.

Activities

The following activities are suggested to expand your knowledge of the subjects covered during this hour:

☐ To see a home page created with Claris Home Page 2.0 Lite, load your Web browser and take a look at this book's site: `http://www.prefect.com/home24`. All the features were created by using the software.

☐ Part of the peculiar charm of the World Wide Web is the unpredictability of its publishers. Visit the Web page `http://www.boutell.com:80/announce/` to find out about some of the newest sites to become available on the Web.

1

Hour **2**

Creating and Editing a Page

Now that you have reviewed the history of the World Wide Web, you're ready to take the first step towards making some history of your own. You will be using Claris Home Page 2.0 Lite for the first time to create a Web page—in this case, the home page of British writer Edward George Bulwer-Lytton. Bulwer-Lytton never created his own page, unfortunately, because he died 120 years before the popularization of the World Wide Web. You'll correct this iniquity and learn about the following topics during this hour:

- ☐ Running Home Page
- ☐ Creating, titling, and saving documents
- ☐ Adding text
- ☐ Saving your first page
- ☐ Trying it out with a browser

Making Space for Your Pages

Before getting started today, you need to create a folder on your system where your Web pages can be stored. Create a folder called Webwork. This folder will be the starting place for all the projects you undertake in coming hours.

Next, you need to create a subfolder called "Stormy" inside the Webwork folder. It will be the storage place for today's project, Bulwer-Lytton's home page. You'll understand the significance of the folder name about 12 minutes past the hour.

Running Claris Home Page 2.0 Lite

When you create your first home page during this hour, you'll be using Claris Home Page 2.0 Lite. With this software, you can design a Web page in the same way you would design a document with a word processor: Type in some text and then dress it up with special formatting, different fonts, and other stylistic flourishes. Today, you'll focus on the first part—typing in text where you want it to show up on a page.

At this point, you should have installed Home Page on your system. Go ahead and run the program, and if you see a title window introducing the software, bypass it by clicking the OK button.

After the title window has closed, Home Page creates a blank document in a large gray-shaded window that fills most of the screen. The document is given the default name Untitled.htm.

This gray window is a Web page, although at the moment it isn't a particularly interesting one—there's nothing on it. Unless you're a big fan of minimalism, you'll want to put something on this first page. For starters, you should give your page a title.

A Title for Your Page

Every Web page can be given a title—a short line of text that identifies the page's purpose or contents. The title is a bit of a loner, because it isn't displayed along with the other parts of the page. Instead, it's shown at the top of the browser in the frame of the window itself.

To give your page a title using Home Page, you need to choose the Document Options feature. You can use a button or a pull-down menu command to do this. The Document Options button is shown in Figure 2.1, which displays the top part of the Home Page window as you're running the program for the first time.

2

Figure 2.1.

The Document Options button on the main Home Page toolbar.

The Document Options button

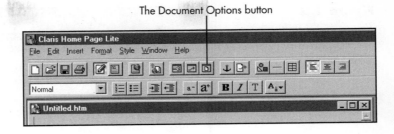

If you would prefer to use the pull-down menu, choose Edit | Document Options.

When you choose the Document Options feature, you can set up several things for your home page. During this hour, the only component you'll be modifying is the Document Title field. Enter the following text in the field: Edward George Bulwer-Lytton's Home Page. Click the OK button when you're done.

COFFEE BREAK

If the name Edward George Bulwer-Lytton sounds familiar, and you're not an aficionado of nineteenth-century British writer-poet-politicians, you probably have heard of the Bulwer-Lytton Fiction Contest. This yearly event is a contest for writers to pen the worst opening sentence possible for a novel (writing the rest of the novel is optional). Bulwer-Lytton's name graces the competition because he was the first writer to begin a book with the line, "It was a dark and stormy night." For contest details, visit its official home page at the following Web address:

http://www.best.com/~sbr/

Choosing a good title for a Web page might not seem important, considering that it isn't displayed very prominently on a Web browser. When you're surfing to a Web site, you might never notice the title atop the browser window as you get caught up in a point-click-scroll, point-click-scroll frenzy.

However, the title becomes important when your pages have been placed on the Web because a descriptive title can help people find you. Popular Web searching tools, such as AltaVista, display page titles as the result of a search. Figure 2.2 shows an example of AltaVista searching for titles containing the words *Bulwer-Lytton*. The title of each page is underlined above the text of the page and its Web address. You'll learn more about AltaVista and other searching tools during Hour 24, "Telling the World."

Figure 2.2.

*Results of a search using
the Netscape Navigator
Web browser.*

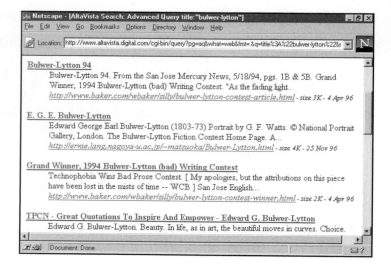

Before taking a look at your home page's new title, you should put something on the page
itself.

Placing Text on a Page

On the Home Page software running on your system, you should see a large window with
`untitled.htm` as the caption. This is where you'll put everything that should be displayed on
your home page.

You should see a blinking cursor near the upper-left corner of the untitled.htm window. (If
not, click your mouse there and a cursor will appear.) Enter the text of Listing 2.1 into the
area, making sure to press Enter only when you see a ¶ mark in the listing. Don't type in the
line numbers and colons at the beginning of the lines; they're included so that specific line
numbers can be referred to.

TIME SAVER

On behalf of carpal tunnel nerves everywhere, all the sample Web pages
from this book are on the CD-ROM that accompanies it. There's an
Examples folder on the CD-ROM with subfolders for each hour. If you'd
like to use these pages to cut-and-paste text, or to avoid typing entirely,
you can start with the file index.html in the Examples\Hour2 folder of the
CD-ROM.

Listing 2.1. The text of Edward's home page.

```
 1: A Dark and Stormy Site¶
 2:
 3: The Edward George Bulwer-Lytton Home Page¶
 4:
 5: Welcome to the home page of Edward George Bulwer-Lytton, the
 6: British novelist and poet who lived from 1803 to 1873. I am
 7: best-known today for beginning the 1830 novel Paul Clifford with
 8: the following line:¶
 9:
10: "It was a dark and stormy night and the rain fell in torrents
11: -- except at occasional intervals, when it was checked by a
12: violent gust of wind which swept up the streets (for it is in
13: London that our scene lies), rattling along the housetops, and
14: fiercely agitating the scanty flame of the lamps that struggled
15: against the darkness."¶
16:
17: However, what I would prefer to be known for is my dislike of
18: the residents of Greece:¶
19:
20: "Those who look back to classic days of Greece would be greatly
21: disappointed at its present state.... and would be astonished to
22: find any resemblance still exists between the Greek who fought
23: at Marathon and Thermopylae, and the one who is at present
24: contending on the same field as his ancestors." -- An Autumn in
25: Greece, 1826¶
```

After typing in the text, you need to give the page a filename and save it to disk. Choose File | Save As (which is on the File pull-down menu), and you'll get a chance to select a filename and the folder to store the page in. The folder should be Stormy, which you created earlier. Make the filename index.html.

All Web pages that you create should be named with the extension .html or .htm, which indicates that the file is an HTML document—a text file that has special formatting commands for display as a World Wide Web page.

JUST A MINUTE

You might be wondering why the name index.html is chosen when something like edward.html seems more descriptive. The reason is that index.html is the most common filename for the main page of a Web site. In a Web browser, typing the address http://www.broccoli.com is the same as typing http://www.broccoli.com/index.html—you get the main home page of Broccoli Town U.S.A. in either case. When you type a Web address without a filename, as in http://www.broccoli.com, most Web sites go looking for a page to present called index.html.

Trying Out the Page

There are two ways to preview Edward George's home page—within the Home Page software and with your favorite Web browser. The fastest way to see the page is with Home Page's Preview Page feature. The Preview Page button is shown in Figure 2.3, and it can also be selected with the menu option Window | Preview Page.

Figure 2.3.

The Preview Page button on the main Home Page toolbar.

The Preview Page button

The Preview Page feature gives you a chance to see what the home page looks like. It's a simple Web browser that displays the page according to its own rules for how HTML documents should be shown.

TIME SAVER

If you ever want to see what one of the buttons represents in Home Page, hold your mouse cursor over the button for a few seconds. A text box appears that describes the button's function.

While you are using Home Page's Preview Page feature, you can't make any corrections that are needed. To get back into the mode where changes can be made, choose the Edit Page feature. It's the pencil-and-paper button immediately to the left of the Preview Page button. You can also select this feature by choosing Window | Edit Page from the menu.

In addition to previewing a page within the Home Page software, you can take a look at the page with your system's primary Web browser by using Home Page's Preview in Browser feature. Click the button immediately to the right of the Preview Page button or choose the File | Preview in Browser menu option.

If your system has a default Web browser set up, such as Microsoft Internet Explorer or Netscape Navigator, the Bulwer-Lytton home page will be loaded in that browser. Figure 2.4 shows what the page looks like in a current version of Internet Explorer.

2

Figure 2.4.

The Edward George Bulwer-Lytton Home Page.

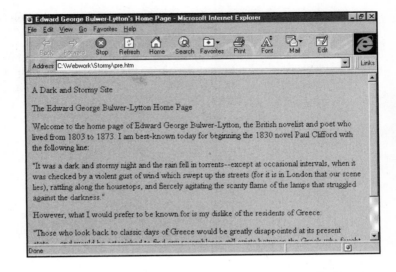

While you have your new page displayed with a browser, change the size of the window running the browser. When you make the browser smaller or larger, watch the text on the Bulwer-Lytton page. The margins will change so that all of the page's text can still be read, no matter what the size. Each paragraph will remain separate from the other paragraphs.

Web pages can be extremely flexible in this regard, allowing users to configure the browser in different ways on their systems. This flexibility is especially true of text, the simplest thing you can put on a page.

With the Preview in Browser feature, you can test your home pages with the browser you want it to look best with. Many Web page designers choose a current version of Navigator or Internet Explorer as the target audience because those browsers are the two most popular ones in use today. Also, a page that looks good in a current version of Navigator is likely to look good in a current version of Internet Explorer because the browsers have similar functions and features.

JUST A MINUTE

If your Home Page software doesn't load a Web browser when you choose the Preview in Browser feature, or it loads a browser you don't want to use, choose Edit | Preferences from the menu. This choice opens a window where you can change the behavior of the Home Page program. Click the Browser Preview tab and you'll see a Set button. Click it to find the Web browser you want on your system, and set it for use with page previews.

Summary

Edward George Bulwer-Lytton now has his own home page, composed entirely of text, and you have finished your first Web page in record time. Adding text to a Web page is simply a matter of typing it in where you want it to appear in relation to other things on the page. Home Page 2.0 Lite offers two ways to check your work—inside Home Page's Preview Page feature and with your own preferred Web browser.

As you saw when you changed the size of your Web browser's window, text doesn't always appear in the same place. Like all elements of a Web page, text can move around, based on the Web browser being used, the system running the browser, and the human doing the browsing.

During the next two hours, you'll get a chance to make Edward's page a little more exciting by adding images and links to other pages on the World Wide Web.

Q&A

Q When choosing a name for a Web page, is there a reason to use the file extension .HTML instead of .HTM?

A Both .HTML and .HTM can be used to identify HTML documents, but you should probably use .HTML unless your system can use only three-character file extensions. It's the most common way to identify that a file is a Web page, and many Web surfers assume that a page has the .HTML extension when they're trying to call it up with a browser.

Q I have seen page titles displayed when I search for a Web page, but how is that helpful? Do searching tools on the Web give titles more weight than the text on a page when a search is being conducted?

A Different searching tools, such as AltaVista and WebCrawler, have their own rules for what's important on a Web page. Some tools have a way to search the titles only, and it often is a good way to find what you're looking for on the Web. Go to the Web page http://www.altavista.digital.com and choose the Advanced Search option. In the Selection Criteria field, enter the text title: Bulwer-Lytton. This will re-create the search shown previously in Figure 2.2. On AltaVista, you'll find listings for several pages that mention the author, including a version of this hour's Edward George Bulwer-Lytton home page on the *Teach Yourself to Create a Home Page in 24 Hours* Web site at http://www.prefect.com/home24.

2

Q Do I have to go through Home Page Lite to see the pages I create with this book?

A Not at all—once you have saved a copy of a Web page created with Home Page, you can load it directly. With most systems, this is simply a matter of double-clicking the filename of the page you want to view. Go to the Webwork\Stormy folder on your system and double-click index.html. It should load with your preferred Web browser.

Quiz

Test your knowledge of this hour by taking this brief three-question test.

Questions

1. Where does the title of a Web page appear when it's viewed with a browser?

    (a) In search engines

    (b) At the top of the page

    (c) Atop the browser window

2. What's the most commonly used filename for the main page of a World Wide Web site?

    (a) default.html

    (b) index.html

    (c) totally_nude.html

3. True or False: All text looks the same no matter what Web browser you use.

    (a) True.

    (b) False.

    (c) I'm not answering until I talk to my lawyer.

Answers

1. c. The title appears atop the browser window in the same place a program's name appears. It's also displayed with many search engines when they find your pages on the World Wide Web.

2. b. Some Web sites use default.html or default.htm instead, but index.html is the most common choice for a site's main page.

3. b. Even text, the simplest element of a Web page, varies depending on the browser being used.

Activities

The following activities are suggested to expand your knowledge of the subjects covered during this hour:

☐ If you have more than one browser installed on your computer system, load the same Web page simultaneously on each browser. Choose a complicated page, such as http://espnet.sportszone.com, to see the differences in presentation between the browsers.

☐ Create your own home page, with a short description of yourself. If you dislike the residents of a particular nation-state, be sure to point that out—there's nothing like controversy to attract people to a home page. Create a new Webwork\MyHome subfolder and store your home page in it under the name index.html.

Hour 3

Adding Links to Other Pages

In the last hour, you created the home page of British writer Edward George Bulwer-Lytton—several paragraphs of text featuring two quotes from his books. However, the page differs from most home pages on the World Wide Web in one important respect: It's a dead end.

That observation isn't a slam against Bulwer-Lytton; it's a comment about the page itself. A Web surfer who reaches the page has nowhere to go but backward. During this hour, you'll learn how to correct this problem by adding links to other pages. The following topics are covered:

- ☐ Adding new pages to your home page
- ☐ Creating links to those pages
- ☐ Creating links to pages on the Web
- ☐ Organizing lists of links
- ☐ Receiving e-mail using a link
- ☐ Testing the links

Like It? Link It

The World Wide Web wouldn't be very webby if there were no links. One of the things that makes this medium unique is the haphazard way in which the audience experiences it. The Web is the least orderly form of communication on earth, with the possible exception of my pre-calculus professor in college. On the Web, you can jump from one place to another with no rhyme or reason to your choices—start out with a sports site in Seattle, jump from there to the Dorothy Parker poetry archive, and end up with a recipe for garlic chutney (it "makes a great gift," according to http://www.cyber-kitchen.com).

A *link* is a connection from one Web page to another. Links can be represented by text, graphics, or both. You click a link to go from the current page to a new one.

Anything that can be found on the World Wide Web can be linked to. You can create links to other Web pages, image files, audio files, or other types of information.

One of the first items most people put on their home page is a list of their favorite Web sites. To see how links work, you'll do that during this hour for Edward George Bulwer-Lytton.

COFFEE BREAK

If ever a nineteenth-century politician-bard cried out for a nickname, it's Edward George Bulwer-Lytton. His name sounds like a prestigious law firm, and one wonders what surname would result from a union between his descendant and an heir to Olivia Newton-John or Claude Levi-Strauss.

Creating a Page for Links

There are two ways you can link to another page on the Web:

- ☐ Linking to another page or file on your own site
- ☐ Linking to something on someone else's site

During this hour, you'll create a second page for the Edward George Bulwer-Lytton home page as a place to keep his favorite links. This gives you a chance to see how two pages on the same site can be linked together.

To get ready to create the links page, load Home Page if it isn't already running and close the index.html page if it's still open.

You will be creating a new page to house Bulwer-Lytton's collection of links. Click the New Page button on the Home Page toolbar, which is the leftmost icon indicated in Figure 3.1, or use the File | New Page menu option.

Figure 3.1.
The New Page button.

The New Page button

A new window opens with the default title Untitled.htm, which you can change when you save the page for the first time. To start off the page, enter the text of Listing 3.1. Don't forget to press Enter only when you come to each ¶ mark.

Listing 3.1. The introductory text of the links page.

```
1: Edward George Bulwer-Lytton's Favorite Web Sites¶
2: Though I was never able to surf the Web, these are a few
3: places I would have worn out my carpal tunnel nerve
4: visiting: ¶
```

After you have entered these four lines of text, go ahead and save the page by clicking the Save Page button—it's the diskette icon near the New Page button. You can also choose File | Save from the menu.

Before you can save the page, Home Page asks you to do two things. The first is to give the page a title. Enter the text Edward George Bulwer-Lytton's Favorite Links as the title and click OK.

CAUTION

Home Page makes sure you have a title of some kind to avoid a common malady on the Web—people leaving default text or no text at all as a page's title. The search engine AltaVista reports that more than 10,000 Web pages have the title "your Document Title here," which is the default text used by another Web-page creation tool that shall remain nameless.

After you have given the page a title, Home Page asks you to select a filename for the page and a folder to store it in. Choose the folder Webwork\Stormy and the filename links.html.

Adding a List of Links

When you are putting together a group of links, you don't have to present them in paragraph form as you did with Edward George's main page. Lists of information can be grouped in two ways:

☐ Unnumbered lists, which are indented and marked off with a bullet symbol (a circle or square)

☐ Numbered lists, which are indented and automatically numbered when the page is presented

Click your mouse to the right of the text visiting: on the page you're working on. The cursor should appear there. Before entering any text, click the Make Numbered List Entry button, which is indicated in Figure 3.2. You can also use the Format | Numbered List menu option.

Figure 3.2.

Click this button to begin a numbered list.

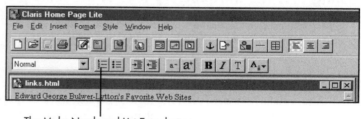

The Make Numbered List Entry button

After you choose to begin a numbered list, the indented text #. appears next to the cursor. This sign is replaced with a number when the page is displayed, as you will see in a few minutes.

The first numbered item will be text describing the Bulwer-Lytton Fiction Contest, the annual competition selecting the worst first sentence of imaginary novels. With your cursor to the right of the text #., enter the following:

```
The Bulwer-Lytton Fiction Contest — I can't think of a reason
why they named it after me, but I'm deeply honored¶
```

Once you have added the text, you're ready to add a link. Using your mouse, highlight the text that reads Bulwer-Lytton Fiction Contest. You do this by clicking the mouse when the cursor is slightly to the left of the word *Bulwer*, holding down the mouse, and dragging it until the cursor is to the right of *Contest*.

When the text is highlighted, you can add a link with Home Page's Insert Link feature by choosing Insert | Link to URL from the menu. You can also click the Link Editor button, which is immediately to the left of the Document Options button on the toolbar.

When you choose to add a link, a dialog box opens where you can enter the address you're establishing a link to. The address, a URL, can be to a Web page, a graphic, or anything else that's on the Web. In this case, enter `http://www.best.com/~sbr` and press Enter. There's no OK or Close button on this dialog box, so you have to close it yourself, just as you would close any window or folder. (On Windows 95 systems, close the box by clicking the × button in its upper-right corner.)

The text of the page should now have the words *Bulwer-Lytton Fiction Contest* underlined. You can test out this link by opening the page with your preferred Web browser. Click the Preview in Browser button to load the page you are working on. When it has loaded, click the `Bulwer-Lytton Fiction Contest` link to see the page.

CAUTION

Because the World Wide Web is in a constant state of change, some of the links used during this hour might not be valid by the time you read this book. If you experience any problems using the links here or elsewhere in the book, visit the Web page `http://www.prefect.com/home24/linkstatus.html`. It will contain the status of the links used in the book and recommend changes or substitutes when needed.

After you finish testing your first link, return to Home Page to add the rest of Bulwer-Lytton's favorite sites.

Finishing the List

Your next task is to add a few more items to the list after the Bulwer-Lytton Fiction Contest entry. There should be a second indented `#.` after the first list entry, which indicates that Home Page is ready to receive the text of a new list item. (If not, place your cursor to the right of the word *honored* and press Enter once.)

When your cursor is to the right of the second `#.`, you're ready to add some entries to finish off the list. Enter the following text:

```
A page about my life and links from professor Mitsuharu Matsuoka¶
Frank's Creative Quotations lists five of my noteworthy quotes¶
The home page of my side of Parliament, the Conservative Party¶
The Internet Scone Page¶
```

When you hit Enter after the Scone entry, there will be another `#.` on the following line because Home Page expects you to add another item to your numbered list. This `#.` prompt causes a number to appear on the page, even if it doesn't have a list entry beside it. To remove it, you must change the format of the current line from numbered list to normal text. You can do that by choosing Format | Normal from the menu or using a special formatting choice drop-down list on the toolbar, which is indicated in Figure 3.3.

Figure 3.3.
Use this list to select a
type of text formatting.

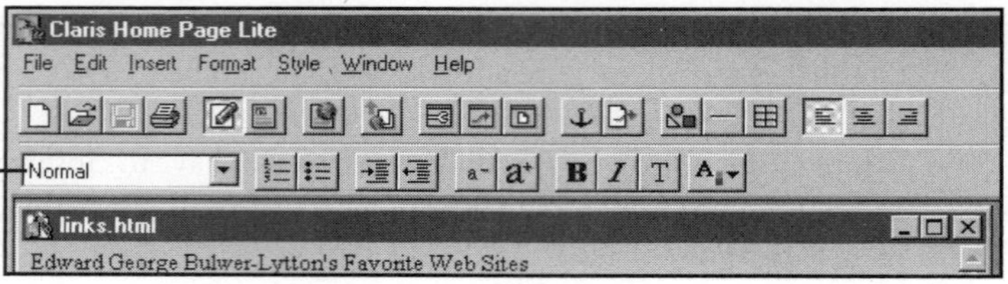

Claris Home Page Lite
File   Edit   Insert   Format   Style   Window   Help

Normal

The formatting drop-down list —

links.html
Edward George Bulwer-Lytton's Favorite Web Sites

After switching back to normal formatting, you need to add the links to the four items in the list. To do that, highlight the text and use the Insert URL feature, as you did with the first item. Table 3.1 indicates the text to highlight and the link that should be used.

Table 3.1. The links to add to the page.

Text to Highlight	Link
my life and links	http://ernie.lang.nagoya-u.ac.jp/~matsuoka/ Bulwer-Lytton.html
noteworthy quotes	http://www.bemorecreative.com/one/22.htm
Conservative Party	http://www.conservative-party.org.uk
Internet Scone Page	http://home1.gte.net/stbooth/scones.html

Removing the Numbers from the List

Although it makes sense to number the list of Bulwer-Lytton links, especially if he's ranking them from most-best to least-best, there are going to be times when you would prefer not to number each item in a list. For instance, if you're creating a Web page listing your grandchildren, numbering them could get ugly—the No. 1 kid is going to get a false sense of superiority, and the lowest-ranked kid might turn to a life of mail fraud to boost his self-esteem. Going alphabetical with no numbered items would save thousands in therapy bills.

Creating unnumbered lists is just like creating numbered ones. An unnumbered list is called a bulleted list, because the circle or square placed next to each list entry is bulletlike in appearance. To start an unnumbered list, click the Make Bullet List Entry button or choose the Format | Bullet List menu option.

You can also turn existing text into a list. To try this, highlight all five entries in the list of Bulwer-Lytton's favorite links by using the mouse's click-and-drag ability.

Make sure that the text of all five list items is highlighted (don't worry if the first #. is not highlighted). Click the Make Bullet List Entry button or choose Format | Bullet List from the menu to convert the list from a numbered list to a bulleted one.

3

Creating Links to Your Own Pages

In many cases, the Web site you create will consist of more than one page. To connect these pages, you need to create links between them.

One way to connect them is to use the full Web address of each page. If your main page is stored at `http://www.noplace.com/index.html` and you have a guest book page at `http://www.noplace.com/visitors.html`, you can use these full Web addresses in your links.

However, it's more convenient to use local links between items that are part of your own home page. A local link includes just a reference to a filename and possibly the directory where you can find the page. In the previous example, index.html and visitors.html are in the same directory. If you wanted to add a link from the index.html page to the guest book, all you would have to use as the link is the filename visitors.html. No long Web address is needed because the page is part of the same Web site.

Using local links is more convenient because you can test the pages without putting them somewhere on the World Wide Web first. You can also move your home page to a new Web address without having to change a bunch of links between your own pages on the site.

Create a link at the bottom of the Bulwer-Lytton page that connects it to the main page you created last hour. First, with your cursor after the last entry on the list of links, enter the following text:

```
Return to the Main Page of this Site¶
```

Highlight this text and use the Link Editor feature of Home Page to associate a link with this text. You can use the Link Editor feature by clicking the button indicated in Figure 3.4 or choosing Insert | Link to URL from the menu.

Figure 3.4.
Creating a link.

The Link Editor button

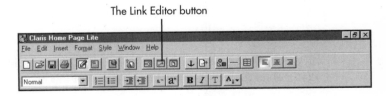

Instead of typing in a Web address to use with the link, click the Browse Files button, which allows you to pick the file on your system that should be loaded when this link is clicked. Find the index.html file in your Webwork\Stormy folder. Select it and close the dialog box.

Surfing Around Your Own Pages

If a Web site you're working on is made up of several different pages, you might find it cumbersome to open, close, and save each file just to make small changes.

One way to go from page to page while working on them is to use the Preview Page feature you learned about during Hour 2, "Creating and Editing a Page."

After saving the links.html page, click the Preview Page button. While previewing the page, you can't edit text, but you can use the links that are connected to other parts of your own Web site.

Click the link you just created, which is labeled `Return to the Main Page of this Site`. The index.html page will be loaded, and you can edit it by clicking the Edit Page button.

JUST A MINUTE

> As you might already have discovered, the Preview Page feature doesn't work for links that aren't part of your home page. To test them, you have to preview the page with a Web browser.

Once you can edit index.html, add the following line of text at the bottom of the page:

`Some of My Favorite Links¶`

Use this text as a link to the Web page links.html in the Webwork\Stormy folder. You can now jump back and forth between the two pages of the Bulwer-Lytton home page, as you can test with Home Page's Preview Page feature.

Sending Mail with a Link

As stated previously, links aren't restricted for use only with Web pages. You can link to a graphics file, a text file that isn't formatted for the Web, or any other type of information.

One special kind of link makes it easier for people visiting your page to send you e-mail. It's called a Mailto link, and the following is an example:

`mailto:home24@prefect.com`

If you used this text for a link on one of your pages, it could be clicked to send e-mail to `home24@prefect.com`, the address for the author of this book. You're encouraged to try it for any reason as you're going through the book, unless you'd like me to join your multilevel-marketing pyramid of prosperity.

When a Mailto link is clicked, your system calls up the preferred program you use to send e-mail, if there is one. Some systems are configured to use a built-in mail program in the Web browser.

3

Returning to the index.html page, put your cursor on the bottom of the page and add the following text:

```
Send Us E-mail!
```

Highlight this text by clicking and dragging your mouse, and turn it into the following link:

```
mailto:dmayhew@iquest.net
```

COFFEE BREAK

> The Mailto link is pretty straightforward, but if you'd like to test it, please click on `Send Us E-mail!`. When your mail program loads, pen a short note about how you're really getting your money's worth out of the first hour and 45 minutes of this book. Say you're enjoying yourself so much that it seemed like only 50 minutes and 12 seconds went by. This Mailto link ends up with David Mayhew, an acquisitions editor at Sams.net Publishing. If you're looking for a job, David might be looking to replace a writer once he finds out I'm passing out his e-mail address.

Summary

Now that you can add links to your Web pages, you're ready to join the millions of people who catalog their every interest as a list of links. You should join Edward George Bulwer-Lytton in exhibiting this aspect of your personality—never before has it been possible to tell a worldwide audience about your love of something such as scones.

Using local links to connect your pages makes them easier to use, and you can encourage visitor feedback with a Mailto link.

In the next hour, you'll finish the Edward George Bulwer-Lytton home page by adding some images to it. In the process, you'll get a chance to see how links can be added to images instead of text.

Q&A

Q Before I create a link to a Web page, do I have to ask permission from the person whose page I'm linking to?

A There are no rules—you'll have to be guided by how many gifts you want from Santa based on his assessment of your behavior. As a point of courtesy, you might want to inform the publisher of the other Web page about the link, but that doesn't appear to be the norm. Most people consider anything to be fair game for a link if it's accessible over the Web. Heloise and Emily Post have yet to weigh in on the issue.

Q Can you link to a local page that isn't in the same directory as the page you're linking from?

A Home Page handles this automatically with the Browse Files option, which allows you to choose the linked page (or file) with your mouse. You can also do this manually by specifying the directory along with the name of the file. For example, if you want to link to a graphics file called picture.gif that's in a subdirectory called Images, the link would be `Images/picture.gif`.

Q How do I send e-mail directly from a Web page, as I have done on some sites I visit?

A Sending mail from a page is done by including a type of program on your site called a *CGI gateway*. Using a CGI program involves getting special access to the site hosting your Web pages in most cases, and because CGI can be difficult to learn even for experienced programmers, it's beyond the scope of this book. Most Web surfers can make use of a Mailto link, so you're still making it possible for people to contact you with questions or comments.

Quiz

Test your knowledge of this hour by taking this brief three-question test.

Questions

1. What are the two components that make up a link?

    (a) Text and graphics

    (b) Text and URLs (Web addresses)

    (c) Sugar and spice

2. When you want to add a link to your favorite page on the Web, what should you probably do first?

    (a) Go to the page with your browser and use cut-and-paste to get the address.

    (b) Create text on your page for the link to be associated with.

    (c) Ask permission of the Web site's publisher.

3. If you don't put any links on a page, what have you done?

    (a) Forced most visitors to use their browser's Back button to leave the page.

    (b) Created a dead-end.

    (c) Missed the opportunity to lead visitors to other parts of your home page.

3

Answers

1. b. You must have a Web address or local filename and some kind of text or image to use it with.

2. Anything but c. Web addresses are often unwieldy, so it usually is easier to paste them in directly from your browser. Home Page requires that you have something to link to, such as text, before creating a link.

3. a., b., or c.

Activities

The following activities are suggested to expand your knowledge of the subjects covered during this hour:

☐ If you have built your own home page, as recommended during Hour 2's "Activities" section, create your own mylinks.html Web page with your own favorite sites and link it to your main page. Make sure to add a link to this book's site at `http://www.prefect.com/home24` so you have it handy.

☐ Visit the Yahoo! directory at `http://www.yahoo.com` and type in a subject that's interesting to you—anything from aardvarks to zymurgy. Visit at least five sites related to your selected topic and create a page of links to them, with short one- or two-line reviews of the sites.

Hour 4

Putting Images on Your Page

One of the more oft-quoted remarks of the past decade comes from tennis pro Andre Agassi: "Image is everything." Andre might not really feel that way, especially given the really bad haircuts he has gotten in recent years and the fact he was paid to say it. However, it's a popular saying, and "image is everything" has been used to describe the growth of the World Wide Web.

Once it became possible to put images on Web pages, the World Wide Web was on its way towards being a mass medium. Images are a way to make pages seem more dynamic, and they can also be used to present information that can't be offered effectively in text form. During this hour, you'll learn how to use Claris Home Page 2.0 Lite to place images on a page. The following topics are covered:

- ☐ Placing an image on a page
- ☐ Centering images
- ☐ Using images with links
- ☐ Choosing text to identify an image
- ☐ Aligning text alongside an image
- ☐ Expanding the border of an image

Working with Images

Before starting any of the examples in this hour, you need to handle a few preparatory tasks. First, go to the Webwork\Stormy folder that has been used to store the other pages from the Bulwer-Lytton Web site. Create a new subfolder called "images" for storing all the image files you include on the site.

After creating the images folder, retrieve the files cover.gif, chpmade.gif, and w.gif, which are in the Resource folder of this book's CD-ROM.

Copy all three of these files into the Webwork\Stormy\images folder, and you're ready to continue.

During this hour, you'll be using images to spruce up one of the pages you worked on during past hours—Edward George Bulwer-Lytton's home page.

Inserting an Image

To get back to the main page of the Bulwer-Lytton Web site, take a look at the options on the File menu of Home Page. Documents you have worked with recently should appear as menu options, and one of these is probably C:\Webwork\Stormy\index.html. Load this page.

To make space on the page for the first image you're going to work with, insert a blank line after the line that reads The Edward George Bulwer-Lytton Home Page. With your cursor positioned at the beginning of that line, click the Insert Image button, shown in Figure 4.1. You can also use the Insert | Image menu option.

Figure 4.1.
Making space for an image.

The Insert Image button

A dialog box opens where you can select the filename of an image. Find the cover.gif file that you placed in the Webwork\Stormy\images folder at the beginning of the hour. Select this file to place it on your Web page at the current position of the cursor.

The image, Edward George's solemn visage over storm clouds, will be displayed on the page.

4

JUST A MINUTE

You can use Home Page to display three types of image files: GIF files, JPEG files, and bitmap files. GIF files have the file extension .GIF, and they are well-suited for smaller images with fewer colors. JPEG files have the file extension .JPG or .JPEG, and they are often used to display photographs on a Web page because they can show a lot of detail without being large files. Bitmap files, which have the extension .BMP, convey a lot of visual detail but are also very large. They're not used often on the Web.

The image of Bulwer-Lytton will probably look better if you center it horizontally on the page. While you're doing this, you can center the top two lines of text on the page, too.

Highlight the top two lines of text and the image by doing the following: Click your mouse down at the spot where you should begin highlighting, drag it, and release the mouse when you have highlighted the text and cover.gif image.

While the highlighted area is being displayed, click the Align Text Center button, which is four buttons to the right of the Insert Image button. (You also can choose Format | Align | Align Center from the menu.)

When you use the Align Text Center feature, the text and images at the top of the page are centered when Web browsers load the page. Figure 4.2 shows the page in the Internet Explorer browser.

Figure 4.2.

An image centered on the Bulwer-Lytton page in a browser window.

When you're designing Web pages, it's easy to forget how many different ways people can view a page. The image you have put on the Bulwer-Lytton page will look great to those using browsers such as Navigator and Internet Explorer, but some Web surfers don't have software that can display graphics on pages. Others are using pages for the textual information only.

For the benefit of non-graphical users, there are some things you can do. First, you can provide a text description of the image, which will be shown only to those users who aren't receiving the image. This feature is called the *Alt Label*, short for *Alternative Label*.

Setting the Alt Label requires using Home Page's Object Editor tool. In Home Page, an *object* is considered to be anything on a Web page that isn't text—graphics, Java programs, and the like.

Click once on the image you just placed on the Bulwer-Lytton page; a black border should appear around it to indicate that it's been selected. Click the Object Editor button on the toolbar, which is indicated in Figure 4.3. (You also can use the Window | Show Object Editor menu option.)

Figure 4.3.

Using the Object Editor tool.

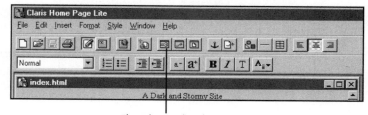

The Object Editor button

After you choose the Object Editor tool, a dialog box opens that you can use to modify the object. If you choose either the Basic or Both tab, you will see a place to choose an Alt Label for the image. Enter the text Edward's Head in the Clouds in this field. Press Enter, and then close the dialog box by clicking the × button in the upper-right corner.

If you're using a graphical browser, you might not see the benefit of the Alt Label because you never see it. Web browsers are starting to display it occasionally along with graphics. When the page is loading, some browsers display the Alt Label until the image or other object has finished loading. Also, in browsers such as the current Internet Explorer, if you leave your mouse over an object, its Alt Label appears, if one has been set up.

You also can use the Alt Label with Java programs on a Web page, for the benefit of those using browsers that can't run Java programs. This topic is covered during Hour 14, "Adding Animation to a Page."

Benefits of Alt Labels

Many Web page developers use Alt Labels infrequently or not at all, even on professional sites that get thousands of visits each day. However, Alt Labels are a way to open up your Web pages to an audience that couldn't use them any other way—sight-impaired Web surfers. If a user can't see a menu graphic on a page, using an Alt Label or an all-text menu somewhere else is the only way to make the page usable to some visitors.

Also, some people using the Web choose to turn off all graphics as a way to make pages load more quickly. This method can be highly beneficial for users connecting to the Web with slow dial-up modem connections.

If you've never seen what the Web's like for some non-graphical surfers, with some browsers you can turn the image display off. In Internet Explorer, choose View | Options from the menu and uncheck the Show Pictures checkbox. When you see a page that's on the Web, Alt Labels will be displayed in place of graphics and other objects.

Figures 4.4 and 4.5 show the difference between the graphics-on and graphics-off versions of Switchboard, a popular site offering address and phone number directories for businesses and individuals at `http://www.switchboard.com`. Because Switchboard uses Alt Labels to identify each graphic, it's possible to use the site without seeing the graphics, if you want.

Figure 4.4.

The Switchboard people and business directory with graphics on.

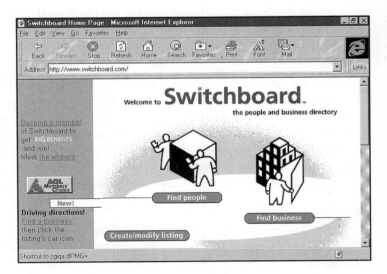

Figure 4.5.

The Switchboard people and business directory with graphics off.

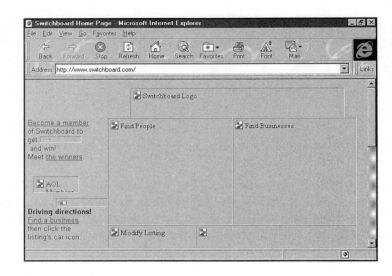

Displaying an Image in Different Ways

With the Object Editor tool, you can also change the display size of an image. By default, images are shown at their exact size, but you can make them smaller by specifying either the exact height and width you want or a percentage of each. The changes you make don't alter the image in any way, so it's still possible to use it normally.

With the image on the Bulwer-Lytton page highlighted, select the Object Editor tool and click the Advanced tab in the dialog box. You will see fields where you can change the height and width of the displayed image. Click the drop-down lists next to the Height and Width fields that currently read Pixels, and change each of them to Percent. After you do that, you can choose any number from 1 to 100 for both the Height and Width fields. These fields don't have to correspond with each other, so you can stretch an image to any dimensions you seek. Set the image to display with a width of 90 percent and a height of 50 percent. Close the Object Editor dialog box, and use the Preview in Browser tool to check out the page.

CAUTION

Displaying an image at an altered size often causes a lot of its quality to be lost. None of the current browsers can scale an image with the same skill as a graphics program, so you might prefer creating a scaled-down image on your own instead of changing the Height and Width values of an image with the Object Editor.

4

If you ever change your mind and decide to display an image at its normal size, click the Reset Size button in the Object Editor's Advanced dialog box to clear out the changes you have made to the Height and Width fields.

Using Images with Links

Like any other element of a Web page, images can be used as links. To see how that works, insert a blank line at the bottom of the Bulwer-Lytton page, below the text Send us e-mail!.

Click the Insert Image button to open a dialog box where you can choose an image to display on the page. Choose the file chpmade.gif from the Webwork\Stormy\images folder and it will appear on the page. This is a "Made with Claris Home Page" graphic for use on any Web pages you design with the software. If the image isn't centered, highlight it and click the Align Text Center button on the toolbar.

Click the "Made with Claris Home Page" image once so that a border appears around it. To attach a link to this image, click the Link Editor tool or use the Insert | Link to URL menu option.

Enter the following Web page address for the link:

http://www.claris.com/support/products/clarispage/

A border will appear around the image, indicating that it's a link. If you preview the Web page in a browser and click the image, you'll be taken to the official page for users of Claris Home Page.

If you would like the image to appear without any kind of border or with a larger border, choose the Object Editor tool while the image is highlighted. In the Basic and Both tabs of the dialog box, you get a chance to set the border width in pixels. You can select either of the tabs to make a change.

By default, this field is blank, which makes a standard border appear around the image. Experiment with this field by changing the border width to 0 pixels, which removes the border entirely, or changing it to 10 pixels, which adds a thicker border than the standard one.

Lining Up Images and Text

The images that you have added up to this point are laid out in their own areas of the page. The image of Bulwer-Lytton with his head in the clouds is centered with no text to the left or right, and the same is true of the "Made with Claris Home Page" graphic.

You can also lay out images so that text appears to their left or right. For example, try adding a graphical flourish to the text—a big graphical *W* to replace the letter *W* that starts off the page's text.

In the text Welcome to the home page, place the cursor to the left of the letter *W* in the word *Welcome* and click the Insert Image button. Choose the graphics file w.gif from the Webwork\Stormy\images folder. An ornate black *W* will appear on the page, so you should delete the first *W* in the text—otherwise, you'll be "wwelcoming" people to the page.

CAUTION

Unlike most aspects of Home Page, text lined up with images isn't always displayed in Home Page the same way it shows up on a Web browser. The Lite version of the software doesn't have all the features of the full version, and lining up text with images is one of the differences between the two. For this section, use the Preview in Browser tool to see what a page will look like in a browser.

After you add the W graphic, it will be displayed with the bottom of the image aligned close to the bottom of the text. Figure 4.6 shows what this alignment looks like in the Internet Explorer browser.

Figure 4.6.

Displaying an image alongside text on a page.

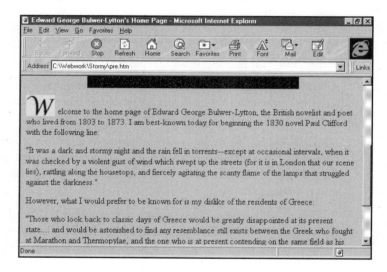

You can modify the alignment of the text around the image by using the Object Editor tool. Select the W graphic, choose the Object Editor tool, and go to the Basic tab of the dialog box. One of the options in this box is changing the alignment, which currently shows a value of `Bottom`. Other options are `Top`, `Middle`, `Left`, and `Right`.

JUST A MINUTE

While you're using the Object Editor on the W graphic, set its Alt Label to `W`. If you don't, people who don't see the images on this page will be "elcomed" to the Edward George Bulwer-Lytton home page instead of "welcomed." You should be more hospitable to people whose browsers aren't as cool as yours.

4

The first two values, Top and Middle, work best when there's only one line of text to the right or left of the image. Top alignment causes the top of the image to be aligned with the top of the text alongside it, and Middle causes the image to be aligned with the center of the text.

Because the text you're placing the graphic next to is more than one paragraph in length, the two best options to choose from are Left and Right. Right alignment causes the graphic to appear along the right edge of the page and the text appears around it to the left. Figure 4.7 shows what the W graphic looks like in the Internet Explorer browser with Right alignment selected.

Figure 4.7.

Displaying an image aligned to the right of text.

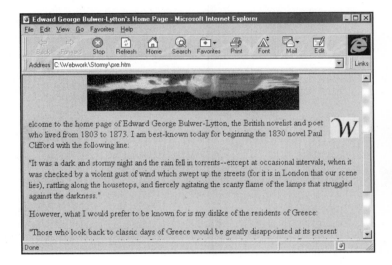

Detail-oriented readers might question whether it makes sense to put a big *W* to the right of the text, when it was intended to be used as part of the word *Welcome*. This is an intentional gaffe to show the Right alignment option in action.

COFFEE BREAK

This is the only intentional error in the book, but there might be some unintentional ones to keep it company. Detail-oriented readers who find those gaffes are encouraged to send e-mail to the author at home24@prefect.com and visit the book's corrections and clarifications page at http://www.prefect.com/home24/errata.html.

Perhaps the best way to display the W graphic is to use the Left alignment choice. Select it, and preview the page in a Web browser. Figure 4.8 shows the result.

Figure 4.8.

*Displaying an image
aligned to the left of text.*

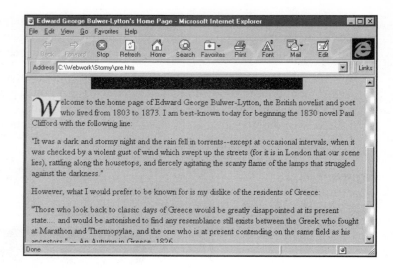

Considering the Size of Images

When you're putting images on a Web page, keep in mind the amount of time they'll take to view. As you have probably noticed when surfing the Web, image-packed pages can take a while to load (especially if your definition of "while" is "six minutes less than forever"). Staring at a blank screen while you wait for a page to finish loading makes Amish life look better and better.

Home Page has a feature that makes it easier to determine whether your page has too many images on it. Choose the Edit | Document Statistics menu option, and you'll see a report estimating how long your page will take to load. You can also choose specific elements of a page to check their loading times.

These figures are estimates of the minimum amount of time the page will take for people with Internet connections at the 14,400-baud and 28,800-baud speeds. Although some people are using faster Internet connections, the majority of today's Web users can't connect faster than 28,800 baud. If your page takes several minutes to load under a best-case scenario, you might want to consider using fewer images.

You can also shrink an image or use JPEG files instead of GIF files because they take up less file space. The cover.gif file on the Bulwer-Lytton page is 45K in size, and it's the main reason the page takes 31 seconds to load.

A JPEG file of the same Bulwer-Lytton image could be as small as 6K in size, but you'd lose a lot of image quality. If you'd like to see whether the tradeoff is worth it, copy the file cover.jpg from the Resource folder where you retrieved the other images at the beginning of this hour. Put cover.jpg in the Webwork\Stormy\images folder. From within the Home Page editor, delete the cover.gif image to make room for cover.jpg in its place (don't delete the actual file—just the element on the Web page you're editing). Use the Insert Image tool to put cover.jpg on the page.

JUST A MINUTE

When you choose the Insert Image tool, a dialog box opens where you can select the image's filename. When you go to the images subfolder and don't see cover.jpg, you might think you copied it to the wrong folder earlier. Check the "Files of type" drop-down list at the bottom of the dialog box, and make sure it's set to JPEG File or All Files.

Using a JPEG file in this case changes the minimum 28,800-baud loading time from 31 seconds to 6 seconds—a sizable difference. There's always some loss in image quality, which will be especially acute in this example if your monitor is set to display more than 256 colors.

The general rule of thumb for graphics on the Web is this: GIF files are good for menus, logos, and other elements that have few colors, and JPEG files are good for photographs and other complicated images with a lot of different colors.

Summary

This hour was your first chance to work with the visual side of home page design. Adding images to the Bulwer-Lytton home page makes it look more like pages you see on the Web.

Images can add a lot to a Web page, especially if they convey some type of information that adds value to the rest of the content. It's debatable whether the "Edward in the Clouds with Storms" image adds much, but I worked a long time on it, and my sixth-grade teacher said I showed potential as an artist. That ought to count for something.

However, using images has a downside because they can take time to load on a page, as you learned at the end of the hour. You'll have to decide how many images to use, or whether to use them at all, when you're putting together your own home page.

Now that you've learned how to improve the image of your home page with graphics, you'll spend time during the next hour improving the look of text.

Q&A

Q **Can images be aligned along the right side of the page instead of being centered or aligned along the left?**

A In addition to the Align Text Center tool, which can be used for images as well as text, there are Align Text Left and Align Text Right tools. They have buttons alongside the Align Text Center button, and you can also use them with the Format|Alignment menu option.

Q **What determines the color of a border around an image that's being used as a link?**

A The color corresponds with the color of the text that's being used as a link. The colors are selected with the Document Options tool, and they change, depending on whether the link has been used previously.

Q **What programs can be used to scale an image to a different size?**

A Many image-editing programs are available that can change the size, or the format, of a graphic. The most popular one among Web developers is probably Adobe Photoshop, a tool for modifying photographic images and creating original graphics. Other programs include Micrografx Webtricity, Micrografx Picture Publisher, and Paint Shop Pro.

Q **Can a link include both an image and adjacent text?**

A Yes, it can—in many cases, it's good to include text along with a graphic so that everyone can make use of the link. If you'd like to try this, add a line of text below the "Made with Claris Home Page" graphic and give it the same text as the image. Highlight the image and the text together, and use the Link Editor to set the Web address the link should connect to.

Quiz

Test your knowledge of this hour by taking this brief three-question test.

Questions

1. What tool can be used to change the display area of an image?
   - (a) Link Editor
   - (b) Object Editor
   - (c) A socket wrench

2. What kinds of text are most suitable for use with the Top and Middle image alignment options?

    (a) Text that's no longer than a single line

    (b) Text that's longer than a single line

    (c) One- or two-word items

3. What type of graphics file is best to use when documenting Andre Agassi's bad hair decade?

    (a) GIF files

    (b) JPEG files

    (c) Bitmap files

Answers

1. b.

2. a. Text that's longer than a single line in length won't format well with the Top or Middle options.

3. b. Assuming that Andre's hair will be shown in photographs, JPEG is the best format to select. Pen-and-ink illustrations might work as GIF files.

Activities

The following activities are suggested to expand your knowledge of the subjects covered during this hour:

☐ If you have built your own home page, as recommended previously, find some of your favorite image files from your hard drive and use them to liven up your home page. If you don't have any handy, steal some from this book's Web site at http://www.prefect.com/home24. Windows 95 users can do this by clicking their right mouse buttons over an image while viewing it on the Web.

☐ Adventurous readers can find some images to play around with by using the File|Open Library menu option to view the library of clip art that's included with Home Page. The library is covered fully in Hour 13, "Using Material from Libraries," but you can experiment with it now fairly easily. The library has images you can drag-and-drop onto your own Web pages.

4

PART

II

Home Page Text and Color

Hour

Hour 5

Presenting Text in Different Ways

During the first year of the World Wide Web's existence, it was used primarily by the high-energy physics community. To keep up with the speedy pace of developments in that field, and other technical fields of study, Web founder Tim Berners-Lee wanted a way for information to travel around the world quickly.

The Web initially focused on the information being communicated, not on the way the information looked. During this hour, you'll learn some of the techniques created to present textual information on the Web. The following topics are covered:

- ☐ Using headings of different sizes
- ☐ Making text bold, italicized, or underlined
- ☐ Indenting text with the Blockquote feature
- ☐ Creating superscripts, subscripts, and other unusual text
- ☐ Marking text as an address

Focusing on the Content

When you created the text of the Bulwer-Lytton home page, you entered several paragraphs describing the page and quoting from the author's books. That text was relatively short and easy to read, but viewing a page becomes more difficult if there's a lot of text.

The most common way to break up a long textual piece into digestible chunks is through headings. *Headings* are the equivalent of headlines on a newspaper, and you can use six different sizes of headings on a Web page.

In Claris Home Page 2.0 Lite, you use headings through the Format menu. To get ready to try it out, create a new subfolder of Webwork called Text, and run Home Page. Then create a new document in Home Page, and enter the text of Listing 5.1.

TYPE   **Listing 5.1. The text of index.html.**

```
1: Rogers Cadenhead: His Life and Times¶
2: Part 1: Oops! The Story of My Birth¶
3: Chapter 1: Everything I Am I Owe to Schlitz Malt Liquor¶
4: Chapter 2: "Are Babies Supposed to Look Like That?"¶
5: Section 2-1: Born to Belch¶
6: Section 2-2: The Only Toddler in Rehab¶
```

The text of this page can be compared to a table of contents in a book because it indicates the different sections that represent a Web site called Rogers Cadenhead: His Life and Times.

It's a bit difficult to determine how the text is organized, but it should be more clear with some of the lines indented, as follows:

```
Rogers Cadenhead: His Life and Times¶
                Part 1: Oops! The Story of My Birth¶
                        Chapter 1: Everything I Am I Owe to Schlitz Malt Liquor¶
                        Chapter 2: "Are Babies Supposed to Look Like That?"¶
                                Section 2-1: Born to Belch¶
                                Section 2-2: The Only Toddler in Rehab¶
```

You can use headings as a visual cue about the structure of this outline. Highlight the first line, Rogers Cadenhead: His Life and Times. This is the title of the Web site, so it's fitting to give it the largest possible heading. Do this by choosing the Format|Heading 1 menu option. When you make this change, it's reflected immediately in the Home Page editing window, and the text will be larger and bolder.

Headings are numbered from 1 to 6, with 1 being the largest and 6 the smallest. Highlight the second line of text, Part 1: Oops! The Story of My Birth, and make it a Heading 2 size. The text will be slightly smaller than the heading above it.

5

The next two lines of text are chapter headings for chapters 1 and 2, which are included in part 1. Highlight these two lines and make them a Heading 3 size. The final text to format is the section headings 2-1 and 2-2. Highlight those two headings and make them a Heading 4 size.

Save this page as index.html in the Webwork\Text folder, giving it the title Headings. Then take a look at this page with your preferred Web browser by clicking the Preview in Browser button. The different headings give you a visual cue to the hierarchy of headings on the page. Figure 5.1 shows what these headings look like with the AOL Web browser.

Figure 5.1.
The index.html Web page displayed with AOL's browser.

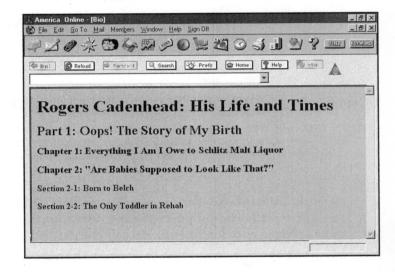

Headings are a good way to break up a page that has a lot of text on it, and they can also be used to better organize the document.

If you decide to change text from a heading back into normal text, you can choose Format|Normal from the menu.

Bold, Italicized, and Underlined Text

With Home Page, you can emphasize specific words and phrases by using some features common to word processing software: bold, italicized, and underlined text.

To see how these features work, start a new document in Home Page and enter the following text:

```
I only drove the car. I was cleaning the gun when it went
off. I didn't inhale. It's not my fault; I was bottle-fed.¶
```

This will give you some text to experiment with. You can make text bold, italicized, or underlined by choosing options from the Style menu. For bold and italicized text, you can also click buttons on the Home Page toolbar. The Bold and Italic buttons are shown in Figure 5.2.

Figure 5.2.

The Bold and Italic buttons on the main Home Page toolbar.

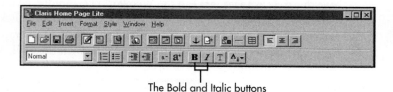

The Bold and Italic buttons

CAUTION

When underlining text, it's important to note that text links are automatically underlined with most Web browsers. Although links are usually a different color than the surrounding text, in many cases people visiting your page see underlined text and expect it to be a link. In the example you're working on now, the text I didn't inhale. might frustrate visitors who expect it to link to another page on the Web. Because of this confusion, many home page developers don't use underlined text.

Highlight the text drove the car and click the Bold button, and then italicize the text cleaning the gun. Highlight the sentence I didn't inhale. and use the Style|Underline menu option to underline it.

Take a look at this page with a Web browser, using Home Page's Preview in Browser feature. You can mix-and-match these features, so text can be both bold and underlined, for example, or bold and italicized.

Other Ways to Emphasize Text

There's another way to call attention to text on a Web page besides bold, italics, and underlining features. If you choose Style|Other|Emphasis from the menu, that option places an emphasis on the text. If you choose the Style|Other|Strong menu option, that tells a Web browser to place a strong emphasis on the text. Browsers define how text should be emphasized and what a strong emphasis should look like.

With the current versions of the Netscape Navigator, Microsoft Internet Explorer, and America Online browsers, a strong emphasis is shown by displaying bold text, and an emphasis is shown with italicized text.

The Strong and Emphasis formatting commands aren't used often on Web pages because you get the same result with the Bold and Italics features, respectively, and the latter commands are easier to remember. Strong and Emphasis are consistent with one of the original goals of the Web: The information being displayed was much more important than what it looked like. As the Web has become more design-oriented, most page designers are choosing Bold and Italics to specify exactly what they want text to look like when it's emphasized.

Superscripts, Subscripts, and Strikethrough Text

Three other features you can use for text are superscripts, subscripts, and strikethrough text, all of which are available from the Style menu.

Superscript is text that's slightly raised above a line, such as what you use for an exponential number. *Subscript* is the opposite—text that's slightly lowered from the rest of a line, which is used often by chemistry students and mad scientists (which might be a little redundant). Return to the sample page you've been working on, and add a new line at the bottom with the following text exactly as shown:

```
E = mc2. Choosy mothers choose JifThorium230.¶
```

After typing in this text, highlight the 2 in the text mc2. Choose the Style | Superscript menu option, and the number *2* will appear slightly above the rest of the text on that line.

Next, highlight the text Jif and choose Style | Strikethrough from the menu. The text will be shown with a line crossing through it, as though you're correcting an error.

Finally, highlight the text 230 and choose Style | Subscript. This option causes the selected text to appear below the rest of the line.

Save the page with the title Features and the filename features.html in the folder Webwork\Text. Figure 5.3 shows the Web page displayed with Microsoft Internet Explorer.

5

Figure 5.3.

The features.html page shown in Internet Explorer.

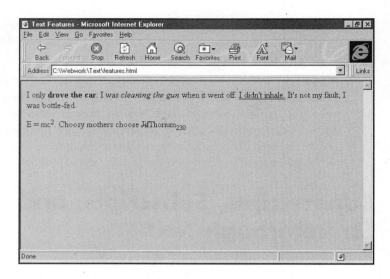

Other Unusual Formatting Choices

Several other types of formatting can be applied to text by using Home Page; many of them are duplicated by the options you already know about, and others are rarely used.

The following choices are also available under the Style menu of Home Page or the Style | Other menu option:

- ☐ **Teletype:** A monospace font similar to one a typewriter can produce; it's sometimes used for computer code listings and other technical information. Sample, Keyboard, and Code also look the same as Teletype on a Web page.

- ☐ **Citation:** A citation attributing the source for information, as seen in an academic paper or similar scholarly project. Most Web browsers italicize a citation the same way other text is italicized.

- ☐ **Inserted and Deleted:** These two formatting choices aren't supported by current versions of the Microsoft Internet Explorer, Netscape Navigator, or AOL browsers. You can see in Home Page that they function identically to Underline and Strikethrough, respectively, so use those formatting styles instead.

- ☐ **Raw HTML:** This style is used for HTML formatting tags in a Web page, which is described during Hour 12, "Experimenting with HTML Commands."

Another formatting option doesn't display text any differently. Instead, the Style | Reset menu option removes all other formatting from text. Because you can combine several different types of formatting at one time, using the Reset option is faster than removing each type of formatting individually.

5

Indented Text and Other Formatting

The last project during this hour demonstrates three more text formatting commands: block quotations, addresses, and preformatted text.

Create a new page in Home Page, and enter the text of Listing 5.2.

TYPE   **Listing 5.2. The text of fullpage.html.**

```
 1: "Anyone who has lost track of time when using a computer knows
 2: the propensity to dream, the urge to make dreams come true,
 3: and the tendency to miss lunch." -- Tim Berners-Lee¶
 4: The World Wide Web is a great way to look busy at your
 5: deskget work done. One of the reasons for its success
 6: is how easy it is to create Web pages. Originally, pages
 7: were created using HTML tags such as the following:¶
 8: <B>70 percent of the Earth is covered with
 9: H<SUBSCRIPT>2</SUBSCRIPT>O</B>¶
10: On a Web page, this line looks like the following:¶
11: 70 percent of the Earth is covered with H2O¶
12: Rogers Cadenhead <home24@prefect.com>¶
```

Save this page in the Webwork\Text folder with the title The Web and the filename fullpage.html.

The first feature you'll use on the page is Blockquote formatting, which is used when you'd like to set a long quotation off from the rest of text by indenting it on both sides. It's also used on Web pages any time you want to push the margins of text inward.

Highlight lines 1 to 3 of Listing 5.2, the quote about the computer by Tim Berners-Lee. To indent this text with the Blockquote command, choose the Format|Blockquote menu option. You can also make use of the Blockquote feature with the Indent and Outdent buttons, shown in Figure 5.4.

You can use either the Format|Blockquote menu option or the Indent button to push the margins of text away from the left and right edges of the page. You can do this more than once, making the width of the selected text narrower each time.

To remove the indentation, or make the text less indented, just click the Outdent button.

JUST A MINUTE   As you will see during Hour 7, "Dressing Up Your Page with Color," you can use the Blockquote feature with a background image. You can indent text and then put a graphical column on the right and left edges of the page.

Figure 5.4.

The Indent and Outdent buttons on the main Home Page toolbar.

The Indent and Outdent buttons

Preformatted Text

By now, you might have discovered that you don't have precise control over how Web pages are laid out. Although different Web browsers handle pages a bit differently, in general they all put blank lines between paragraphs, start new paragraphs at the left margin, and remove more than one blank space or blank line in a row.

If you want to make sure that text on a page will appear exactly the way you typed it, you can designate the text as *preformatted*. Lines 8–9 of Listing 5.2 show an example of HTML tags being used on a Web page. You can use them to preformat your text; simply highlight the text and choose the Format | Preformatted menu option.

This menu option makes the text appear in a different size. Unlike other text in the Home Page editing window, the preformatted line doesn't wrap around—text extends beyond the right margin of the page. That happens when the page is displayed in a Web browser, too, if the browser window isn't wide enough.

JUST A MINUTE

You'll see during the next hour, "Resizing Text and Using Fonts," how to change the size of text. You could use this feature to shrink the size of preformatted text, minimizing the chance that it will extend beyond the right margin of a Web browser window.

Other Changes

As stated previously, you can apply more than one formatting command to text. To see this technique in action, highlight Line 11 of Listing 5.2, `70 percent of the Earth is covered with H2O`, and make it boldface text. Next, highlight the `2` in `H2O`, and make it subscript text with the Style | Subscript menu option. The 2 is then displayed as bold, subscripted text.

Another formatting command is used to denote the part of a Web page that's an address. In this case, Line 12 of Listing 5.2 shows the name and e-mail address of this page's creator: `Rogers Cadenhead <home24@prefect.com>`. Highlight this text and use the Format | Address menu option.

5

With most Web browsers, text that has been identified as an address is italicized. You could also italicize it directly. It has become standard practice on Web pages to provide an e-mail address, and sometimes a name, of the person in charge of updating the page.

JUST A MINUTE

Because you're using a name and e-mail address, you also should make this text into a Mailto link, as you learned during Hour 3, "Adding Links to Other Pages." Highlight the name and address and click the Link Editor button or choose Insert | Link to URL from the menu to add a link to the text. Enter the following as the link: `mailto:home24@prefect.com`. With any browser that can handle a Mailto link, clicking this text begins an e-mail letter addressed to `home24@prefect.com`.

As the finishing touch on the page, highlight the text `look busy at your desk` and mark it as strikethrough text. Figure 5.5 shows what the page looks like when you preview it with a Web browser.

Figure 5.5.

The fullpage.html page with AOL's browser.

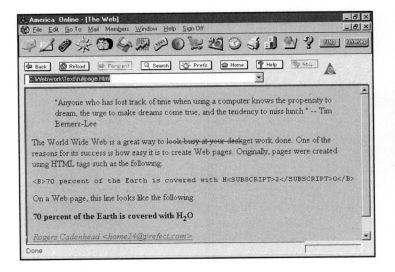

Summary

Using headings and changing the formatting of text make a page more readable, especially if the page has a lot of textual information. They're also used to make a page more visually appealing.

As you create some of your own pages and experiment with these features of Web page design, you'll get a feel for how much special formatting and how many headings to use.

Q&A

Q Does text that includes HTML commands such as `Party on, <B>Garth</B>`! require the use of preformatting to prevent the HTML tags from actually being displayed?

A Home Page prevents any HTML tags from being turned into HTML, so you can use the open bracket < and close bracket > signs without worrying that they'll change the way the page is displayed. Preformatting is more commonly needed with HTML editors that let you use HTML tags as you're editing a page.

Q Why can't I make a heading bold?

A Headings are automatically displayed in bold in the most popular browsers, so you can't modify that feature in Home Page with the Bold button or a menu option. You can use italics, underlining, and other formatting with headings, however.

Q Is there a limit to the number of times text can be indented?

A There's no restriction to clicking the Indent button a dozen times or more, but with most text you'll reach a point where only one character is displayed on each line. Because Web pages are displayed at different sizes on different computer systems, there's no specific rule for the maximum number of times text can be effectively indented. It's probably best not to do it more than three or four times.

Q Is there a way to use superscripts or subscripts on a line without affecting the vertical space between lines of text?

A Unfortunately, Web browsers can't handle superscripts or subscripts without creating an uneven amount of spacing between two lines of text. To see what this spacing looks like, load the fullpage.html page in Home Page and change the word success into subscript text. The amount of space above and below that line will look unbalanced. The only way to minimize that look is to use superscripts and subscripts only on paragraphs that aren't more than one line.

Quiz

Test your knowledge of this hour by taking this brief three-question test.

5

Questions

1. Which element of a Web page is a good way to break up a text-heavy document?

   (a) Italicized text

   (b) Preformatted text

   (c) Headings

2. With most Web browsers, Strong formatting is equivalent to what other type of text formatting?

   (a) Italicized text

   (b) Bold text

   (c) Underlined text

3. Which group of researchers were the first to stake a claim to the World Wide Web?

   (a) Non-stick deodorant developers

   (b) High-energy physicists

   (c) Sabrematricians

Answers

1. c.

2. b.

3. b. If the sabrematricians had been there first, we'd be drowning in statistics about nineteenth-century baseball players, the death of the drag bunt, and the ratio of sock height to slugging percentage.

Activities

The following activities are suggested to expand your knowledge of the subjects covered during this hour:

☐ Create a page for your own home page with some of your favorite quotations, and make sure to put your e-mail address and name at the bottom of the page. Use the formatting covered during this hour and the Mailto link.

☐ Use the formatting options covered during this hour on Edward George Bulwer-Lytton's main page, index.html in the Webwork\Stormy folder. Indent the quotations from Bulwer-Lytton's books, italicize his book titles, and make Edward's name boldfaced.

5

Hour 6

Resizing Text and Using Fonts

The techniques taught during the past hour are the most common ways to modify text on the Web. They are standard parts of Web design, and some of the techniques were intended to identify the type of information being formatted. For example, the Blockquote formatting option can set aside a block quotation, and the Address option can indicate a Web page publisher's e-mail address. Today, you'll focus on what the text looks like, learning how to change the size of text and the font it's displayed with.

These features aren't as widely available to Web surfers as Hour 5's techniques, but they're becoming more commonplace as users adopt browsers such as Netscape Navigator and Microsoft Internet Explorer. The following topics are discussed during this hour:

☐ Making text larger and smaller

☐ Using different text sizes to organize a page

☐ Learning which browsers support text resizing

☐ Using different fonts for text

☐ Considering compatibility issues

Changing the Size of Text

One of the ways to differentiate your Web pages from many others on the Internet is to alter the text size. You might do this to call attention to text, as when presenting a news article with its first paragraph enlarged for emphasis. You might also change text size to call attention away from text, as in the long legal disclaimers included with any consumer product ("Manufacturer not responsible for any accidental death, dismemberment, or other unpleasant occurrence that may result from use of product. This includes, but is not limited to, being dissolved into a cloud of noxious vapor.").

In Claris Home Page 2.0 Lite, you use the Style | Size menu option to set the text size. You have seven possible sizes to choose from, ranked from 1 for the smallest size to 7 for the largest.

These numbers, however, aren't associated with a specific, physical size—as you might be accustomed to with word processing software, where text can be set to a point size. Instead, the numbers are used to determine how much bigger or smaller text should be than the default size, which is 3. Figure 6.1 shows the seven text sizes in a Web browser. They look similar in Home Page's editing window.

Figure 6.1.

The seven possible font sizes in Netscape Navigator 3.01.

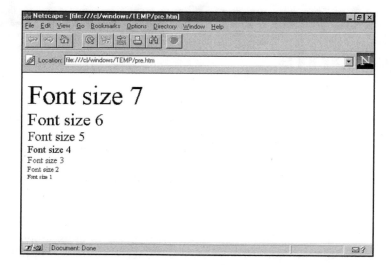

A Working Sample

To get ready for your first project of the hour, go to the Webwork folder on your system and create a new subfolder called "Eod." After running Home Page, create a new document that will be used to show the different text sizes. Enter the text of Listing 6.1 into the document, and save it with the filename `index.html` in the directory Webwork\Eod. When Home Page asks what title to give the document, enter the text An Entirely Other Day. This Web page will use text sizes to distinguish parts of the document from each other.

Listing 6.1. The full text of index.html.

```
 1: Thanks for Sharing¶
 2: November 22nd, 1996¶
 3: So it's late -- or, rather, it's eight-thirty, which we've begun
 4: to consider late -- and Joanne and I are out doing our
 5: demographically responsible duty and going to see a movie. On
 6: the way, we pass a man driving a car with a customized license
 7: plate.¶
 8: "I FX DKS" it says.¶
 9: And, of course, we figure he's a waterfowl veterinarian.¶
10: This excerpt is adapted from An Entirely Other Site, the Web musings of
11: Greg Knauss. Visit it at http://www.eod.com.¶
```

COFFEE BREAK

As stated in the listing, this page's text is adapted from the Web site An Entirely Other Day at http://www.eod.com. Greg Knauss is using his strand of the Web to share humorous asides and other vignettes from his daily life. It's a great example of the kind of intriguing oddness that could exist only on the World Wide Web.

Before changing any of the text of the page, make the top line of the document into a heading. Highlight the text Thanks for Sharing and choose the Format | Heading 1 menu option.

Next, highlight the last paragraph, which begins with the text This excerpt is adapted from. Use the Style | Size menu to set the paragraph text to 1, the smallest possible size.

Then, highlight the date November 22, 1996 and set it to size 2. While it's still highlighted, use the Style | Italic menu option to make the text italic.

The final change to the text size is to the text I FX DKS. Because it's the tag of a license plate and the focus of the vignette, it makes sense to call attention to it.

Instead of using the Style | Size menu, you'll use a button on the Home Page toolbar to modify the text size. Figure 6.2 shows the Smaller Text and Larger Text buttons.

6

Figure 6.2.

The Smaller Text and
Larger Text buttons on
the main Home Page
toolbar.

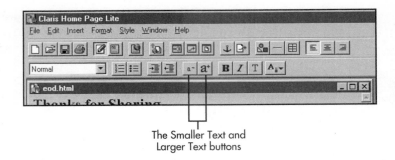

The Smaller Text and
Larger Text buttons

Highlight the text I FX DKS and use the Smaller Text and Larger Text buttons to cycle through the possible sizes. Each button affects the size by 1, and you start from the default size of 3. Change the text to a size of 5, which is about the same size as the heading "Thanks for Sharing."

To make the last change on the page, you ought to turn the text http://www.eod.com into a link to that Web page.

TIME SAVER

Home Page supports the Copy, Cut, and Paste features you might be familiar with from other programs. Turning the URL into a link can be speeded up by using Ctrl+C to copy http://www.eod.com to the Clipboard and Ctrl+V to paste the Clipboard text into the Link Editor's URL field.

Some of the changes you have made to this page aren't as evident in Home Page as they would be in a Web browser, so use the Preview in Browser feature to see what the page looks like with your preferred browser. Figure 6.3 shows the finished product in Navigator 3.01.

Side-Effects of Text Resizing

Although changing the size of text can be a useful tool, you need to keep some things in mind when you're using this feature on your own Web pages.

The most important issue is whether Web surfers will benefit from your toil. Resizing text makes use of an advanced HTML tag that became implemented with Web browsers in the past two years. It's fully supported by current versions of Microsoft Internet Explorer, Netscape Navigator, and America Online's built-in browser, and both Internet Explorer and Navigator have supported it for more than a year.

Figure 6.3.

A preview of index.html in Netscape Navigator 3.01.

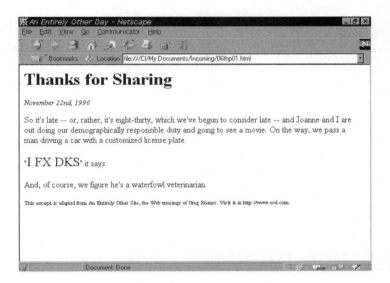

Current statistics show that up to 90 percent of Web surfers are using versions of the Big Two—Internet Explorer and Navigator—so it's likely that people who visit your page can see size changes in text. However, users with non-graphical browsers, such as Lynx and older software, will see all the text at the same uniform size. In the case of Thanks for Sharing, that shouldn't make too much of a difference. Figure 6.4 shows this page with a version of Lynx.

Figure 6.4.

The index.html page in Lynx 2.7 for Windows 95 and NT users.

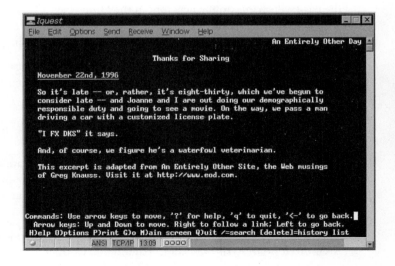

Where to Use Resizing

Avoid resizing text within long paragraphs and as a substitute for headings. For example, when you resize a few words in a paragraph that's more than a line long, the spacing between lines is affected—the line with the resized text takes up a different amount of vertical space than the other lines do. To see this, enlarge the text `demographically responsible` in index.html to size 5, and take a look at it with a Web browser.

Resized text can be as large—or larger—than headings, so you might be tempted to use it for a headline instead of one of the headings. You should avoid doing that, however, because headings are a feature that's universally supported on Web browsers. Also, some search engines that index Web pages consider headings to be more important than text when a Web surfer is looking for pages. If those headings were replaced with resized text, the search engine's database wouldn't consider anything on the page to be a headline.

Using Different Fonts

A new and somewhat controversial feature of Web page design is the ability to use different fonts. With Home Page, you can change text and headings to any font that's installed on your system.

Try this out on the Web page you've worked on so far during the hour. Highlight the entire page—a quick way to do this is to press Ctrl+A while your cursor is anywhere on the document. To change the font, choose the Style | Font menu option and a list of fonts on your system will be shown. Choose Courier New or Courier, if they're available. The text of the page will change to the new font in the Home Page editor, and you can also see it when you preview the page with a browser. Figure 6.5 shows the result in a Web browser using Internet Explorer and a system with the Courier New font installed.

Anyone who has the same font installed on his or her system can see the page the way you've designed it. Others see the page with the default font for their browsers.

Because the page can be viewed by Web surfers in either case, you can experiment with different fonts on your pages. However, the difficulty is finding fonts that are likely to be on enough systems to make it worthwhile to use them.

Versions of the Helvetica, Courier, and Times Roman fonts are available on most computer systems used to surf the Web, but they often have slightly different names on different systems. The fonts you use on a page must have exactly the same name as a user's font to be seen.

Microsoft lists the following fonts as being common to all Windows 95, NT, and 3.1 systems: Arial, Arial Bold, Arial Bold Italic, Arial Italic, Courier New, Courier New Bold, Courier New Bold Italic, Courier New Italic, Times New Roman, Times New Roman Bold, Times New Roman Bold Italic, Symbol, and Wingdings.

6

Figure 6.5.

The index.html page displayed with a different font.

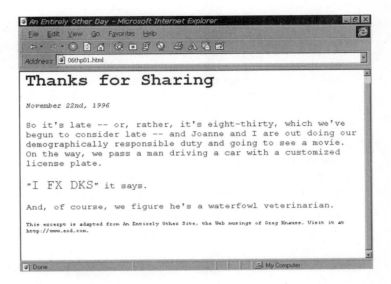

Macintosh System 7 users should have the following fonts on their systems: Courier Regular, Courier Regular Bold, Courier Regular Bold Oblique, Courier Regular Oblique, Helvetica Regular, Helvetica Regular Bold, Helvetica Regular Bold Oblique, Helvetica Regular Oblique, Symbol, Times Roman, Times Roman Bold, Times Roman Bold Italic, and Times Roman Italic.

Microsoft, which introduced the use of fonts in Web browsers, is trying to expand the number of universal fonts that can be used. Versions 3 and higher of Microsoft Internet Explorer supply the following fonts: Arial Black, Comic Sans MS, Comic Sans MS Bold, Impact, Verdana, Verdana Bold, Verdana Bold Italic, and Verdana Italic. These fonts are also available for free download at the following Web page:

```
http://www.microsoft.com/truetype/fontpack/
```

If the font you've selected isn't available, a substitute can be selected on the user's system—usually the default font.

JUST A MINUTE

The controversy over using different fonts is that it prevents users from selecting their own. When Web browsers could display text in only a single font, some browsers offered the option of choosing a different default font to improve pages' readability. Selecting your own font for a page overrides the user's ability to do so, which causes some Web designers to call for using the default font only.

Specifying More than One Font

To increase your odds of finding a workable font, you can specify more than one font when changing text by using the Style | Font | Other menu option. Try using this option on the index.html Web page after highlighting the entire page. A dialog box opens, where you can enter a list of font names, separated by commas. Enter the following:

```
Arial, Helvetica, helvetica
```

This entry specifies the list of fonts to choose from when the page is loaded in a browser. The first available font on the list is used, and you can specify as many as you want. If the first font isn't available, the second is used if it's found on the Web surfer's system, and so on—until a match is found or there are no more fonts in the list to look for.

For users who can see different fonts on their Web browsers, it's another way to call attention to the page. Figure 6.6 shows the index.html page with Verdana text and an Impact heading.

Figure 6.6.

Using different fonts on a page in Netscape Navigator 3.01.

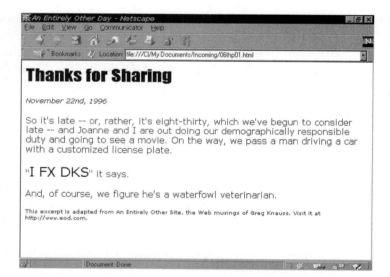

Summary

Resizing text and changing its font bring some of the features of printed documents to Web pages. Font changes represent a departure from the way text has been presented on the Web. Instead of focusing on what the text is—such as a code example, a quotation, or an address—they're based entirely on looks.

If you're not worried about creating a vain home page, you can use Home Page to present text with some visual panache.

Q&A

Q If there's an unusual font I'd like to use on a page, is there a way to make it available?

A Some Web designers are encouraging visitors to download special fonts that are used on a page, which you can do if you have the license to make the font available. However, many Web surfers would find the download a cumbersome request just to see a Web site and would ignore it or skip the page entirely. As an alternative, you could create a graphics file of the special font and offer the text that way. The disadvantage to this method is that there's no way to provide anything other than an Alt Label as an alternative, and the graphic text won't be considered part of the page's text.

Q What font is available if I need the text to be of a fixed width?

A Variations of the Courier font are the best bet when you're looking for a fixed-width font. If you want to accommodate as many visitors as possible, use the Style | Font | Other feature and specify the fonts as `Courier New, Courier Regular, courier`.

Q How can I change the default font used with my Web browser?

A Using a current version of Microsoft Internet Explorer, choose the View | Options menu option and select the General tab of the dialog box. One of the buttons at the bottom of the box is Font Settings, and it can be used to select the default font and fixed-width fonts to use on Web pages. With Netscape Navigator, choose Options | General Preferences from the menu and select the Fonts tab of the dialog box. You can select both default and fixed-width fonts for this browser, too.

Q Is there a way to increase the size of a few words in a paragraph without altering the vertical spacing between lines?

A Spacing is going to be adversely affected by mixing different font sizes in a single paragraph. The line with the largest font will take up more space than other lines, and it will look a bit uneven. As a rule of thumb, you might want to use different-sized fonts only on short paragraphs that won't be displayed over several lines.

6

Quiz

Test your knowledge of this hour by taking this brief three-question test.

Questions

1. What's a quick way to highlight the entire contents of a Web page in Home Page?

   (a) Press the Home key.

   (b) Press Ctrl+A.

   (c) Click the right mouse button.

2. Which browser does not support the use of different fonts on a page?

   (a) Lynx

   (b) Microsoft Internet Explorer

   (c) America Online's browser

3. Which of the following is not a standard Microsoft Windows 95 font?

   (a) Courier New Bold Italic

   (b) Times New Roman Bold

   (c) Helvetica Old Bold Do Not Spindle Mutilate or Fold

Answers

1. b.

2. a. Lynx is a text-only browser, so it doesn't include support for any font selection.

3. c. What does "spindle" mean, anyway?

Activities

The following activities are suggested to expand your knowledge of the subjects covered during this hour:

☐ Visit Microsoft's Typography Web site, mentioned earlier in the hour, at the address http://www.microsoft.com/truetype/fontpack/. Read the pages related to "Typography on the Web" for tips on how to incorporate fonts into your Web pages and download and install the free fonts that are available.

☐ Getting back to your own home page, re-create the pages you have created so far with some common fonts. Be sure to specify more than one font for each choice, and use some different text sizes on the pages.

Hour **7**

Dressing Up Your Page with Color

There was once a time when humans and dogs could experience the World Wide Web on even footing (or should that be pawing?). The color-blind nature of canines wasn't a disadvantage when using a Web browser because the first pages could be shown in black, white, and various shades of gray without losing much.

However, there's a whole cornucopia of colors on display when you visit a Web page today. Using Claris Home Page 2.0 Lite, you can change the color of several elements of a Web page: the text, the links, and the background.

If you're not worried about alienating man's best friend, you can use this hour to learn about the following topics:

☐ Selecting a background color for a page

☐ Choosing the default color for text

☐ Selecting three colors for links

☐ Understanding the different types of links

☐ Choosing colors for selected text

A Colorful Lesson

To get ready for this hour's project, go to the Resource folder on the book's CD-ROM and copy the file planet.jpg into a new folder called Webwork\Space.

You will be creating a home page about astronomical information on the World Wide Web, and this spacebound image of Earth will be the central feature of your site.

Create a new document in Home Page, and insert an image onto the page. Select the planet.jpg image from the newly created Webwork\Space folder, and this large graphic will be displayed in the editing window. Center this graphic on the page by clicking once on the graphic and then clicking the Align Text Center button. Also, you might want to maximize the editing window so that there's more space to work on this page and its large graphic.

Selecting a Background Color

The image of Earth has a solid black background on all sides. You can take advantage of this attribute by making the page's background black, also.

You can set a page's background color with the same Home Page feature you use to change a page's title: Click the Document Options button on the Home Page toolbar or choose Edit | Document Options from the menu to open the Document Options dialog box.

One of the choices in this dialog box shows the label "Background" alongside a colored box. This box indicates the currently chosen background color, which will probably be the same light gray used as the dialog box's background.

COFFEE BREAK

> Before the use of background and text colors, the World Wide Web was a sea of black text on light gray pages. At the time of this writing, one of the only popular Web sites that doesn't impose a color choice on the Web surfer is Yahoo! Visit http://www.yahoo.com, and you'll see a page with the color designated by your browser as its background color. Most people see light gray.

To change the background color of this page, click the colored box next to the Background label. A dialog box opens, giving you 48 basic colors to choose from and 16 boxes for additional colors you can specify.

Figure 7.1 shows this dialog box in black and white, which is exactly how it would appear to dogs. When you're looking at the real thing in Home Page, you'll see each of the colors that can be immediately chosen as the page's background color.

7

Figure 7.1.
*Picking a color for
selected text.*

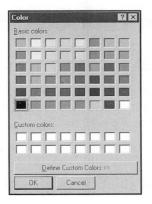

For this example, choose the solid black box and click OK. Click OK again to exit the Document Options dialog box and finalize the change.

When you return to the editing window, you won't be able to tell where the image ends and the rest of the page begins because the black background extends outward in all directions.

Selecting a Color for Text

You're now ready to add some text to the page underneath the image. Click the mouse anywhere on the Earth graphic and a border will appear, showing you the edges of the image. Click the mouse outside this border and the cursor should appear at the lower-right area of the image. Press Enter once and the cursor will move below the image so that you can begin entering the following text:

Web Sites That Leave the Wide World Behind

As you begin entering this text, you'll probably think that something is wrong. You can't see what you're typing! That's because the standard color for text in Home Page is black, and black text on a black background is, of course, impossible to see.

Return to the Document Options dialog box and click the colored box next to the Text label to choose a new default color for all text on the page. Select light blue as the color. When you exit the Document Options dialog box, you'll be able to see what you were trying to type.

Correct any typos so that the text correctly reads Web Sites That Leave the Wide World Behind. If it isn't already centered, center it and make it into a Heading 2 size by highlighting the line of text, clicking the Align Text Center button, and choosing the Format | Heading 2 menu option.

7

Choosing Link Colors

The remainder of this page will be a list of interesting astronomical sites on the Web. Each site listing will include a link, a short description, and a rating of 1 to 4 stars.

With your cursor below the heading you just created, click the Align Text Left button so that text is no longer centered. (You could also have used the Format | Alignment | Align Left menu option to align the text.)

Enter the text of Listing 7.1 onto the page.

Listing 7.1. The site listings to add to the page.

```
 1: The Hale-Bopp Home Page: Russell Sipe's extensive image-packed
 2: site about the comet. ***¶
 3: NASA: The space agency's official home page, updated regularly
 4: with news and images from current missions. ****¶
 5: Astronomy Magazine: A starting point for the magazine's readers
 6: and other astronomy buffs. **¶
 7: Babylon 5: The official Warner Bros. home page for the science
 8: fiction TV series and cult classic. ***¶
 9: Heaven's Gate: A copy of the San Diego cult's official site
10: detailing their UFO-based beliefs. *¶
```

Before making the title of each listing into a link, you should designate some colors to use for links. Links are the only element of a page that can readily change color.

Using the Document Options dialog box, you can choose colors for three types of links: normal links, visited links, and active links. Web browsers can keep track of the pages that have been visited recently, and this tracking determines whether a link is normal or visited. A *normal link* hasn't been loaded with the browser recently, and the opposite is true of a visited link.

JUST A MINUTE

> The amount of time a visited link still shows up as a visited link depends on the Web browser being used and how it's configured. By default, the current version of Netscape Navigator causes a visited link to expire after nine days, which makes it a normal link again. Internet Explorer visited links have a default of 20 days.

The first color to designate for this page is the normal link color. Select the color white.

The second color to choose is for visited links. Select the color dark green.

The final color for links is a bit of an odd one, because it's so infrequently seen during a Web surfing session. The active link color is shown for a brief moment after a link is selected, but before the browser loads the page associated with that link. Choose bright yellow as the color for active links.

Now that you have chosen all the default colors you can designate for a Web page, you're ready to turn some site titles into links. Add the following links to the page:

☐ The Hale-Bopp Home Page should link to http://www.halebopp.com.

☐ NASA should link to http://www.nasa.gov.

☐ Astronomy Magazine should link to http://www.astronomy.com.

☐ Babylon 5 should link to http://www.babylon5.com.

☐ Heaven's Gate should link to http://www.heavensgatetoo.com.

To make it a little easier to read these listings, highlight all five listings and indent the text twice.

Adding Colors to Selected Text

In addition to choosing a default color for all the text on a page, you can use different colors for selected text. Highlight the three-star rating for the Hale-Bopp Web site—the text *** at the end of the listing.

To choose a color other than light blue for this text, click the Text Color button from the Home Page toolbar, as shown in Figure 7.2, or choose Style | Color from the menu.

Figure 7.2.

Picking a color for selected text.

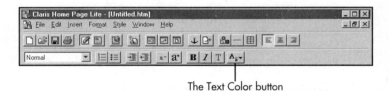

The Text Color button

When selecting a text color, you can choose from one of five set colors: red, blue, green, yellow, and black. You can also choose the default color for text that has been changed. If you want to select a different color from the ones normally available, you can choose the Other option to pick from the same colors that were available when designating background, default text, and link colors.

In this example, choose yellow as the color for the Hale-Bopp site's star rating. Change the asterisks for the other site ratings to yellow, also.

7

Now that you've completed all the work associated with this project, you're ready to take a look at the finished canvas. Save the page as `index.html` in the Webworks\Space folder and give it the title `Web Sites That Leave the Wide World Behind`. Figure 7.3 shows the page viewed with Netscape Navigator.

Figure 7.3.

The index.html page in Netscape Navigator.

One of the features you should experiment with on this page is the way the links change color. Be sure to watch for a link to be displayed briefly in yellow when you select it.

After experimenting with a page's link colors, you will quickly find yourself with nothing but visited links. However, you can tell the Netscape Navigator and Internet Explorer Web browsers to forget they have visited any pages on the Web. In Navigator, choose the Options | General Preferences menu option and click the Expire Now button. In Internet Explorer, choose View | Options | Navigation and click the Clear History button.

Defining Custom Colors

A wide spectrum of colors is available immediately by clicking Home Page's Text Color button and using the dialog box containing 48 colors. If none of these colors fits what you're trying to do with a Web page, you can define 16 additional colors in the color selection dialog box. They are called *custom colors*.

There's a huge number of color combinations you can use to fill these 16 custom colors—more than 16 million, in fact.

To see how custom colors are defined, click the Text Color button and select the Other option from the drop-down menu that appears. This choice opens the color selection dialog

7

box, showing 48 colors to select from, above a row of 16 custom color boxes. Unless you have already defined a custom color, all 16 of these boxes are white.

Click one of the custom color boxes, and a border appears around the box. To designate a color for the box you have selected, click the Define Custom Colors button. The dialog box will expand, as shown in Figure 7.4.

Figure 7.4.

The expanded color selection dialog box.

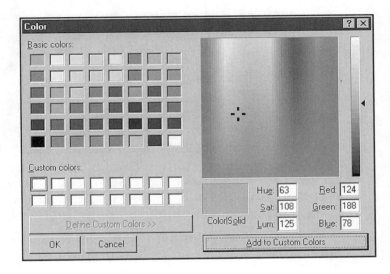

There are two ways you can use your mouse to select a color. The first way is to click your mouse somewhere inside the large multicolored square on the dialog box. A gunsight-style cursor (also called a *cross hair*) appears at the spot where you've clicked, and a box labeled Color | Solid is then updated in response to your choice. The Color|Solid box indicates what your custom color currently looks like.

Another part of the dialog box changes when you click in the multicolored square—a vertical bar along the right edge of the dialog box displays a range of similar colors based on your choice. This vertical bar determines the brightness of your custom color. Click the mouse anywhere on this bar, and the Color|Solid box changes to reflect the new brightness level.

Use the multicolored square and brightness bar to create a custom color that looks like a red piece of chalk—a faded color that's somewhere between white and light red. To do this, click the multicolored square in the upper-right corner, and click the brightness bar somewhere close to white at the top.

Figure 7.5 shows where the gunsight and brightness bar cursors can be placed to choose a chalky red color.

7

Figure 7.5.

Defining a custom color with the dialog box.

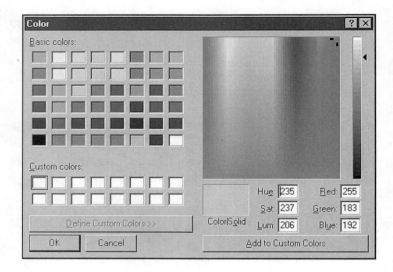

Click the Add to Custom Colors button to make this color one of your 16 custom colors. This choice will be saved so that you can use it any time you use the color selection dialog box in Home Page.

Another common way you can define a custom color is to use its RGB or HSB values. They're easier to understand if you know what the acronyms stand for—*HSB* is Hue, Saturation, and Brightness, and *RGB* is Red, Green, and Blue.

If you don't know a color's RGB or HSB values, you won't need to use this feature because you can select colors visually with your mouse. However, if you do know one of these values, you can enter it in the fields of the expanded color selection dialog box.

Click one of the empty custom color boxes so you can make it into a custom color. Enter the values of 255 in the Red field, 204 in the Green field, and 102 in the Blue field, then click the Add to Custom Colors button. You now have a butterscotch yellow that can be used on your Web pages.

Summary

As most non-canine readers can see, color is a way to increase the visual attractiveness of a Web page. It can also be used to call attention to specific parts of a page and improve the readability of text.

If you've spent some time surfing the Web, you also know that color can be a complete hindrance to a page's readability. You might need to use font sizes and other text changes, as well as colors, to create the most usable site for people who visit.

Q&A

Q **The color I want to use on a page isn't available. Is there a way I can use it?**

A In the Document Options dialog box where 48 colors can be selected, you can pick an alternative by clicking the Define Custom Color button. You can use the RGB values, if you know them, of the color you want, or choose a color manually by sliding a cursor around a swath of different colors and brightness levels.

Q **Is there a way I can find out the RGB or HSB values of a color I like on a Web page?**

A Most image-editing tools display the RGB or HSB value of a currently selected color, either as a range of 0 to 255 or a range of 0 to 100. Home Page uses a range of 0 to 255, so you might have to do a little math to convert the values. The Web page http://www.mhri.edu.au/~pdb/colour/RGBlist.html shows RGB values for several dozen colors, along with names that describe the colors, such as slate_blue, cobalt_green, and my personal favorite, papaya_whip.

Q **Are colors supported by all the popular browsers?**

A All the features described during this hour are supported by Netscape Navigator, Microsoft Internet Explorer, and America Online's built-in browser. Using colors raises some of the same issues as fonts for users who define their own colors to increase readability, so it's a question of deciding whether using color is worth the possibility that some visitors might not be able to use the site. It's standard on the Web to use colors for backgrounds, and colored text is being used with increasing frequency.

Q **Is there a way to create a multicolored background?**

A You can't create a multicolored background using the background color feature demonstrated during this hour, but you can create a graphics file that represents each of the colors you want to use in a background. That technique is covered during the next hour, "Putting Images Behind Your Pages."

Quiz

Test your knowledge of this hour by taking this brief three-question test.

Questions

1. Which of the following colors isn't available from the Style | Color menu?

   (a) Black

   (b) Orange

   (c) Red

7

2. Which of the link colors are you going to see the least often?

    (a) Visited links

    (b) Active links

    (c) Normal links

3. What percentage of American citizens is color-blind?

    (a) 1

    (b) 5

    (c) 25

Answers

1. b.

2. b. Active links are displayed only at the moment the link is selected, so they're the link least seen.

3. a.

Activities

The following activities are suggested to expand your knowledge of the subjects covered during this hour:

☐ Find some crayons, either by borrowing them from a child, raiding your own toy box, or visiting a restaurant that puts paper down so you can color on the tables. Pick a few of your favorites and try to re-create them as custom colors. Send e-mail to home24@prefect.com if you come up with a particularly fetching interpretation of burnt sienna.

☐ Take one of the pages you have already created and go nuts with colors, experimenting with different background and text color combinations. Also, try out the following effect: Make the visited link color the same as the background color.

Hour 8

Putting Images Behind Your Pages

During the past hour, you learned how to choose a background color for your page. However, many pages on the World Wide Web have more sophisticated backdrops for their content; to do this, you need to use background images.

Putting a graphic behind a Web page's text and images has become a standard feature supported by Web browsers, and it's a simple way to improve the look of your Web pages.

During this hour, you'll learn how background images are used in Claris Home Page 2.0 Lite, and also how they can be misused. The following topics are covered:

☐ Putting a background image on a page

☐ Understanding how background images are displayed

☐ Using a background tile effectively

☐ Making a page readable over backgrounds

☐ Using a vertical background image

☐ Creating an area for text over a background

Behind the Scenes

One of the most often used—and most often abused—features of the World Wide Web is the background graphic. Displaying a background image is a standard part of Web pages today, as well as a useful feature. A well-designed background graphic can organize a page and highlight specific sections, and it can also increase a page's visual appeal.

The drawback is that a misused or poorly designed background graphic can render a page unusable. Many pages on the Web today practically require the use of psychics to read. The text color and background color run together or clash with each other dramatically, which makes it hard for visitors to use the page.

Fortunately, it's easy to use background images successfully. You'll learn how to do so during this hour as you create pages that work with two different types of background graphics.

An Intricate Background

Create a new folder for your system called Webwork\Back to house all the Web pages and related files used during this hour. Go to the Resource folder on the book's CD-ROM and copy the following files into Webwork\Back: groovy.gif, herald.jpg, and city.gif.

You will be creating a Web page that uses a dark, intricate background graphic. This type of image gives you a chance to deal with some of the issues involved in using a complex graphic.

Create a new Web page in Home Page, and start off by defining the colors you will use for text and links. Using the Document Options dialog box, which is available as a button on the main Home Page toolbar, make the following changes to the colors for the page:

- ☐ Text: the brightest, most neon purple
- ☐ Normal link: light blue
- ☐ Visited link: bright green

After you've made those changes, enter the text of Listing 8.1 on the page.

Listing 8.1. The text of the Web page.

```
1: A ¦ n ¦ d ¦ I ¦ Q ¦ u ¦ o ¦ t ¦ e¶
2: "There's something to be said for the stress that makes us
3: all want to kill each other and make really cool web pages."¶
4: > R.U. Sirius, CTheory¶
```

8

After entering the text, highlight the line A ¦ n ¦ d ¦ I ¦ Q ¦ u ¦ o ¦ t ¦ e and change the color to white. While the text is still highlighted, change the size to a Heading 2.

Also, highlight all the text on the page and choose the Style | Font | Other menu option. A text field opens, where you can choose a new font for the page's text. Enter the following as the font value:

```
Verdana,Arial,Helvetica,Helvetica Regular,helvetica
```

This setting gives Web browsers a list of fonts to choose from when displaying the text. The first listed font that's available on a system is the one displayed, so Verdana is the most likely font to be shown on visitors' systems.

As the final changes to the text, highlight all the text from the first quotation mark to the end of the text. Set this text to size 4 by using the Style | Size menu option, and indent it five times with clicks of the Indent button.

Adding a Background

To add a background image to the page using Home Page, click the Document Options button or choose the Edit | Document Options menu item. You'll see the same dialog box used to set colors for the page.

To pick a graphics file to display as the background of the page, click the Set button next to the Background Image label. Go to the Webwork\Back folder and select the groovy.gif file as your background image.

After you click OK to exit the Document Options dialog box, the editing window is immediately updated with the image you've selected. You'll see a purple image that might be better described as a flashback instead of a background.

Background images are displayed underneath the text and graphics on a page. An image that's smaller than a Web page is repeated again and again underneath the page's text—this process is called *tiling*, because it's comparable to laying tiles on a kitchen floor.

Figure 8.1 shows the background image that you have put on this page (in black-and-white, unfortunately—color printing on this project wasn't possible because of cost overruns at Sams.net Publishing on the project *Teach Yourself to Save Money in 24 Hours*).

Save this page as index.html in the Webwork\Back folder, and give it the title And I Quote.

Figure 8.1.

The background image file groovy.gif.

COFFEE BREAK

This psychedelic graphic was designed by Jeffrey Zeldman, a Web developer and advertising writer who co-created the *Batman Forever* and *Batman & Robin* Web sites. Zeldman's home page at `http://www.zeldman.com` offers many resources for free use on your own pages, and it's also a great example of the kind of inspired lunacy possible on the Web.

Because an image is tiled over a page, you can create an intricate background image that loads quickly. The groovy.gif file is only 9K in size.

Making a Page Readable

You must also consider the readability of the page when you're using a background image. Text can be difficult to read over a dark or intricate background. As a Web surfer, you have probably wiped out on several pages that were impossible to look at because of mismatched text-and-background combinations.

Several choices make the current page legible over its background graphic, however. The following techniques were used:

☐ Bright colors were chosen for the text and links because dark colors would fade into the background.

☐ The fonts selected for the page are all sans-serif fonts, which generally are easier to read over a graphic.

☐ A larger heading and larger text size were used.

Figure 8.2 shows the result in the Microsoft Internet Explorer browser.

Figure 8.2.

The index.html page viewed in Internet Explorer.

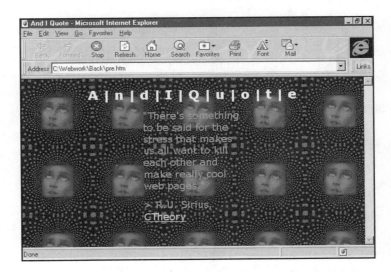

This example shows that you can take steps to make a complex background and text work together. An unusual background graphic is an attention-getting feature, especially when the image is displayed several times on a page.

Another Type of Background

As you have discovered with the first project of this hour, using a dark or intricate background can make it more challenging to create a page. For this reason, some Web page designers prefer to split the background into a vertical graphic and a plain single-colored area. Text and other elements on the page are placed over the single-colored area, which is much like using a background color for a page.

The vertical graphic can run along the left edge of a page, the right edge, or both. In your next project, you will be working with one of these vertical background images.

Create a new page in Home Page and start it off by inserting an image on the page (not as a background). Select the file herald.jpg from the Webwork\Back folder, and center the image on the page by selecting it and clicking the Align Text Center button.

When you're done, you'll see a picture of Herald Square, a New York City block around the *New York Herald* building. The cursor should be along the lower-right corner of the image. Use the Insert | Line Break menu option to send the cursor to a new line in the editing window.

JUST A MINUTE

> Depending on how your computer monitor is equipped to display colors, you might see orange speckles in the image of the city. These speckles don't show up when the page is previewed with a Web browser because Home Page doesn't have the same image-handling abilities that browsers do. Some problems you might see with an image in Home Page are caused by this difference. Always preview a Web page with a browser if you're confused by the appearance of an image within Home Page.

After the cursor is on a new line, enter the text of Listing 8.2 on the page.

Listing 8.2. Starting text for the page.

```
1: Herald Square, New York City, circa 1908¶
2: The New York Herald, which later became the Herald-Tribune,
3: is considered one of the great newspapers in U.S. history.
4: Founded by James Gordon Bennett in 1835, the Herald became
5: known for aggressively pursuing news stories. In 1869, the
6: Herald sent Henry Morton Stanley to Central Africa to find
7: the missionary David Livingstone, a hunt that captivated readers
8: around the globe for two years. The Herald-Tribune closed in
9: 1966.¶
```

Highlight Line 1 of this listing so you can make some formatting changes to it. Center this line of text with the Align Text Center button, make it italicized with the Italic button, and reduce the font size by 1 with the Smaller Text button.

Placing the Background

Now you're ready to add a background image to this page. Using the Document Options dialog box, click the Set button and select the file city.gif from the Webwork\Back folder. The background consists of a vertical picture of city buildings along the left edge of the page and solid white on the remainder of the background.

When you're using a background graphic, the background color you have chosen for the page isn't used with Web browsers that display background images. You don't have to designate a background color if you're using a graphic in its place.

Adjusting the Text

The background you have chosen for this page doesn't obscure the picture of Herald Square, and it doesn't block the line of text that identifies the picture. However, it does make it impossible to read the rest of the text because the black letters can't be seen easily over the background image, as shown in Figure 8.3.

Figure 8.3.

The Web page with text displayed over the background image.

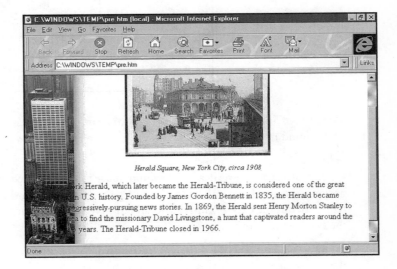

Herald Square, New York City, circa 1908

...rk Herald, which later became the Herald-Tribune, is considered one of the great ...n U.S. history. Founded by James Gordon Bennett in 1835, the Herald became ...gressively-pursuing news stories. In 1869, the Herald sent Henry Morton Stanley to ...a to find the missionary David Livingstone, a hunt that captivated readers around the ... years. The Herald-Tribune closed in 1966.

Instead of changing the font in any way, highlight all the text from Lines 2 to 9 and use the Blockquote feature to indent the selected text three times.

JUST A MINUTE

Using the Blockquote feature to indent text is useful for moving a page's contents away from a vertical background image, but it also reduces the available space for text by indenting the page's right-hand margin, too. You'll learn some other methods for handling vertical backgrounds during Hour 13, "Using Material from Libraries."

Save the page as `herald.html` in the Webwork\Back folder with the page title `New York Herald`. Preview the page in a browser to see how the contents of the page are displayed with the background image. Figure 8.4 shows the result with America Online's built-in browser.

Figure 8.4.

The herald.html page viewed in America Online's browser.

The city.gif image is 46K, which is more than twice the size of many graphics used as background images. What makes this file so large is that the vertical image is several inches tall.

Often, you can find a vertical background image that's displayed in several tiles, just like other background graphics. If the contents of a page are taller than the graphic, then the image is repeated, but the background image isn't displayed in tiles from left to right if it's wider than the browser window.

In the current project, the solid white portion of the background graphic is much wider than the city image, which leaves no room for the image to tile horizontally.

JUST A MINUTE

The photo of Herald Square comes from *Touring Turn-of-the-Century America: Photographs from the Detroit Publishing Company, 1880-1920.* This Library of Congress collection comprises more than 25,000 photos in a searchable subject index. The online exhibit is available at the following Web address:

`http://lcweb2.loc.gov/ammem/detroit/dethome.html`

You'll get a chance to work with a much smaller vertical background during Hour 13.

8

Summary

Whether your tastes in imagery are sedate or psychotic, you should now be able to make use of background images for the Web pages you're working on. Home Page makes it easy to preview the effects of a background you have selected, and you can change things immediately until you get the results you want.

In keeping with the metaphor that a World Wide Web site is a home, you can think of a background graphic as wallpaper. However, this wallpaper's a bit more visually assertive than its non-electronic equivalent, so you have to do more to avoid shrinking into it.

Q&A

Q Why do some tiled backgrounds appear seamless, but others show the edges of the graphic very clearly?

A Whether you can see the image's edges is a result of how the graphic was designed. Many background images are developed so that the left and right edges and top and bottom edges match each other. They are called *seamless* background tiles because you can't tell easily where one tile ends and the next begins. The groovy.gif image used during this hour is an example of this kind of image.

Q Can any image file be used as a background?

A Any JPEG or GIF file that you can put on a page can be put underneath it, too. If you see a Web page graphic that would make a good background and you have permission to use it on your own pages, you can make use of a special feature of some browsers to grab it. With Netscape Navigator or Microsoft Internet Explorer, right-click your mouse over an image and you'll be given an opportunity to save the graphic on your system.

Q How do you make a background tile?

A Using any image-editing tool, you can make your own tile by creating a graphic and saving it as a .GIF or .JPG file. That's all there is to it, but there are some things to keep in mind as you're developing a tile. First, it should be seamless, if possible, because it makes the contents of the page easier to see over the background, and it generally looks better. Second, a vertical tile must be wider than the width of any browser windows used to view the page, or the tile won't be displayed vertically. It's impossible to know all the widths of browser windows because site visitors use different monitor sizes. However, if you make your image 1,500 pixels wide, you should get the results you want for almost all visitors to your Web page.

Q Can you use transparent graphics with a background?

A No, and there's no real reason to do so. The background color of the page can be included instead of transparent pixels on a GIF image, creating the same effect in the same amount of disk space.

Quiz

Test your knowledge of this hour by taking this brief three-question test.

Questions

1. What's the term used to describe how background images can be displayed repeatedly on a Web page?

    (a) Redundancy

    (b) Tiling

    (c) Redundancy

2. For a background image to tile downward but not rightward, what has to take place?

    (a) The Document Options dialog box must be used to change a setting.

    (b) A steady vigil of prayer and fasting must be followed.

    (c) The image used must be wider than the browser window.

3. Who was quoted on the hour's first Web page project?

    (a) I.M. Angry

    (b) R.U. Sirius

    (c) Y.U. Ask

Answers

1. b.

2. c. Different browser windows have different widths, so a background image of this kind is usually 30–50 percent wider than a normal window.

3. b. Sirius is a musician, writer, the co-founder of *Mondo 2000* magazine, and a profoundly quotable person.

Activities

The following activities are suggested to expand your knowledge of the subjects covered during this hour:

☐ Reload the first page you worked on during this hour, which featured the quotation and the hallucinatory background image. Change the text color and font to different color combinations and see how they affect the page's readability.

☐ Using background images from an archive such as www.zeldman.com, experiment with them on some of the Web pages you have created so far. Try tiled and vertical background graphics, if both are available to you.

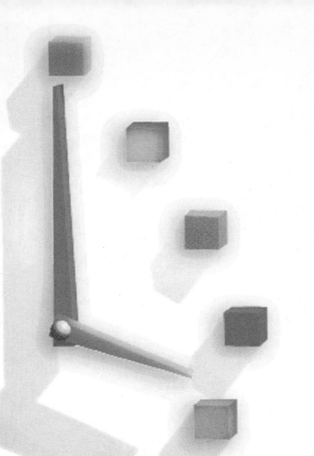

PART
III

Home Page Design

Hour

Hour 9

Using Numbered and Unnumbered Lists

As David Letterman and Santa Claus can attest, nothing beats making a list. Letterman has been chronicling the top 10 everything for more than a decade, and Santa keeps two huge databases of good and bad children.

The subject matter of this hour should appeal to Dave, Santa, and anyone else who wants to make a list and check it twice. You will learn how to create two kinds of lists in Claris Home Page 2.0 Lite: numbered lists and unnumbered ones. The following topics are covered:

☐ Creating lists on your pages
☐ Numbering lists
☐ Building unnumbered lists
☐ Putting one list inside another
☐ Changing a list

Making a List

Lists are a way to group related items on a Web page. Each item in a list is usually brief, but there's no limit on the amount of text each item can contain.

There are no restrictions on what each list item can contain: Graphics and other information can be included with text or used in lieu of text. However, text works most effectively, and other types of information don't always format correctly when put into a list on a Web page.

Lists can be numbered—perhaps you're ranking the all-girl singing groups of the '60s from best to worst, and you want to reserve the #1 spot for Martha and the Vandellas.

Lists can also be unnumbered—in case you want to note your love of the Shangri-Las, Crystals, and Ronettes, but don't want to risk offending any of them by ranking them.

Lists aren't a flashy feature compared to some other things you have learned to do. However, there are times when a list conveys information more coherently than another format would. Lists are useful for the following purposes:

☐ When you want to emphasize something

☐ When you have a list of related items that would be confusing as a single sentence

☐ When you want to break up a lot of text

This book isn't immune from the lure of lists, either. You'll have to decide which of the preceding three items applies in this section.

One thing you don't have to worry about with a numbered list is the numbering. When you specify that a list should be numbered, all you have to worry about is supplying the list items. They're numbered automatically when loaded into a Web browser.

Numbered Lists

Your first project of the hour is to present a numbered list: the first round of the 1982 NFL draft.

COFFEE BREAK

There's no particular significance to using this NFL draft instead of something else, but the author is a Dallas Cowboys fan who can't forget this particular draft despite years of aversion therapy. The Cowboys used their pick in this round to select Rod Hill, widely considered to be their biggest draft blunder of all time.

Before you start this project, create a new folder on your system—Webwork\Lists—to store the pages you create during the hour.

To begin, create a new page in Home Page. To begin a numbered list, you can click the Make Unnumbered List Entry button or use the Format|Numbered List menu option. The button is shown in Figure 9.1.

Figure 9.1.

Creating an unnumbered list.

The Make Unnumbered List Entry button

When you start a numbered list, a number sign and period appear to the left of the cursor. The number sign is a placeholder that's replaced with a specific number when the Web page is displayed. Numbered lists on a Web page begin with 1 and count upward—there's no way to modify this numbering.

After you have begun a numbered list, enter the text of Listing 9.1 on the page. When you press Enter each time you encounter a ¶ symbol in the text, you will be ending one list item and beginning a new one.

Listing 9.1. The list to put on the page.

```
 1: 1982 NFL Draft, First Round¶
 2: New England Patriots: Kenneth Sims, DE, Texas¶
 3: Baltimore Colts: Johnnie Cooks, LB, Mississippi State¶
 4: New Orleans Saints (supplemental pick): Dave Wilson, QB, Illinois¶
 5: Cleveland Browns: Chip Banks, LB, USC¶
 6: Baltimore Colts (from Los Angeles Rams): Art Schlichter, QB, Ohio State¶
 7: Chicago Bears: Jim McMahon, QB, Brigham Young *¶
 8: Seattle Seahawks: Jeff Bryant, DE, Clemson¶
 9: Minnesota Vikings: Darrin Nelson, RB, Stanford¶
10: Houston Oilers: Mike Munchak, G, Penn State¶
11: Atlanta Falcons: Gerald Riggs, RB, Arizona State¶
12: Oakland Raiders: Marcus Allen, RB, USC *¶
13: Kansas City Chiefs: Anthony Hancock, WR, Tennessee¶
14: Pittsburgh Steelers: Walter Abercrombie, RB, Baylor¶
15: New Orleans (from San Diego Chargers): Lindsay Scott, WR, Georgia¶
16: Los Angeles Rams (from Washington Redskins): Barry Redden, RB, Richmond¶
17: Detroit Lions: Jimmy Williams, LB, Nebraska¶
18: St. Louis Cardinals: Luis Sharpe, T, UCLA¶
19: Tampa Bay Buccaneers: Sean Farrell, G, Penn State¶
20: New York Giants: Butch Woolfolk, RB, Michigan¶
21: Buffalo Bills: Perry Tuttle, WR, Clemson¶
22: Philadelphia Eagles: Mike Quick, WR, North Carolina State¶
23: Denver Broncos: Gerald Willhite, RB, San Jose State¶
```

continues

Listing 9.1. continued

```
24: Green Bay Packers: Ron Hallstrom, T, Iowa¶
25: New York Jets: Bob Crable, LB, Notre Dame¶
26: Miami Dolphins: Ray Foster, G, USC¶
27: Dallas Cowboys: Rod Hill, CB, Kentucky State¶
28: Cincinnati Bengals: Glen Collins, DE, Mississippi State¶
29: New England Patriots (from San Francisco 49ers): Lester Williams, DT, Miami¶
30: * - Active player in 1996 season.¶
```

Two lines in this listing are included in the numbered list, but don't really belong in it. You can remove text from a list by highlighting the line and choosing Format|Normal from the menu. Do this to Line 1, the title of the page, and Line 30, which indicates what an * means next to a draft pick's listing.

After making these changes, save the page with the title 1982 NFL Draft and save it under the filename draft.html in the folder Webwork\Lists. Use Home Page's Preview Page feature to see the numbers appear on the list, which allows you to check the numbering and make sure it looks OK. Figure 9.2 shows the page in the Microsoft Internet Explorer browser.

Figure 9.2.

The draft.html page viewed in the Internet Explorer browser.

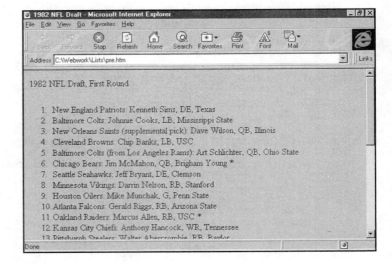

Unnumbered Lists

An unnumbered list replaces the numbers preceding each item with some kind of bullet character—usually a circle or square, depending on the browser being used. Because unnumbered lists use these bullets in front of each item, they are also called *bulleted lists*.

Working with an unnumbered list in Home Page is exactly the same as working with a numbered one. You start an unnumbered list by clicking the Make Bullet List Entry button or using the Format | Bullet List menu option.

You can also create lists within other lists and mix and match numbered and unnumbered lists when using them together. If you're having trouble visualizing what a list within a list would be, think of the structure of this book. There are six parts, numbered from 1 to 6. Within each of these parts are four chapters, and each set of four chapters could be numbered from 1 to 4 if Sams.net was willing to title this book *Teach Yourself to Create a Home Page in Six Four-Hour Parts.*

To see how to create lists within lists, start a new Web page in Home Page and use Listing 9.2 as the starting text.

Listing 9.2. The starting text of the new page.

```
 1: Sitcom Siblings
 2: Bradford
 3: David
 4: Mary
 5: Joannie
 6: Susan
 7: Nancy
 8: Elizabeth
 9: Tommy
10: Nicholas
11: Brady
12: Greg
13: Marcia
14: Peter
15: Jan
16: Bobby
17: Cindy
18: Walton
19: John Jr. ("John-Boy")
20: Jason
21: Mary Ellen
22: Ben
23: Erin
24: James ("Jim-Bob")
25: Elizabeth
```

After entering the text, highlight all of the text except for the first line, Sitcom Siblings. Turn the highlighted text into an unnumbered list. This list will be easier to understand when you break it into smaller lists. The text you have entered makes up two lists: a list of specific family surnames, and a list containing the first names of family members.

You need to use the Indent feature to identify a list within another list. Highlight all the individual members of the Bradford family, beginning with David and ending with Nicholas, and click the Indent button. The text is then indented, and the type of bullet identifying each list item changes in the Home Page editing window. Do the same for the Bradys—beginning with Greg and ending with Cindy—and then the Waltons—starting with John Jr. and concluding with Elizabeth.

After indenting the individual family names, turn each list of family names into a numbered list by clicking the Make Numbered List Entry button or choosing Format | Numbered List from the menu. The number sign (#) will appear in place of the bullets in front of each list item.

Make the names of the Brady and Walton siblings into their own numbered lists also, and indent them once as well.

Save the file as char.html in the Webwork\Lists folder, and give the page the title Characters. Preview the page with your preferred Web browser, and the finished product should resemble Figure 9.3.

Figure 9.3.

The char.html page viewed with Netscape Navigator.

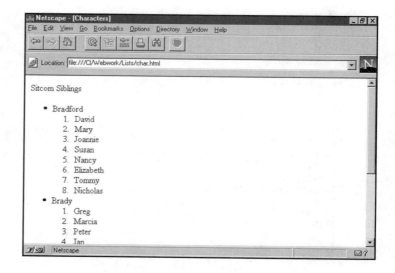

Different browsers handle unnumbered lists differently in terms of the bullets used in front of each item and how they are used. In the current example, Netscape Navigator displays a solid bullet in front of the main list item—the last names of the sitcom families—and hollow bullets are used when the individual names were in unnumbered lists.

Summary

If you have gone through the first half of this book with plans of creating a personal home page, you might not be able to resist the urge to list things there. There are dozens of CD collections listed in great detail on the World Wide Web, and if you have the urge to exhaustively document your own possessions, you can use lists to do so.

Lists also serve a practical purpose because they can be used to break up a text-heavy page and make it more readable. Lists are also useful for outlines, a book's table of contents, and other information that can be presented as a group of short items.

Q&A

Q If I want to consolidate a list I've recently indented into its own list, how can I do that?

A The Outdent feature, available by clicking the Outdent button, merges one list into another by widening the list's margin toward the right and left edges of the page. This technique is comparable to removing the Blockquote feature from text. Also, you can change the list to normal text and then turn it into the kind of list you want.

Q There's no spacing between some numbers in a numbered list and the list items. Is there a way to change this?

A With current versions of popular Web browsers, the spacing and numbering of numbered lists are determined by the browser. These things can't be changed when you're developing the page that contains the list. Although Home Page doesn't support the feature, using HTML programming and some other Web editors, you can change the way a list is numbered and the number it begins with.

Q Is there a way to make the bullets next to an unnumbered list not appear?

A There's no way in Home Page to suppress the display of the bullets, but there's no advantage to making a list of items into a list without displaying the bullets. Using the Indent feature and a line break at the end of each line, you could make a list of items look the same as an unnumbered list without the bullets.

Q Who were the standouts to come from the first round of the NFL draft in 1982?

A Marcus Allen, a 15-year veteran going into the 1997 season with the Kansas City Chiefs, has been the standout. Jim McMahon also rates high because he led the Bears to a Super Bowl win while still a young player, and Luis Sharpe and Mike Quick had long and successful NFL careers, too.

Quiz

Test your knowledge of this hour by taking this brief three-question test.

Questions

1. What's another term for a bulleted list?
   - (a) An unnumbered list
   - (b) A numbered list
   - (c) A hit list
2. What text is used as a placeholder for the number in a numbered list item?
   - (a) No
   - (b) #
   - (c) >
3. Which fictional television siblings provided the most tax relief for their parents?
   - (a) Bradfords
   - (b) Bradys
   - (c) Waltons

Answers

1. a.
2. b.
3. a. The unexpected arrival of Nicholas gave the title of most prodigious sitcom spawners to Tom and Joan Bradford, winning by one over John and Olivia Walton. Mike and Carol Brady trailed by two.

Activities

The following activities are suggested to expand your knowledge of the subjects covered during this hour:

- ☐ Put together a Web page listing your five favorite news, sports, and entertainment-related sites. Organize the information into three lists, each with five items in it, and be sure to include links to each site.

- ☐ Find something you have compiled far too much of in your home and document it in great detail. Use this information to create a list on the home page you've been working on in previous hours.

9

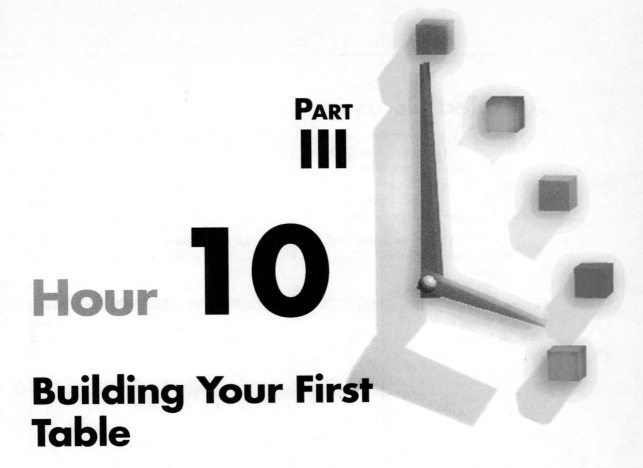

Hour 10

Building Your First Table

The title of this hour makes it sound like the chapter of a home-improvement book for the Amish. No error has been made, however—the table you will be learning to build is made of data, not of wood.

Tables are grids on a Web page that hold information. Claris Home Page 2.0 Lite makes it easy to create and modify tables, and it's one of the strong suits of the software, compared to using HTML programming to design Web pages.

You will create a table during this hour as the following topics are covered:

- ☐ Creating the initial settings for a table
- ☐ Putting information into table cells
- ☐ Understanding how tables are displayed
- ☐ Creating tables without borders
- ☐ Using tables to organize a Web page

A Tabled Discussion

A *table* is a grid of rectangles, each of which can hold text and images. Each rectangle in a table that can hold information is called a *cell*, a term that's borrowed from spreadsheet software. If you use Quicken or another bank-account management program, you ought to be familiar with cells. Every time you enter a check into Quicken, you put the check number into one cell, the recipient into another, and the amount of the check into a third. A fourth cell keeps count of how much money you have left, no matter how depressing the total.

The cells of a table are arranged vertically into *columns* and horizontally into *rows*. Figure 10.1 shows a table with 9 rows and 7 columns. This table is being used to display rotisserie baseball statistics.

Figure 10.1.

A table displayed with Microsoft Internet Explorer.

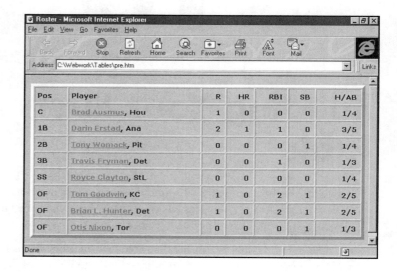

Pos	Player	R	HR	RBI	SB	H/AB
C	Brad Ausmus, Hou	1	0	0	0	1/4
1B	Darin Erstad, Ana	2	1	1	0	3/5
2B	Tony Womack, Pit	0	0	0	1	1/4
3B	Travis Fryman, Det	0	0	1	0	1/3
SS	Royce Clayton, StL	0	0	0	0	1/4
OF	Tom Goodwin, KC	1	0	2	1	2/5
OF	Brian L. Hunter, Det	1	0	2	1	2/5
OF	Otis Nixon, Tor	0	0	0	1	1/3

COFFEE BREAK

That's my rotisserie team I've shown in Figure 10.1, and it shows why I've chosen book writing as a career over sports wagering.

As you can see in Figure 10.1, each cell in a table doesn't have to be the same size. Cells in the same row and cells in the same column are given the same amount of space, which maintains the table's rectangular shape, but you can vary the width of different columns to make room for the text and images inside a cell.

Making a Table

Before starting the first project of this hour, create a new folder on your system called Webwork\Tables. Go to the Resource folder on the book's CD-ROM, and copy the file pills.gif into Webwork\Tables. The Tables folder will also be used to store the Web page you're going to create.

The first step in building a table with Home Page is to click the Insert Table button, shown in Figure 10.2, or choose Insert | Table from the menu.

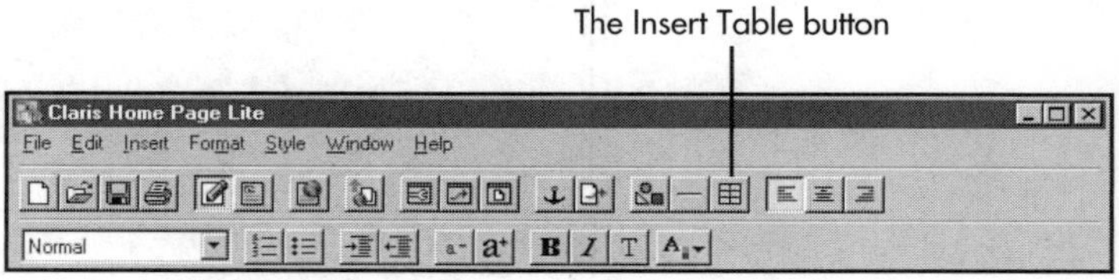

Figure 10.2.

Click this button to begin creating a table in Home Page.

The Insert Table button

Start a new page in Home Page and insert a table onto the page. A grid appears on the page, and the Table dialog box opens where you can set up the table.

Three settings need to be established for a table:

☐ The border width of the table's grid, or 0 if no border should be displayed

☐ The number of rows in the table

☐ The number of columns in the table

Give this first table a border size of 5, and set it to have 5 columns and 11 rows. Close the dialog box, and you should see a 5×11 grid of cells on the Web page. A blinking cursor and blue border are shown in one cell—the one in the upper-left corner of the grid.

This border indicates that you can modify this cell. You will be using this table to re-create part of the 1982 NFL draft, which you put on a page with a numbered list during the previous hour, "Using Numbered and Unnumbered Lists."

The leftmost column is used to hold the order of draft picks in the table. With your cursor in the upper-left cell, enter the text Order.

Click the mouse in the cell immediately to the right—the cell in row 1, column 2. Enter the text Team. The next three cells to the right should have the following text: Selection in the center cell of row 1; Position in row 1, column 4; and School in the last cell of row 1. Figure 10.3 shows what the table should look like after you enter all this text into the cells of row 1; note that the blue selection border is surrounding the cell in row 1, column 5.

Figure 10.3.

The table with row 1 completed.

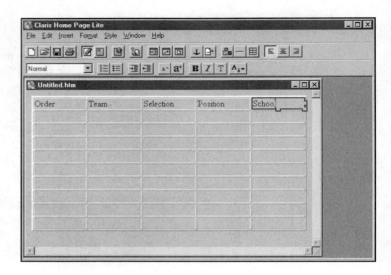

Using the information from Table 10.1, fill out the remaining 10 rows of the table on your new Web page. To go from one cell to another without using your mouse, press Tab after you finish entering the text in a cell.

Table 10.1. 1982 NFL Draft picks.

Order	Team	Selection	Pos.	School
1	New England Patriots	Kenneth Sims	DE	Texas
2	Baltimore Colts	Johnnie Cooks	LB	Miss. St.
3	New Orleans Saints	Dave Wilson	QB	Illinois
4	Cleveland Browns	Chip Banks	LB	USC
5	Baltimore Colts	Art Schlichter	QB	Ohio St.
6	Chicago Bears	Jim McMahon	QB	Brigham Young
7	Seattle Seahawks	Jeff Bryant	DE	Clemson
8	Minnesota Vikings	Darrin Nelson	RB	Stanford
9	Houston Oilers	Mike Munchak	G	Penn St.
10	Atlanta Falcons	Gerald Riggs	RB	Arizona St.

The Flexibility of Tables

Tables are an extremely flexible tool on a Web page. If you don't do anything to change the width or height of columns and you don't change the way cells are displayed, the table will take up only as much space as it needs to display each cell item.

JUST A MINUTE

Changing certain aspects of a table, such as modifying a column's width or height, is discussed during the next hour, "Creating More Sophisticated Tables." You will be using the default table during this hour to see how it works, then getting into more advanced tables afterward.

Save the current page with the title Draft Picks and the filename picks.html, and store it in the folder Webwork\Tables. When you preview the page with your preferred Web browser, it should resemble Figure 10.4.

Figure 10.4.

The picks.html page displayed with Microsoft Internet Explorer.

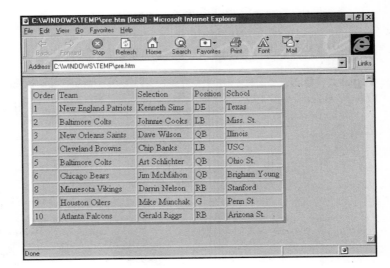

Order	Team	Selection	Position	School
1	New England Patriots	Kenneth Sims	DE	Texas
2	Baltimore Colts	Johnnie Cooks	LB	Miss. St.
3	New Orleans Saints	Dave Wilson	QB	Illinois
4	Cleveland Browns	Chip Banks	LB	USC
5	Baltimore Colts	Art Schlichter	QB	Ohio St.
6	Chicago Bears	Jim McMahon	QB	Brigham Young
8	Minnesota Vikings	Darrin Nelson	RB	Stanford
9	Houston Oilers	Mike Munchak	G	Penn St
10	Atlanta Falcons	Gerald Riggs	RB	Arizona St.

If you display the picks.html page in a maximized window, all the rows should have the same height. The columns will vary in width depending on the widest text item in one of the column cells. For instance, the Team column is slightly wider than the text New England Patriots because that team name takes up the most space.

This feature makes it easier to use tables. All you worry about is entering the text and choosing the right font and color, and the rest is taken care of.

Modifying a Table

To change how a table is displayed, you need to select the entire table for editing instead of a specific cell. Normally, a blue border surrounds the table cell you're currently working on. To select the table for editing, move your mouse directly over the outer edge of the table. Your mouse pointer should change from a cursor or two-headed arrow into the normal cursor—the white arrow—unless you have configured your system to use a different one. Click the mouse, and the blue border should appear around the entire table.

To edit the table once it's selected, use Home Page's Object Editor feature by clicking the Object Editor button or choosing the Window | Show Object Editor menu option. A Table dialog box then opens where you can configure the table. Click the Both tab so that all the configuration options can be modified.

Change the border of this table to 0, and then close the dialog box. The border of the table will change in Home Page's editing window, but you should preview it with your browser and the Preview Page feature.

In each case, the table is displayed without any borders. A borderless table can be used to line up tabular information, which isn't usually possible just by entering text on a page. Figure 10.5 shows the picks.html page after this change is made to the table.

Figure 10.5.

The picks.html page with no border around the table.

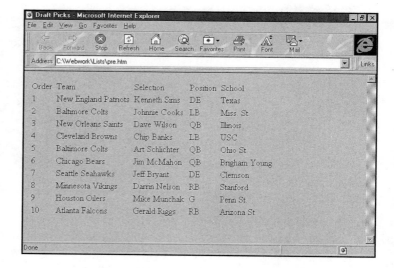

Organizing a Page with Tables

You can also use tables to create a framework for the elements to display on a Web page. As you have learned during previous hours, it isn't possible to describe exactly how text and

10

images should be laid out on a page. The Web browser and the width of the user's browser window can both determine where elements appear on a page in relation to other elements. However, by using tables, you can exercise more control over a page's layout.

CAUTION

> Although all popular Web browsers fully support tables, some Web surfers are still using browsers that can't display tables. Lynx, for example, displays each table cell on its own line. Other browsers display each cell with a space between it, making the table difficult to understand.

As a short example of how you can use tables for formatting, create a new page in Home Page. Use the Document Options feature to select a background image for this page, and select the graphics file pills.gif from the Webwork\Tables folder. A vertical row of pills will be displayed in a column along the left edge of the page.

During Hour 8, "Putting Images Behind Your Pages," you learned how to use the Blockquote feature to indent text. You could use this feature to move text off the background image, but you can also use a borderless table to get the same effect.

Insert a table on this page, setting the border to 0 and specifying 1 row and 2 columns. Close the Table dialog box after entering these values. Before entering any text inside the table, you need to make the left-hand cell much thinner than the right-hand cell. To do this, move your mouse over the border between the two cells. A two-headed arrow appears when the cursor is over the right place. This arrow means you can drag the column border to the left or right. Drag it to the left by clicking and holding down the mouse, then moving the border until it's within a quarter-inch of the pill background image. When you release the mouse, your editing window should resemble Figure 10.6.

Now that you have moved the border, the right-hand cell can hold the text and images of your page. Enter the text of Listing 10.1 into the cell at row 1, column 2.

Listing 10.1. The text to enter into the cell.

```
 1: Sneeze-B-Gone¶
 2: The fabulous new product from Dubious Pharmaceuticals!¶
 3: Allergies are nothing to sneeze at. This affliction reduces more
 4: people to tears than a Meryl Streep Film Festival, and it turns
 5: the coming of spring into a season of discontent.¶
 6: Say goodbye to watery eyes and nasal drip with Sneeze-B-Gone.
 7: Only four easy payments of $19.95.¶
 8: No warranties expressed or implied. Manufacturer makes no
 9: promises that this product is safe for human consumption. Do not
10: store in a hot area or pills may spontaneously burst into flame.¶
```

Figure 10.6.

Moving the border between two rows.

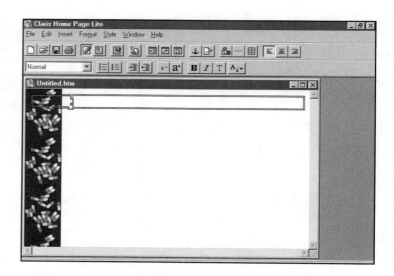

After entering this text, highlight all the text in the last paragraph (from lines 8–10) and make it the smallest size possible, in the grand tradition of all legal disclaimers. Figure 10.7 shows the page with Microsoft Internet Explorer.

Figure 10.7.

The Sneeze-B-Gone page in Microsoft Internet Explorer.

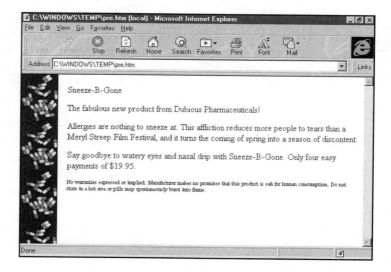

Save this page as `pills.html` with the title `Sneeze-B-Gone`, and store it in the folder Webwork\Tables.

10

Summary

Even though you can't serve breakfast on them, the tables you learned to build during this hour have their own uses. If you're presenting a lot of data on a page, such as statistics or other reports, you can use Home Page to quickly arrange this material into a table.

As you will see in the next hour, you can modify tables in several different ways to increase their usefulness. They're a type of furnishing that can fit in many types of Web pages.

Q&A

Q Can I use the Alignment feature to center a table?

A Yes you can, but you can't do some of the things you can normally do with other objects. For example, using Home Page, you can't set up the alignment of text so that it wraps around tables. This is possible using HTML programming, but it's not supported in the Lite version of Home Page.

Q Can you put one table inside of another?

A Give it a try—you can put anything inside a table cell that you could put on a Web page. It could be difficult to work with the cells of a table within another table, but by adjusting the column borders as needed, you should be able to create enough space to work.

Q Can I use a table with only one row and one column?

A There's no restriction against it, and using a single-cell table makes sense in some page layouts. You might place a text item or graphic in a single-cell table to put a thick border around it. The table can also be used to make sure that parts of a page don't go outside a specific margin. Tables are an effective way to lay out a complex Web page.

Q Should I use tables even though some Web surfers won't be able to see them correctly?

A At the time of this writing, all popular Web browsers support tables in their current versions. Unless you're specifically targeting an audience that's unlikely to have current browsers, you can probably use tables without worrying about how they will be viewed. As with other advanced features, you can offer an alternative page that doesn't make use of tables, thus supporting both groups of visitors.

10

Quiz

Test your knowledge of this hour by taking this brief three-question test.

Questions

1. What do the contents of a table and the Godfather of Soul, James Brown, have in common?

    (a) They both got their groove back.

    (b) They both feel good, like you knew that they would.

    (c) They both have been in cells.

2. What is used to change the number of rows and columns in a table after it's created?

    (a) The Document Options feature

    (b) The Object Editor

    (c) The mouse

3. Which of the following isn't a feature of tables on Web pages?

    (a) Every cell in a row has the same size.

    (b) Rows are only a little bigger than the widest item in any of their cells.

    (c) Every row has the same size.

Answers

1. c.

2. b.

3. c. Rows can vary in size with other rows, but all the cells in a single row must have the same height.

Activities

The following activities are suggested to expand your knowledge of the subjects covered during this hour:

☐ Experiment with different border sizes for the tables created during this hour, and preview the pages with a Web browser to see how the borders are displayed.

☐ If you have created your own home page, create a table to display some biographical information about yourself: name, age, birthplace, favorite authors, turn-ons, and turn-offs. Feel free to add rows regarding any body measurements if you don't have modesty issues.

10

Hour 11

Creating More Sophisticated Tables

During the past hour, you learned how to build a basic table that holds many of the things you'll want to organize on your own Web pages. You're now ready to try some advanced features of Claris Home Page 2.0 Lite's table-editing tool. Getting back to the home-improvement motif of the previous hour, if this really were a furniture-building tutorial, you would be moving from simple four-legged tables into lathework during this hour.

You'll learn more about tables as the following topics are covered:

☐ Modifying the size of cells in a table

☐ Making table cells larger than other cells

☐ Changing the size of a table

☐ Changing the space between table cells

☐ Modifying the blank space inside cells

Putting It All on the Table

If you're still wondering why the table-editing features of Claris Home Page 2.0 Lite are useful, take a look at a small table created with HTML programming codes:

```
<TABLE BORDER=5>
<TR><TD>
<P>1
</TD><TD>
<P>New England Patriots
</TD><TD>
<P>Kenneth Sims
</TD><TD>
<P>DE
</TD><TD>
<P>Texas
</TD></TR>
</TABLE>
```

Tables are one of the hardest things to create with HTML programming, and they're extremely difficult to modify after they have been created. As Web page editing tools have become more sophisticated and software such as Home Page has become available, one of the biggest factors for their success is fear of tables.

Your project this hour gives you a chance to work with the remaining features of Home Page's table-creation tool.

Creating a Useful Table

One type of table that can be useful on a Web page is a calendar. For your project during this hour, you will create a calendar for January 1998.

Figure 11.1 shows the way the calendar falls in that month, beginning with New Year's Day on a Thursday.

Figure 11.1.

The calendar for January 1998.

S	M	T	W	T	F	S
				1	2	3
4	5	6	7	8	9	10
11	12	13	14	15	16	17
18	19	20	21	22	23	24
25	26	27	28	29	30	31

11

You could represent this calendar with a table that's seven columns wide and six rows deep, adding an extra row on top as a place for the month and year. Just follow these steps:

1. Create a new page in Home Page and insert a table by clicking the Insert Table button.

2. In the Table dialog box, set the table border size to 5 and specify 7 rows and 7 columns for the table, and then close the Table dialog box so you can begin entering information in your table.

3. Leave the top row of cells empty, and put the three-letter abbreviations for the days of the week in row 2's cells: SUN, MON, TUE, WED, THU, FRI, and SAT.

4. In the next row, put a 1 in the cell directly under the cell containing THU. Fill in the rest of the calendar with the days of the month, ending with 31 in the rightmost cell of row 7.

Now that you have entered the names of the days and all the calendar dates, you need to modify the table to make room for the label in row 1.

Expanding a Cell's Size

An advanced feature of tables is the ability to make a cell combine with other cells. Click your mouse in the leftmost cell of row 1. Your editing window in Home Page should resemble Figure 11.2.

Figure 11.2.

The calendar page after all dates have been entered.

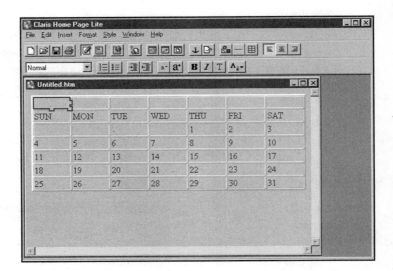

When you clicked your mouse in the cell, a blue border should have appeared around the cell. This border has projections that stick out on the lower-right corner, the right side, and the bottom of the cell. These extensions are *handles* you can use to stretch the cell's size. You grab and stretch a handle by clicking your mouse on it and then holding down the mouse button while you drag the mouse. Releasing the mouse button releases the handle.

Try this technique out by grabbing the handle along the right edge of the blue border and dragging the handle until the blue border surrounds all seven cells in the top row of the table. When you release the handle, the top row will be a single cell instead of seven cells. Enter the text January 1998 into this newly expanded cell.

Modifying the Table Text

Highlight all the text in the table and change the font to Arial Black, Helvetica, Verdana, or another sans-serif font you have available.

Next, highlight the text January 1998 and center it by clicking the Align Text Center button or choosing the Format | Alignment | Align Center menu option, and then do the same to each of the titles for the days of the week. As you're centering the text for the weekdays, make each weekday title two font sizes larger, too, by clicking the Larger Text button twice each time.

Expanding the Table

As a final change to the calendar, click the table along one of the outer edges to select the entire table for editing. The blue border should appear around the table itself instead of surrounding a specific cell.

This blue border has handles that can be used to change the size of the table, but you can also resize a table in two other ways. Using the Object Editor tool, you can modify the dimensions of a table by specifying the exact height or width in pixels. You can also specify a percentage for the width, which determines how wide the table should be in relation to the width of the whole page.

Click an outer edge of the calendar table so that a blue border appears around it. To use the Object Editor, right-click your mouse or click the Object Editor button, and the Table dialog box will appear. Click the Both tab to see all the settings that can be changed. Figure 11.3 shows this dialog box.

Figure 11.3.
The Table dialog box.

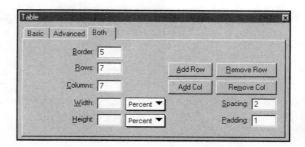

11

The Table dialog box has no values set for the Height or Width, which causes the table to take up only as much space as it needs to hold what's inside the cells.

Next to the Height and Width fields are white buttons labeled Percent. This means you can enter a numeric value in the field to determine what percentage of the Web page the table should take up.

Enter a value of 90 in the Width field and press Enter. If you can see the table in Home Page's editing window, you will notice it shrinking in width to 90 percent of the window's width.

Next, click the Percent button next to the Height field. You can choose between the values of Percent and Pixels. Select Pixels, and you can then specify the exact height of the table in pixels. Enter 280 in the Height field and press Enter.

JUST A MINUTE

Although you can specify the height of a table as a percentage, doing so isn't supported by current versions of Netscape Navigator and Microsoft Internet Explorer. When calculating the size of a table, the width of the browser window is considered to represent 100 percent. There isn't a similar standard to determine the height of a table as a percentage.

Close the Table dialog box and save this page in the folder Webwork\Tables with the filename calendar.html and the title Calendar.

Take a look at the table with your preferred browser. Figure 11.4 shows the page with Microsoft Internet Explorer.

Figure 11.4.

The calendar.html page viewed with Microsoft Internet Explorer.

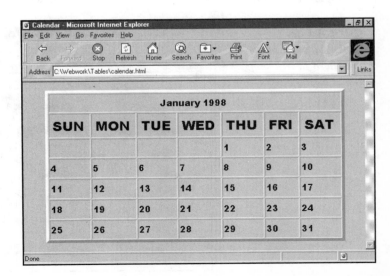

Modifying the Table Cells

By resizing cells, you can use tables to represent information in a variety of ways. In this hour's example, stretching the cells horizontally in the first row made it possible to create space for a table title. You can also stretch cells vertically, giving you more space to describe the contents of the table's cells.

Highlight the entire table again by clicking on an edge, and click the Object Editor button to modify the table. The familiar Table dialog box will appear. You have already used the Object Editor to change the number of rows and columns of a table and to modify the table's height and width. Now you'll use it to change two other settings: padding and spacing.

NEW TERM   *Spacing* is the width of the border between any two table cells. When you increase the spacing, the border becomes thicker. *Padding* is the empty space along the inner edge of a cell. You can't see padding, but it surrounds the contents of a cell. Increasing the padding causes a cell to take up more space.

Change the value of the Spacing field to 5 and then exit the Object Editor dialog box. Home Page immediately displays the result of this change—the space between any two table cells will increase, making the grid lines wider and taller.

Load the Object Editor again and change the value of the Padding field to 5. When you exit the Object Editor, the blank space surrounding the text inside a cell will be larger, pushing the text away from the cell's edges. This result will be most noticeable in the cells containing the names of the weekdays. Some of them might be hyphenated now because the new padding value doesn't leave enough room to keep the text on one line in the cells.

Figure 11.5 shows the result of these changes to the padding and spacing values.

Figure 11.5.

The new calendar.html page viewed in Microsoft Internet Explorer.

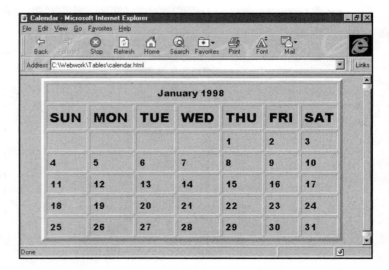

11

Summary

The way you use tables on your Web pages depends largely on the type of pages you create. If you're working on a scientific or statistical project of some kind, tables are probably the most useful way to arrange data. If you're ambitious about Web page design, you might use tables to organize images and text in a compelling way.

In any case, you have all the tools to become a master tablebuilder, and there's no chance you'll accidentally saw off an appendage or hammer a thumb while you're putting one of these tables together.

Q&A

Q Is there a maximum size you can use for the spacing or padding of a table's cells?

A There's no limit, but you'll quickly find out how high a value you can use for each of these settings without making the table unusable. To experiment with different values, keep the Object Editor dialog box open while you're changing values. When you modify a value and press Enter, the editing window immediately changes to reflect the new value.

Q Is there a way to add a row after you have entered text into a table?

A To add a row or column, after opening the Object Editor dialog box, click the mouse inside the table cell that's closest to the place you want the row or column to be added. Click the Add Row or Add Column button, and a new set of empty cells will be added.

Q When I use a spacing value of 0, why don't the lines between cells disappear?

A The default behavior for a spacing value of 0 is to display a thin line between cells rather than dropping the borders entirely. If you'd like the lines to disappear, but you want to keep the table's outer border visible, make the border of your table 0 pixels and put it inside another table that has only one cell.

Q If I expand a cell to cover cells that contain text and images, what happens to that material?

A Home Page lets you cover these cells and wipe out all the information they contain. You will be given a warning message first and asked to confirm it, to guard against inadvertently deleting something you'd like to keep. You can also use the Edit | Undo menu option immediately afterward to undo the cell change and bring back the deleted information.

11

Quiz

Test your knowledge of this hour by taking this brief three-question test.

Questions

1. How do you make a cell combine with a cell that's next to it?

    (a) Use the Object Editor.

    (b) Drag one cell over the other.

    (c) Leave them alone with some pretzels and beer.

2. True or False: You can't modify a table's height and width after it's created.

    (a) True

    (b) True

    (c) False

3. Is there any reason you might want to create a table with one row and one column?

    (a) No.

    (b) Yes, but only if you're weird.

    (c) Yes, as a way to emphasize the table's contents.

Answers

1. b. You can change the size of cells by grabbing the handle of the blue border that appears around a cell when you click on the cell to select it.

2. c.

3. c. The judges will also accept b.

Activities

The following activities are suggested to expand your knowledge of the subjects covered during this hour:

☐ If you have digitized photos of your family available, create a Web page using a table that features cells containing the pictures and cells describing your relatives. If you put the page on the Web, be advised that your descriptions could affect the kind of gifts you get next Christmas.

☐ Return to one of the Web pages you have created from past activities, and use a table around several different links as a way to emphasize the information.

11

Hour 12

Experimenting with HTML Commands

One of the reasons for using a program like Claris Home Page 2.0 Lite is to avoid learning HTML programming, which is a more complex way to develop Web pages.

However, even though you can use Home Page Lite to create sophisticated pages, the Web reinvents itself faster than Dennis Rodman changes hair colors. There will always be new features that aren't fully supported in page editors, and using these new features requires HTML.

This hour serves as a brief introduction to HTML by covering the following topics:

- ☐ Marking up pages with HTML tags
- ☐ Putting information between two tags
- ☐ Changing the attributes of an HTML tag
- ☐ Learning more about HTML

Using Raw HTML

One of Home Page's menu options, Style | Raw HTML, hasn't been used yet, and you might have wondered what it does. The option makes HTML sound like something chafed (raw knees), uncooked (raw meat), or unedited (raw footage).

None of those options seems particularly inviting, but HTML isn't quite that ferocious. It's harder to design a Web page with HTML than with an editing tool such as Home Page, but it's still something you can learn quickly.

COFFEE BREAK

Dick Oliver's *Teach Yourself HTML 3.2 in 24 Hours* (Sams.net Publishing), the second cousin to this book, is an excellent primer on designing your own home pages with HTML. It has an official Web site, the 24-Hour HTML Café, at the following address:

`http://www.mcp.com/sams/books/235-8/index.html`

During this hour, you'll learn the basics of HTML and use these skills to create a home page for the nineteenth-century novelist Edward George Bulwer-Lytton. If that name sounds familiar, it's because you already created his home page in a previous hour with Home Page. By using HTML to do the same task, you can compare the two approaches.

NEW TERM *HTML* stands for *Hypertext Markup Language.* The term comes from the World Wide Web being hypertext—a collection of computer-based documents connected by links, which can be used to travel through the document in any direction. Hypertext represents a new type of communications media because of the way the audience can experience it in such random fashion. One of the only things that compares to it is the hallowed male tradition of using the remote control to watch seven channels in rapid succession, stopping only when bikinis or women's beach volleyball is involved.

The *M* in HTML stands for *Markup,* and it refers to the way a document can be marked up with instructions on how the page should be organized. Think of ad executive Darrin Stevens on the television show "Bewitched" showing a proposed newspaper ad to his boss, Larry Tate. Tate could mark up the ad with instructions on where the headline should go, where the model's pearly-white teeth should be displayed, and where the advertiser's trademark belonged.

You use HTML programming to mark up a Web page and determine settings and functions such as the following:

☐ Where a paragraph of text begins and ends

☐ How much space an image should be displayed in

□ What parts of a page should be centered

□ How to link from one page to another

NEW TERM These things are handled by using *tags,* which are HTML commands surrounded by < and > marks. A Web page is filled with tags that work behind the scenes; none of them are actually displayed, but they determine everything about what the page looks like.

Using HTML Tags

One of the most elementary HTML tags is <P>, which determines where a paragraph should begin. Here's an example of how <P> can be used to separate two paragraphs:

```
I'm glad we came to the Grand Canyon to settle our differences,
dear.
<P>Stand right next to that crumbling cliff edge so I can take a
picture.
```

Figure 12.1 shows how this text is displayed on a Web page. Note how the text dear is displayed on the same line as the text that precedes it, even though they are on two different lines in the HTML code used to create the page. The only time a new paragraph of text begins on a Web page is when the <P> tag is encountered.

Figure 12.1.

A simple Web page created with an HTML tag to separate paragraphs of text.

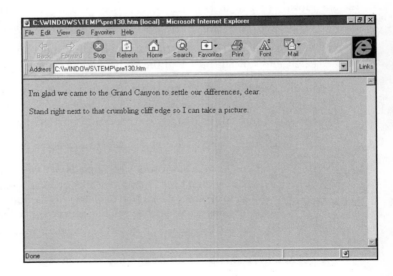

12

On a page, the <P> tag causes a new paragraph to begin after whatever comes before it in the document. It's commonly used right before the text that begins a paragraph.

The <P> tag is called an *opening tag* because it begins something: the display of a new paragraph. A lot of HTML programming consists of using an opening tag and a closing tag. The opening tag begins some kind of markup and the closing tag ends it.

After <P> opens a paragraph, the closing tag </P> is used to end it. Each closing tag has a / character in front of its name, which makes it possible for you to easily match up opening and closing tags. Take a look at <P> and </P>—don't you see the family resemblance?

Another commonly used pair of HTML tags are <TITLE> and </TITLE>. They are used to set up the page's title, which is displayed at the top of the Web browser window. The following is an example of a title set up with HTML:

```
<TITLE>Rural Mountain Cousin Love Ballads</TITLE>
```

Another pair of tags is used to center elements on a page: the <CENTER> and </CENTER> tags. The following example causes a line of text to be centered when the page is displayed:

```
<CENTER>
Free the Bound Periodicals!
</CENTER>
```

Creating an HTML Page

The most basic pair of HTML tags are used to establish a document as a Web page. The <HTML> opening tag is used at the beginning, and the </HTML> closing tag is used at the end.

A Web page is divided into two elements: a heading and a body. The heading is set off with the <HEAD> and </HEAD> tags, and the body uses the <BODY> and </BODY> tags.

The heading doesn't contain anything that should be displayed in the browser window, except for the title—which shows up only at the top edge. The body is where the contents of the page are put; all the images, text, and other material go here.

JUST A MINUTE

> If you have ever taken a look at the HTML tags in a real Web page, you probably didn't see <HTML>, <HEAD>, or <BODY> used in every document. Web browsers such as Microsoft Internet Explorer and Netscape Navigator are flexible enough to handle omissions like this.

One HTML tag can be used inside another, as in the following example:

```
<BODY>
<P>Why are there always vacancies at Norman's motel?</P>
</BODY>
```

In this partial page example, everything between the <BODY> and </BODY> tags is the content of the page, and everything between the <P> and </P> tags is the content of a paragraph.

When you're putting one pair of HTML tags within another, you have to make sure that one really is inside the other. For example, take a look at the following:

```
<TITLE>
<HEAD>
Dallas Cowboy Crime Blotter
</TITLE>
</HEAD>
```

In this example, which pair of tags is on the inside and which is on the outside? The answer is neither, which will cause the page containing these tags to work incorrectly when loaded into a browser.

To correct the error, the `<TITLE>` and `</TITLE>` tags must both be placed between the `<HEAD>` and `</HEAD>` tags, as follows:

```
<HEAD>
<TITLE>
Dallas Cowboy Crime Blotter
</TITLE>
</HEAD>
```

 Putting one set of HTML tags inside another is called *nesting*—the inner tag pair nests inside the outer pair, like an egg in a bird's nest.

Your project this hour will give you a better idea about how these tags are used with each other.

CAUTION

> Don't let this sample project intimidate you. The purpose is to introduce you to HTML programming and how to use it in Home Page, so you're more comfortable tackling it in earnest later on.

12

Using Raw HTML in Home Page

In Home Page, you can't just type in HTML tags and have them work correctly. You have to establish that the text includes HTML programming in it. Start a new page in Home Page and enter the text of Listing 12.1.

Listing 12.1. The text of eddie.html.

```
1: <HTML>¶
2: <TITLE>The Edward George Bulwer-Lytton Home Page</TITLE>¶
3: </HEAD>¶
4: <BODY>¶
```

continues

Listing 12.1. continued

```
 5: <P><CENTER>A Dark and Stormy Site</CENTER></P>¶
 6: <P><CENTER>The Edward George Bulwer-Lytton Home Page</CENTER></P>¶
 7: <P>¶
 8: <CENTER>¶
 9: <IMG SRC="images/cover.gif" WIDTH=384 HEIGHT=251>¶
10: </CENTER>¶
11: </P>¶
12: <P>Welcome to the home page of Edward George Bulwer-Lytton,
13: the British novelist and poet who lived from 1803 to 1873. I am
14: best-known today for beginning the 1830 novel Paul Clifford with the
15: following line:</P>¶
16: <P>"It was a dark and stormy night and the rain fell in
17: torrents--except at occasional intervals, when it was checked by a
18: violent gust of wind which swept up the streets (for it is in London
19: that our scene lies), rattling along the housetops, and fiercely
20: agitating the scanty flame of the lamps that struggled against the
21: darkness."</P>¶
22: </BODY>¶
23: </HTML>¶
```

After entering this text, highlight everything on the page and indicate that it has HTML tags by choosing the Style | Raw HTML menu option. The text will turn red and be displayed in a different font in the Home Page editing window. These changes won't be displayed on the Web page itself—they're just a visual clue that the lines contain HTML tags.

Save the page as eddie.html in the Webwork\Stormy folder. If you're asked to give the page a title, use The Edward George Bulwer-Lytton Home Page.

Home Page Lite doesn't support using the Preview Page feature to see what an HTML page looks like, so you have to preview the page with a browser. Figure 12.2 shows the result.

Figure 12.2.

The eddie.html page displayed with Internet Explorer.

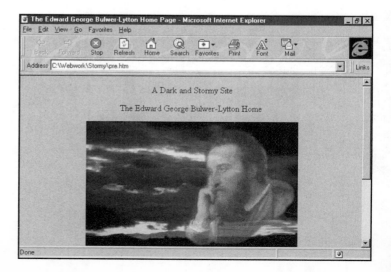

Adding a Link with HTML

The last HTML tag you'll learn to use during this hour is the link. Adding a link with Home Page is a matter of choosing something to attach a link to and then using the Link Editor tool.

With HTML, the first step also involves choosing something to associate with a link. For the eddie.html page, you'll associate a link with the graphic of Bulwer-Lytton. That graphic was displayed on the page by using a single line of HTML:

```
<IMG SRC="images/cover.gif" WIDTH=384 HEIGHT=251>¶
```

The `<IMG>` tag, which doesn't have a companion `</IMG>` tag, describes three things about the image that should be displayed:

- ☐ The filename and location of the image; in this case, it's the file `cover.gif` in a folder called `images`.
- ☐ The height of the image, which is 251 pixels.
- ☐ The width of the image, which is 384 pixels.

A link is associated with something on a Web page by using the `<A>` tag. The *A* stands for *anchor*, and the term was chosen because the tag anchors the link to part of a Web page.

The following is an example of a link that uses the `<A>` tag:

```
<A HREF="http://www.mustardweb.com">Visit the Mustard Museum!</A>
```

This link is attached to the text `Visit the Mustard Museum!`. Figure 12.3 shows what this line of HTML produces on a Web page. Clicking on the text would cause a browser to load the Web page `http://www.mustardweb.com`.

Figure 12.3.

A link associated with text on a Web page.

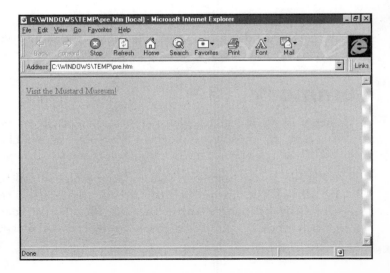

There really is a Mustard Museum at that Web address. It's the official Web site of the Mount Horeb Mustard Museum, home of such features as the Mustard of the Month Club, the Continuous Adventures of Mustard Man, and Poupon U.

An `<A>` tag identifies which Web page to link to by using the HREF attribute. This attribute can be any valid Web address, whether it connects to a page, graphic, or other type of information.

Unlike the `<IMG>` tag, `<A>` has a companion `</A>` tag. The opening `<A>` tag and closing `</A>` tag should have something nested within them: the part of the Web page that's associated with the link. Links can be associated with text, images, other information, or a combination of all three.

For the Bulwer-Lytton page, replace the line referring to the file cover.gif with the following three lines:

```
<A HREF="index.html">
<IMG SRC="images/cover.gif" WIDTH=384 HEIGHT=251>
</A>
```

As you can see, the `<IMG>` tag was not changed. The only modifications are the placement of an opening `<A>` tag before the image and a closing `</A>` after it.

Save the page and test it out with a Web browser. The only difference between this version of eddie.html and the one you created earlier is a thin blue border around the picture. The border indicates that the image is linked to another Web page, and as you have seen in Home Page, this border can be removed.

When you click the image, your browser loads the page index.html from Webwork\Stormy, the same folder that contains eddie.html. The index.html page is a version of the Bulwer-Lytton page you created in an earlier hour with Home Page.

Summary

After working through this hour's subject, you probably have gone into one of two camps. You're either very glad that programs like Home Page exist because they shield you from HTML, or you're interested in learning more about how to program Web pages.

For as long as Web pages are HTML pages, programming will be the first way to try out new HTML tags. The current standard for Web development is HTML 3.2, as described in Dick Oliver's book and many others by authors (Laura Lemay) you might have heard of (Laura Lemay), whose readership is larger than some Pacific Rim nations (Laura Lemay).

12

An advantage of using HTML is that you can use features that aren't yet available in Web-page creation tools, such as Claris Home Page 2.0 Lite. The primary disadvantage is that HTML programming is a more difficult skill for most people to master, and pages can be harder to maintain because of all the tags included in an HTML document.

Q&A

Q How do you leave a line blank by using HTML?

A Using the <P> tag on a line without any text following it displays a blank line. You can't put more than one blank line in a row by repeating the <P> tag, however, because extra lines and extra spaces are both deleted when you're using HTML tags to develop a page. You also can use the <BR> tag, which starts the subsequent material on a Web page on a new line. Using a <BR> tag creates less empty space on a page than a <P> tag does.

Q What is VRML, and is it needed to program pages?

A VRML is Virtual Reality Markup Language, a programming language used to create three-dimensional worlds. It's interesting in its own right and is the subject of several books from Sams.net Publishing. However, it's not directly related to Web page design. VRML is an enhancement, like Java and plug-ins, that you sometimes find on Web pages.

Q What about NORML?

A That's the National Organization for the Reform of Marijuana Laws, a group that can truly be described as "grass roots." You don't need it to design Web pages, and in a technical sense, it can't be considered an Internet enhancement.

Quiz

Test your knowledge of this hour by taking this brief three-question test.

Questions

1. What does the *M* stand for in *HTML?*
    (a) Modeling
    (b) Markup
    (c) Machine

12

2. Which of the following isn't a particularly good reason to use HTML from within Home Page?

    (a) You need to create a complicated page with many images.

    (b) You need to use a new HTML tag that adds sound to a page.

    (c) You need to use a table.

3. What part of a Web page should the <TITLE> tag be used in?

    (a) The heading

    (b) The body

    (c) Anywhere

Answers

1. b.

2. b. c. is particularly wrong because tables are much harder to create with HTML than with a page-editing tool.

3. a.

Activities

The following activities are suggested to expand your knowledge of the subjects covered during this hour:

☐ When you're previewing pages you have completed during the course of this book, use the feature in your browser that allows you to see the HTML tags. In Internet Explorer, use the View | Source menu option, and in Netscape Navigator, choose View | Document Source.

☐ If you're feeling ambitious, try to make eddie.html into an exact duplicate of index.html, using HTML instead of Home Page to add the remaining text, add links, and change the dimensions of the graphic.

PART
IV

Home Page
Special Effects

Hour

Hour 13

Using Material from Libraries

One of the best ways to call attention to your Web pages is to use some graphical icons, a few images, and a creative background. However, it can be time-consuming to create these elements on your own or find graphics from a Web site that offers images for you to reuse.

The first place you should look for graphics is within Claris Home Page 2.0 Lite. During this hour, you'll learn how to use the graphics that come with the software. The following topics are covered:

- ☐ Searching for graphics in a library
- ☐ Pasting graphics onto a page
- ☐ Arranging graphics around other elements
- ☐ Selecting a background image from a library
- ☐ Using a graphic to arrange the page

Starting a New Page

The graphics files that come with Home Page are stored in a graphics library you can search within the program. To get ready for this hour's project, go to the Webwork folder on your system and create a new folder called Kvikhome.

You will be creating a home page during this hour for a strange programming language called Kvikkalkul. This language was supposedly invented in the 1950s to run Sweden's nuclear submarines and create accounting spreadsheets.

Since both the nuclear sub and the spreadsheet date from later than the '50s, Kvikkalkul might be the invention of a demented computer science student.

Is there any other kind?

COFFEE BREAK

To start your Kvikkalkul home page, create a new document in Home Page and enter the text of Listing 13.1 into it. When you're done, save the file as index.html in the Webwork\Kvikhome folder. Give it the title Kvikkalkul home page when Home Page asks for this information.

Listing 13.1. The first draft of the index.html page.

```
1: Kvikkalkul home page¶
2: This Web site is devoted to Kvikkalkul, the secret programming
3: language of the Swedish Navy. On Oct. 20, 1994, the language was
4: described in a Usenet message by an anonymous programmer who worked
5: for the Navy in 1957.¶
6: Programs¶
7: Documentation¶
8: Help¶
9: Send Us E-mail¶
```

Formatting the Text

Before you start adding any graphics, you should modify the text to improve its readability. Do the following:

☐ Highlight the line Kvikkalkul home page and change it to Heading 2 with the Format | Heading 2 menu option.

☐ Highlight the four lines Programs, Documentation, Help, and Send Us E-mail. Change them all at one time into a Heading 3 size.

☐ Insert a blank line above the heading Kvikkalkul home page and a blank line after Send Us E-mail.

Another change you need to make is a little unorthodox. Highlight all the text on the page and turn it into a block quotation with the Format | Blockquote menu option. This text is an entire page instead of a quotation, so it might seem unusual to use the Blockquote option here. What it does, though, is center and indent all the text on the page, which will be helpful later to make room for the background image that borders the page. This technique is similar to one you used in Hour 8, "Putting Images Behind Your Pages."

Opening a Library

If you would like to add graphics to your home page, you have three options: creating a graphic with an image-editing tool, using an existing graphic, such as one from a Web site that offers graphics for your use, and using the graphics that come with Home Page.

Home Page offers more than 100 different graphics for use with Web pages. Most of them are small icons, arrows, bars, and other utilitarian images.

To make these graphics easier to use, Home Page has organized them into a graphics library with different-themed sections. To see this library, choose File | Open Library from the menu. A dialog box opens where you select which library to open. There's only one library included with Home Page's Lite version—the file Clip Art Library.hlb in the Clipart subfolder that was created when you first installed Home Page.

All the files in the Home Page libraries have the .HLB file extension. Highlight the file Clip Art Library.hlb and click the Open button. A window opens, displaying the different sections of the library. The lower half of this window shows a Web page with all the images in the currently selected section. Highlight some of the different library sections and scroll through the lower half of the window, taking a look at the graphics that are part of that section. Figure 13.1 shows some images in the School section.

Figure 13.1.

Browsing through a graphics library in Home Page.

Adding one of these graphics to a page is as simple as dragging the image onto the page. Before you try this out, however, you should make Home Page display the library along with the Kvikkalkul Web page you're working on. To do this, use the Window | Tile Vertically menu option to arrange the two windows side-by-side.

Using Graphics from a Library

The Kvikkalkul page should have a blank line above the heading Kvikkalkul home page; on this blank line, you will add the graphic of a pencil as a visual hint that the page is an educational offering.

Choose the School section of the library and scroll down so that the graphics file pencil.gif is visible. Click the mouse once on this image to make a jagged blue border appear around it. Drag this image by clicking the mouse on the image and holding the button down. After you drop the image in the space above the Kvikkalkul home page heading, you can see it displayed on the page above all the text.

Click once anywhere on the Kvikkalkul page so that you can continue editing that page. Highlight the pencil image and center it by using the Align Text Center button (or the Format | Alignment | Align Center menu option).

To call attention to the headings in the middle of the page, borrow a technique used often on Web pages—putting a small graphic next to each item. To get ready to do this, scroll the Kvikkalkul page until the headings Programs, Documentation, Help, and Send Us E-mail are all visible.

Go to the Yellow library section and scroll down to the bottom of the displayed graphics. You'll see six different yellow squares to put on a page.

Choose the one that has the filename ylsqr10.gif, drag it over to the Kvikkalkul page, and hold it over the line Programs. As you move it over the letters without releasing the mouse button, you should see a cursor that moves on the page. This cursor shows where your graphic will be dropped when you let go of it. Drop the yellow square when the cursor is to the left of the capital *P* in Programs. The square is then displayed alongside Programs with a jagged blue border around it, as shown in Figure 13.2.

Next, click on the word Programs so that a cursor appears between the yellow square graphic and the word Programs. Move the cursor to the left of Programs if it isn't there already, and insert a blank space to put a little room between the yellow square and the heading.

Drop yellow squares to the left of the remaining three headings also, making sure you add a blank space afterward between the graphic and the text.

After these four graphics have been added to the Kvikkalkul page, you should add one more graphic to the page—this time at the bottom instead of the top. Go to the last section of the library, called "Made With Claris Home Page." You will be putting the large "Made With"

13

graphics file chpmade.gif at the bottom of the page. Drag it onto the page and drop it below the heading `Send Us E-mail`. Center this graphic, too.

Figure 13.2.

Dropping library graphics onto a Web page.

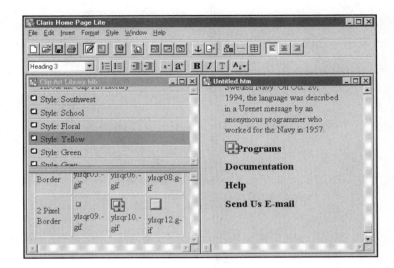

As another formatting touch to the page, indent the four headings (`Programs` and the others) from the text above them. Highlight these four headings, being careful to include all four yellow squares within the highlighted area. To indent this material, use the Blockquote option again by choosing Format | Blockquote from the menu.

To see how these graphics have been incorporated into the home page, use the Preview in Browser tool to see how it looks. Figure 13.3 shows the Kvikkalkul home page in the Netscape Navigator browser.

Adding a Library Background

Selecting a background is more involved than using the other graphics files from a library. You can't drag-and-drop a background onto a page the way you can with other graphics.

The first step in using a library image for a background is to scan through the different library sections and pick a graphics file you think would make a good background. For this example, use one in the Backgrounds: Borders section—a file called plgybord.gif.

To add the background image, click your cursor anywhere on the Kvikkalkul page and then click the Document Options button on the Home Page toolbar. The Options dialog box will open, and you should click the Set button next to the Background Image label. A dialog box opens where you can choose a graphics file. You need to find the plgybord.gif file in one of the folders on your system.

13

Figure 13.3.

Some library graphics on a Web page.

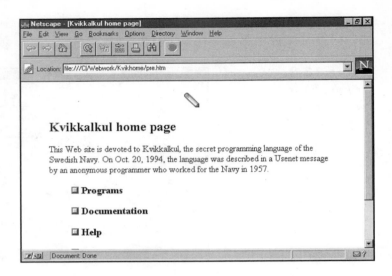

If you have any trouble finding the folder, take a look at the window in Home Page that's displaying the different graphics found in the Backgrounds: Borders library. Scroll to the top of this window if it isn't already visible, and you can see the name of the folder storing plgybord.gif. The Border Backgrounds window shown in Figure 13.4 identifies the folder as Claris Home Page Lite/Clip Art/Claris Clip Art/images/borders/.

Figure 13.4.

Finding a background graphic's folder.

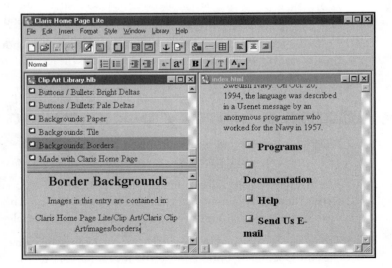

13

You can also use your system's Find File command (or a similar feature) to search for the file when you know its filename.

After you find the background file, highlight it in the dialog box and click the Open button. The name `plgybord.gif` then appears in the Document Options window, and you can click the OK button to make the change permanent. It shows up immediately on your Web page, as shown in Figure 13.5.

Figure 13.5.

The Kvikkalkul page after the background image has been chosen.

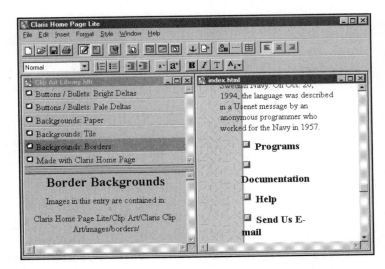

Using an Invisible Graphic

If you take a look at this page with a Web browser that supports background images, you'll see that the text runs onto the vertical gray area that runs down the page. Although this page might be readable because you're seeing black text over a gray area, that's often not the case when the border image is darker or more intricate.

You can use a transparent image from the Home Page library to insert some space between the vertical gray area and the text. This image has the name spacer.gif, but you won't be able to find it in any of the library sections. This graphics file must be added manually.

Click in the editing area of the Kvikkalkul Web page so that the cursor appears to the left of the pencil graphic, and then insert an image by clicking the Insert Image button. A dialog box opens where you can choose the correct image. Select the file spacer.gif from the Clipart/ Claris Clip Art/images subfolder and click Open.

13

At first, you might think you have done something incorrectly, because no image appears on the page. This is normal, however—the spacer.gif file is an extremely small graphic that's entirely transparent. You're not supposed to see anything.

To use this invisible graphic for better spacing between your text and the left-hand border, you need to change its size. To do that, first click the mouse to the left of the pencil graphic until a blue border appears around an empty box. This bordered box indicates that the spacer.gif file has been selected, as shown in Figure 13.6.

Figure 13.6.

Selecting the invisible spacer.gif image.

With this image selected, right-click your mouse once within the blue border and then choose Show Object Editor from the menu that pops up. You can also use the Object Editor by clicking the Object Editor button. When you select this option, it opens an Image dialog box where you can establish different settings for the object—in this case, an image. Click the Advanced or Both tab and you will see fields for modifying the height and width of the object.

Set the image to a width of 40 pixels and a height of 400 pixels. Also, set the Alignment option to Left alignment, which displays the rest of the page to the right of this image.

To make these changes official, close the dialog box by clicking the × in its upper-right corner.

Viewing the Final Result

Because Home Page Lite doesn't display Left and Right alignment within the editing window, you have to view the page in a Web browser to see the result.

Figure 13.7 shows the final version of the Kvikkalkul home page. The completely transparent spacer.gif graphics file has pushed the text further to the right so that it doesn't overlap with any of the gray area.

13

Figure 13.7.

The Kvikkalkul home page.

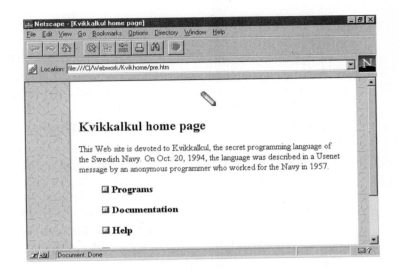

A graphic like spacer.gif is called a *spacer graphic* because it can be used in a variety of ways to put space between elements on a Web page. The graphic itself loads quickly because it's less than 1K, and it can be reshaped to any height and width you need.

TIME SAVER

The size of the spacer graphic in this example was selected through trial-and-error. If you're having trouble picking a good size, it might be helpful to put a 1-pixel border around the spacer.gif file while you're working with it. You can do that with the Object Editor tool in Home Page, and remove the border when you're happy with the size of the graphic.

Summary

Using the Home Page graphics library and some tricks with the Blockquote feature and a transparent graphic, you have turned a relatively simple page into a visually attractive one. The Swedish Navy and the men who served on its nuclear submarines in the 1950s would be very proud, if they actually existed.

By searching through the dozens of graphics that come with Home Page, you should be able to find some that can be useful on the Web pages you create.

13

Q&A

Q Can you use more than one spacer graphic on a Web page?

A Yes, you can—any graphics file can be included more than once on a page. You can also give each spacer.gif file a different height and width, so you can use it in more than one place to arrange a page's layout.

Q Can I add some of my own graphics to a library?

A To add one of your own graphics to an existing library section, use Home Page to open a page that contains the graphic and drag the image to the bottom half of the library window. It will appear there just like pasting an image on a Web page. You also can create a new library section with the New Entry button, which is displayed on the Home Page toolbar when you're using a library.

Q Before I put my pages on the World Wide Web, should I copy image files from a Claris folder into the same folder as my Web pages?

A You don't have to move any files if you're going to use the Publish feature of Home Page, which enables you to put your pages on the Web service hosting your site. If you're using FTP software to publish your pages, you should find the library images you want to use and copy them into folders with the pages they are used on. More information on doing this is available during Hour 22, "Publishing Your Site," and Hour 23, "Sending Your Site Through FTP Software."

Q Where can I find out more about Kvikkalkul?

A Unfortunately, Sams.net Publishing has rejected all proposals to publish *Teach Yourself Kvikkalkul in a Three-Day Weekend*, so you'll have to visit the book's Web site at `http://www.prefect.com/home24`. There's an expanded version of this hour's Kvikkalkul home page on the site.

Quiz

Test your knowledge of this hour by taking this brief three-question test.

Questions

1. What's the file extension used by libraries in Home Page?

    (a) .LIB

    (b) .HLB

    (c) .COM

13

2. What feature of Web page design can you use to indent text on a page?

    (a) Headings

    (b) Alignment

    (c) Block quotations

3. Which type of text alignment can't be seen within Home Page's editing window?

    (a) Top and Bottom alignment

    (b) Chaotic Neutral alignment

    (c) Left and Right alignment

Answers

1. b.

2. c. The Blockquote feature can be used more than once to increase the amount of indentation.

3. c. With the Lite version of Home Page, you can view Left and Right alignment only in a Web browser. Incidentally, answer b is a joke you won't get if you never played the game "Dungeons & Dragons."

Activities

The following activities are suggested to expand your knowledge of the subjects covered during this hour:

☐ Create your own graphic file or make use of one from a Web site that offers graphics for public use. Add this graphic to one of the folders in the Home Page clip art library by dragging it from a Web page into a library folder. As an alternative, you can create a new folder by clicking the New Entry button on the Library toolbar, which looks like a spiral notebook, and drop the image there.

☐ Add a border background to a home page of your own creation, and use the spacer.gif graphic and possibly the Blockquote feature to keep text off the border.

13

Hour **14**

Adding Animation to a Page

In the first several years of its existence, the World Wide Web was often compared to a magazine, a brochure, or another print medium. Browsing a Web site was like leafing through an issue of *Collier's Magazine* in a doctor's waiting room—you view a page, flip to another page, and so on, wondering why the most current magazine at the office is from 1952.

The Web isn't being compared to a magazine any more, and you'll learn two of the reasons why during this hour. Animated GIF files and Java programs are two elements that showcase the Web's uniqueness as a medium of information. During this hour, you'll learn how to use them on the Web pages you create with Home Page. The following topics are covered:

- ☐ Creating animated GIF images
- ☐ Using existing GIFs on Web pages
- ☐ Setting the speed of animations
- ☐ Using Java programs on your pages
- ☐ Finding Java programs to include
- ☐ Modifying the way Java programs work

GIF-Based Animation

If you surf the Web, you have seen animated GIF files, even if you didn't realize what they were. They are images that change as you look at a page, cycling through a series of images to create an animation. Many ad banners at the top of Web pages are animated GIFs, and they're also used to enliven icons—you might have seen spinning arrows and other small animated graphics on personal home pages.

If you're unfamiliar with these graphics or you'd like to see a few more before starting this hour, visit Webmonkey, the Web page developer's resource produced by *Wired* magazine, at http://www.webmonkey.com. That site—like many other parts of the HotWired Web site—frequently features animated banners and other creative uses of GIFs.

The best news about animated GIFs is that you already know how to use them with Claris Home Page 2.0 Lite. Putting an animated GIF on a page is no different than adding any other GIF to a Web page. You use the Insert | Image menu option or Insert Image button to select the GIF file to display, and space is reserved for it on the page.

Using Animated GIFs

To get ready for this hour's projects, go to the Webwork folder on your system and create a new subfolder called Animate. Go to the CD-ROM's Resource folder and copy the files letter.gif, Cube.class, and Cube.java into this new folder.

Creating an animated GIF requires two things: a group of GIF files that can be displayed in sequence and image-editing software that can combine these images into a single animated GIF.

It has been possible to animate GIFs for several years, but it wasn't supported by many image-editing programs until Netscape Navigator 2.0 included support for animated GIFs. Microsoft soon followed suit with Internet Explorer.

If you don't have any software that can combine several GIF files into an animated sequence, you can probably find software for your system that can handle the task. One such program from Microsoft, GIF Animator, can be downloaded for free from the World Wide Web. Visit the following Web page:

```
http://www.microsoft.com/imagecomposer/gifanimator/gifanin.htm
```

Animated GIFs are created by using a sequence of related images. Each of these images can be thought of as a frame, just like a frame that represents a single image in a movie. Figure 14.1 shows GIF Animator with a spinning envelope animation being created. Three of the frames are visible, and they show the envelope at various points as it spins.

Figure 14.1.

Several GIF files being combined to form an animation with GIF Animator.

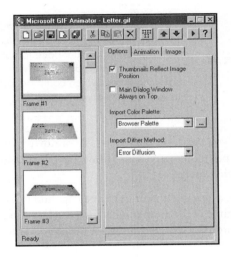

Each of these images is its own GIF image, and software such as GIF Animator merges them together. When you create an animated GIF, you specify the order in which frames will appear and the duration each frame is shown. You could use the duration setting in the envelope animation to make the figure move more quickly, move more slowly, or pause at specific points, for example.

You can also specify whether the image should loop more than once—which is often done to make sure Web surfers have a chance to see an animation at least once. An animated sequence can loop a set number of times or loop indefinitely.

The spinning envelope contains 15 frames, which cover a course of 360 degrees. Each frame is shown for one-tenth of a second before the next is displayed, and the animation loops indefinitely.

14

Putting an Animated GIF on a Page

The spinning envelope, which was created for this book, is in the file letter.gif. You should have already copied it into the Webwork\Animate folder.

COFFEE BREAK

The envelope graphic was created by using Micrografx Picture Publisher to make a 2-D image of a letter, complete with a stamp, and the 3-D development tool trueSpace to put that letter onto an object and spin it. trueSpace created an Audio Video Interleave (AVI) animation of the spinning letter, which could be loaded into Microsoft GIF Animator and converted into an animated GIF.

Once you create an animated GIF or download one from an archive on the Web, you can easily put it on a page with Home Page. Just insert the GIF onto the page as you would with any other image.

Create a new document in Home Page and insert the image file letter.gif onto the page. The first frame of the animation is then displayed in the page's editing window, and Home Page will automatically give the image the correct amount of space to be displayed at its actual size.

Save this page as letter.html with the title Letters. When you preview the page in the browser, you can see the envelope spinning in quick circles, as shown in Figure 14.2.

Figure 14.2.

The spinning envelope on a Web page, shown with Netscape Navigator.

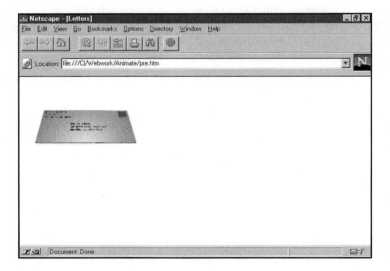

Using Animation Judiciously

Many sites on the World Wide Web offer animated GIF files for use on your own Web pages. Visit the Yahoo! directory at `http://www.yahoo.com` and search for the phrase `animated GIF` to see a listing of more than a dozen animated GIF archives.

As you can see with the envelope graphic, movement catches the eye quickly on a Web page. You can use animated GIFs to bring attention to a particular feature, or just to make a Web surfer stop and take notice of one of your pages.

The cost of using these graphics is slower downloading time for the page that features them. The spinning envelope, for example, is 46K, much larger than a similar static image.

Also, if you overuse animated GIFs, your pages can be distracting for Web surfers to use because their attention will be pulled in several different directions at once.

Whether you're using animated GIFs of your own creation or making use of some from a Web archive, it's important to pick your spots. This point is emphasized on a Webmonkey page about animated GIFs, which warns that overzealous designers "could hardly help themselves" when Netscape made it possible to create animated graphics files.

Putting Java Programs on a Page

Another way you might have seen animation on a Web page is through the use of Java, the programming language from JavaSoft, a division of Sun Microsystems, Inc. However, animation is just a small part of what's possible with Java. Using a special Java program called an *applet*, you can offer interactive programs as part of your Web pages.

Java applets can do many of the same things other software can do. Their only restrictions are used to prevent malicious programmers from using a Java program to damage your system.

Applets are put on pages like any other element. These programs start to run automatically when a page containing an applet is loaded with a browser that can handle Java, such as the current versions of Netscape Navigator, Microsoft Internet Explorer, and AOL's Web browser.

Figure 14.3 shows a Java applet that provides a stereo-like interface to audio files on a Web site. Visitors to the page can use the stereo controls to select a specific song and change the volume. The Web page for this applet is at the following address:

`http://www.goldmall.com/goldstone/gilmore.html`

14

Figure 14.3.

A Java applet that supplies a stereo interface to audio files on a Web page.

Hundreds of Java programs are being offered for use on the World Wide Web. You can add games, informational programs, utilities, and other types of software to your Web pages by using these applets.

To find many of the programs that have been made available, the most comprehensive listing of Java programs and resources is Gamelan at `http://www.gamelan.com`. It offers a searchable database with links to Java-related material on the Web.

Creating a Java Project

Adding a Java applet to a page with Home Page is relatively simple. Create a new document in Home Page to make space for a Java program, and choose the Insert | Applet menu option. When the Applet dialog box opens where you can set up the applet, click the Both tab so all fields of this box are visible. Figure 14.4 shows this dialog box.

First, you need to define the Code field, which identifies the name of the applet you're putting on the page. All applets have the filename extension .class because Java programs are called *classes*.

For this project, the applet is called Cube.class, which should already be in your Webwork\Animate folder. Enter this filename into the Code field.

Normally, the Java applet should be stored in the same folder as the Web page that contains it, as it is in this example. You can also specify that the applet is in a subfolder instead of the main folder. If you put a Java applet into a subfolder, then you must enter the name of the subfolder in the Code Base field. For example, if the applet was in a subfolder called javaprog, the value of the Code Base field should also be `javaprog`. However, because you're putting the Cube applet in the same folder as the Web page you're working on, leave the Code Base field blank.

14

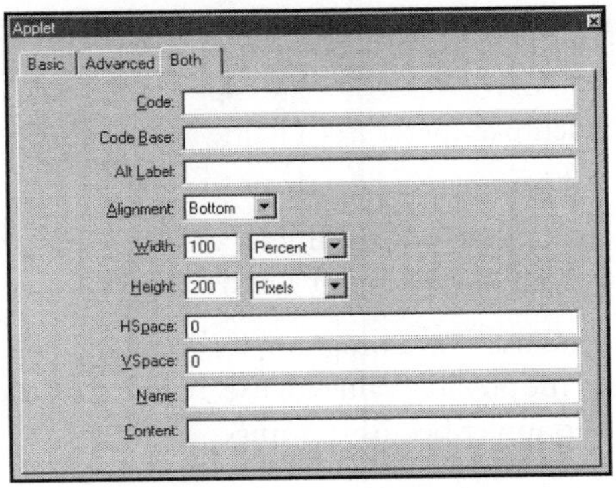

Figure 14.4.

The Both tab of the
Applet dialog box.

Like images and other parts of a Web page, a Java applet can have an Alt Label. This label describes what the applet is and can be viewed by Web surfers who can't run Java programs with their browsers.

Java applets also have height, width, and alignment settings, which establish how much space the program takes up on the Web page and how other elements appear in relation to it. One thing that's important to note with a Java applet is the recommended height and width. Some applets can adapt to any size, but others require a specific height and width. The Cube applet looks best with a height and width of 120 pixels each.

JUST A MINUTE

Although Home Page figures out the correct size to use with images, Java applets aren't automatically put on a page with suitable height and width dimensions. When using a Java program, you have to find the right size through trial-and-error or by consulting the program author's documentation—if any exists.

The last field you need to change is the Content field, where you supply any configuration options used by the applet itself. The Content field requires you to use a little HTML—the programming language used to develop Web pages. Normally, Home Page shields you from HTML by handling it behind the scenes. In this case, however, HTML is used to send a parameter to the Java applet before it begins running. The following should be entered into the Content field:

```
<PARAM NAME="Scramble" VALUE="True">
```

14

You don't have to understand much about the HTML tags in the Content field to use Java applets. All you need to know to use parameters with Java applets is the following:

☐ Each parameter has a name and a value.

☐ All parameters take the form `<PARAM NAME="SomeName" VALUE="SomeValue">`.

☐ More than one parameter can be used in the Content field, as long as each one is within its own set of < and > marks.

When you use a Java program, it should include documentation on what parameters can be sent and the possible values to use. In this case, the Scramble parameter is given a value of True when the applet begins running.

Finishing the Page

Before testing the page in a browser, press Enter after the applet and insert the following text:

```
Unscramble the Cube!¶
Press S to scramble the cube¶
Press R to reset it¶
By Karl Hörnell¶
```

Highlight all the text and the applet and center everything on the page, including the applet. Save the page in the Webwork\Animate folder as cube.html and give it the title Unscramble the Cube.

When you test the page with a Web browser that supports Java, you'll see a page resembling Figure 14.5.

Figure 14.5.

The Cube applet on a page, shown with Netscape Navigator.

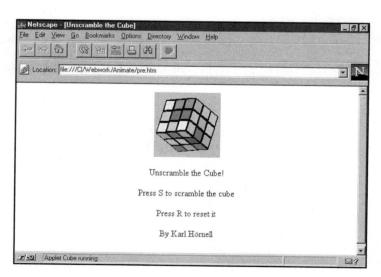

Java can be used to approximate animated sequences, such as the spinning envelope you used earlier this hour as an animated GIF. However, Java animation is more powerful than animated GIFs in the area of users interacting with the graphic.

In this case, a Rubik's Cube–like device is drawn on the screen, and the user can attempt to solve the puzzle by using the mouse. The `Scramble` parameter is used to determine whether the puzzle should be scrambled when it first appears (the value is `True`) or unscrambled (the value is `False`).

COFFEE BREAK

This program was written by Karl Hörnell, a Java programmer in Uppsala, Sweden. If you'd like to get an idea of the creative things that can be done with a Java applet, a good place to start is Hörnell's home page at the following address:

`http://www.tdb.uu.se/~karl`

Summary

Unlike some of the material you'll be discovering in the next two hours, Java and animated GIFs are widely available for your use on the World Wide Web. If you'd like to try these features on your Web pages, you ought to be able to find something to your liking with a few hours of surfing.

You can also develop your own offerings. Java programming is discussed in the Sams.net Publishing book *Teach Yourself Java 1.1 Programming in 24 Hours,* recommended highly because it was written by the author of this book, who has always enjoyed his own work. You can create animated GIFs with any image-editing tool that can prepare a series of related GIFs and merged them with software such as GIF Animator.

Q&A

Q Is it possible to display an animated GIF a few times and then stop the animation?

A Yes, it is—with a tool such as GIF Animator, you can make the animation cycle through a few times and then end. You can also put a long pause in the last frame of the animation and vary the length of time different frames are displayed.

14

Q Are there reasons to use Java for an animated sequence instead of an animated GIF?

A If the animation you envision can be created as an animated GIF, you will probably have better results with that format instead of a Java program. Java applets are a bit slower to load than a comparable animated GIF, in most cases. However, if the animation is complex or random in any way, a Java program is necessary because those effects aren't possible with an animated GIF.

Q Is it safe to run Java programs when surfing the Web?

A Java has security measures in its design that make it difficult for malicious program-mers to do any damage with applets on a Web page. The language also has fewer security risks than JavaScript and ActiveX programs. However, the decision to enable or disable Java programs with your browser depends on what else is on your computer and whether you're backing it up regularly to guard against a catastro-phe. There's no way to guarantee that a Web-based programming language like Java is 100 percent safe from abuse.

Q Can Java be used to create programs that don't require a Web browser?

A Like programming languages such as Visual Basic, C++, and Delphi, Java can be used for any kind of software. A Java program that runs without a browser is called an *application*, to differentiate it from an *applet*.

Quiz

Test your knowledge of this hour by taking this brief three-question test.

Questions

1. Which of the following isn't a way to refer to a Java program?
    (a) An application
    (b) A class
    (c) Dude

2. True or False: Can JPG files be animated like GIF files?
    (a) True
    (b) False
    (c) Put a few drinks in them, and they're plenty animated.

3. What's probably the most common way GIF animations are being used on the World Wide Web?
    (a) Menu choices
    (b) Advertising banners
    (c) Games

14

Answers

1. c.

2. b. A JPG file could be animated within a Java program, but there's no way at present to compile several JPG graphics into an animated sequence.

3. b. Frequently, an ad created as an animated GIF uses few colors and simple images, which makes it quicker to load and display.

Activities

The following activities are suggested to expand your knowledge of the subjects covered during this hour:

☐ Using Yahoo! or another World Wide Web directory, find an archive of animated GIF files available for use on your own Web pages. Pick one of the many animated graphics for a Mailto link: spinning letters, moving envelopes, and the like. Use one on your own personal home page, and attach a Mailto link to it.

☐ Visit Gamelan at `http://www.gamelan.com` and use its search tool to find a Java program to add to a Web page. Download the program's class file and put it onto a page with Home Page.

14

Hour 15

Adding Movies to a Page

There's always a downside to every technology innovation, and this hour's lesson makes that clear. You'll be learning how to put movies on your Web page, and if that doesn't scare you a little, you must not have any relatives or close friends.

Before the Web, someone could inflict their home movies only on a small personal audience—usually immediate family and luckless associates. Now, however, there's no geographic or financial limit to the prospective audience for the video of your trip to the Liberace Museum. If you have some thrilling footage of the world's largest wooden bowl factory, you can make it available on your home page.

During this hour, you'll learn how to present QuickTime movies on your Web pages. The following topics are covered:

☐ Using QuickTime to present images and sound

☐ Putting a QuickTime movie on a page

☐ Different ways to present a movie

☐ Incorporating a movie with other page elements

Lights, Camera, Action

If you're designing pages for an audience of users whose systems can handle the feature, movies are a sophisticated way to enliven a home page. Claris Home Page 2.0 Lite has built-in support for presenting QuickTime files, the most popular movie format used on the Web.

QuickTime is a system devised by Apple, the parent company of Claris, for presenting multimedia, animation, 3-D graphics, and audio files. QuickTime files, which are often called *movies*, have the .MOV file extension. According to Apple, more than 20,000 Web pages currently offer QuickTime content.

The current version of QuickTime is the recently introduced version 3.0. At the time of this writing, most popular Web browsers can support only QuickTime 2.5.

A QuickTime file is presented on a Web page as any graphics file would be—it's displayed around other elements on the page. Before the QuickTime movie can be displayed, however, the Web browser must be equipped with a program that can handle the format.

The ability to display QuickTime files is included as a standard part of the Netscape Navigator and Microsoft Internet Explorer browsers, but your system must have a QuickTime viewer installed on it. Many PCs are shipped with QuickTime preinstalled, or you might have installed it previously along with another software package.

To see whether your browser is already equipped to handle QuickTime movies, you can visit Apple's Web site at the following page:

```
http://www.quicktime.apple.com/sam/
```

This page contains links to sample QuickTime movies. Figure 15.1 shows a QuickTime movie playing on the Netscape Navigator browser.

COFFEE BREAK

The Web page shown in Figure 15.1 is part of the multimedia site We're Making Macbeth! The project details a University of Sheffield class teaching schoolchildren to perform *Macbeth*. The home page is at the following address:

```
http://www.dolphin.org/erik/nethernet/nethertoc.html
```

If you don't have the QuickTime viewer installed on your system, you can download one for free from Apple at the following Web address:

```
http://www.quicktime.apple.com
```

15

Figure 15.1.
A QuickTime movie playing on a Web page.

A QuickTime
movie

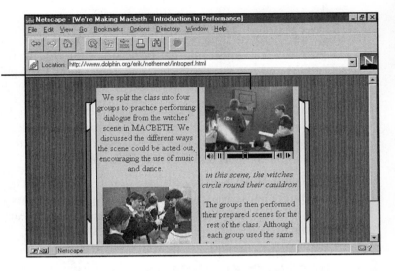

Creating your own QuickTime files requires a developer's kit from Apple or an animation and video software package that can produce QuickTime movies. However, some sites on the World Wide Web offer QuickTime movies and sound files for your own home page. To find them, visit a Web directory service such as Yahoo! and search for quicktime.

Also, visit Apple's QuickTime site at http://www.quicktime.apple.com for more information on the format and to see some examples of it in use.

JUST A MINUTE

The number of Web sites that include QuickTime should increase greatly in the coming year because its current version has added support for Windows authoring. Before QuickTime 3.0, you needed Macintosh systems to create and edit QuickTime files.

Although QuickTime movies have been offered on thousands of pages, their use is limited by the large size of the files. Most are more than 1M in size, and some are as large as 4M or 5M. They also require from 2M to 10M in system memory to display, depending on the size of the QuickTime file being shown. Because of these requirements, QuickTime isn't a feature that's likely to be used by Web surfers with slow modem connections or older computer systems.

Displaying a Movie

To give you a few QuickTime movies to work with, go to the Resource folder on the book's CD-ROM and get the files becker.mov, trailer.mov, tvtop.gif, tvleft.gif, tvright.gif, and tvbottom.gif. Create a new Webwork\Quick folder and copy these files into it.

Once you do that, you're ready to start a new project in Home Page that includes a QuickTime movie. Create a new page and choose the Insert | QuickTime movie menu option. A dialog box opens where you can select a .MOV file to insert on the page. Go to the Webwork\Quick folder and select the file trailer.mov.

You should see a Warner Brothers logo over a cloudy sky on in the page; it's the first frame of the QuickTime movie you have selected. Highlight this box and center it on the page by clicking the Align Text Center button or choosing Format | Alignment | Align Center from the menu.

Presenting a Movie in Different Ways

You can edit some aspects of how QuickTime movies are displayed by using the Object Editor tool. Right-click over the movie to open a QuickTime Movie dialog box where you can change some settings for the movie, such as the following:

- ☐ The height and width taken up by the movie on the page
- ☐ Whether the movie loops back to the beginning and plays again after it's finished
- ☐ Whether the movie plays automatically when it finishes loading
- ☐ Whether a controller is shown to use for playing and pausing the movie
- ☐ Where users can go to download a QuickTime player for their Web browser

Click the Both tab to see all these options. The last of the fields should be set by default to http://www.quicktime.apple.com, the official home page for Apple's QuickTime technology. Don't change this entry, which is labeled Plugin Page, because it gives Web surfers who don't have QuickTime the page they can visit to set up QuickTime on their systems.

The other options can be changed, if you like. For this example, the only thing to modify is the Auto-play checkbox. Check this box so that the QuickTime file plays immediately when it loads on a Web page. If it isn't checked and no controller is shown, the user viewing the page must click on the movie to make it start playing. Figure 15.2 shows the dialog box with the Auto-play box checked. Close the dialog box after making this change.

15

Figure 15.2.

The QuickTime Movie dialog box.

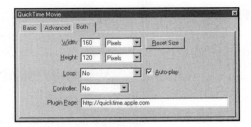

Previewing the Movie on the Page

Before taking a look at the page, use the Document Options feature to change the page's background color to black. This color makes the QuickTime movie hard to find on the page, but if you click in the general area with your mouse, a blue border appears around the movie.

Save the page in the Webwork\Quick folder as `trailer.html`. Give the page the title Coming Soon when Home Page asks you to title it.

Use the Preview in Browser tool to take a look at the page with your preferred browser. If you immediately get a message that your browser doesn't support QuickTime, you're directed to a page at Apple's QuickTime site where you can download and install software to support it. This process is exactly what visitors to your page would go through if they didn't have QuickTime and wanted it in order to see the movie.

When you preview this page with a QuickTime-ready Web browser, you will see a short trailer for the film *Batman & Robin*. Two things heighten the image's presentation: the page's black background and the automatic play feature. Figure 15.3 shows a screen capture from the Web page being displayed through Navigator. QuickTime images are usually small on a page, they can still take up a lot of disk space. This 145-second trailer takes up 8.6M and would be even larger if the QuickTime movie's display area weren't so small.

To get an idea of how you might present a QuickTime file differently, return to the trailer.html page and use the Object Editor tool to change the way the *Batman & Robin* trailer is shown. A fast way to modify options is to right-click on the movie.

Change the Auto-play option so that it's not checked, and set the Controller drop-down list to Yes. Close the dialog box and preview the page again. You should see a gray control bar with several buttons resembling a VCR's controls, as shown in Figure 15.4.

Figure 15.3.

*The trailer.html page
with the QuickTime
movie in progress.*

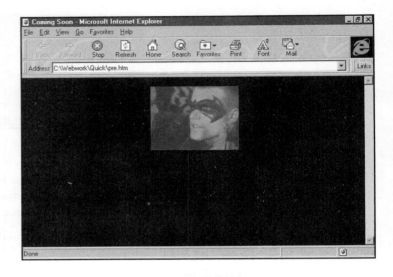

Figure 15.4.

*The QuickTime movie
displayed with controls.*

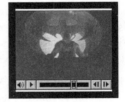

A button with a speaker icon can be used to adjust the volume of the QuickTime movie's sound, if it includes audio. Another button is used to play or pause the movie. These options give the viewer more control over playing the QuickTime movie.

Using Movies with Other Elements

QuickTime movies can be incorporated with the other content on a Web page, as your next project illustrates. You will be incorporating a QuickTime movie into a graphic that includes several GIF files.

Create a new page in Home Page, and make sure your Webwork\Quick folder contains the following files: batman.mov, tvtop.gif, tvleft.gif, tvright.gif, and tvbottom.gif. If it doesn't, copy them from the Resource folder on the book's CD-ROM.

Before putting anything on the page, use the Document Options feature to set the page's background color to white.

15

The first object to put on your new page is the image tvtop.gif. You might not be able to tell what this image is by looking at it, but the filename should be a clue: It's the top of a TV set. For this project, you're displaying a TV set that's showing a QuickTime movie. Although it looks like a single image, the page is composed of five different elements: the movie and four separate parts of the TV graphic that surrounds it.

COFFEE BREAK

Making a movie part of a larger image, as you're doing here, is a trick that's used often in multimedia projects. It helps disguise the small display area of most movie files.

The next part of the TV to add to the page is the left side. Before you can do this, you need to insert a line break that causes the cursor to drop below the tvtop.gif image. Your cursor should be immediately to the right of the tvtop.gif image you have already placed on the page. Use the Insert | Line Break menu option to insert a line break, and then add another image: the tvleft.gif file.

CAUTION

You can't use a paragraph break at the end of a line because it causes a blank line of text to be inserted. The TV graphics wouldn't be displayed as a single image.

Next, add a QuickTime file that represents the area occupied by the TV's screen by choosing Insert | QuickTime Movie from the menu and selecting the file batman.mov. A mostly black frame of the movie will be displayed in the editing window. Next to it, add the right side of the TV image: the tvright.gif file and another line break.

Finally, add the bottom of the TV: tvbottom.gif. You should then be looking at a TV, although the pieces of the image aren't connected yet within Home Page. Press the Enter key after adding the bottom of the TV to insert a paragraph break, and then add the following line of text:

```
Click the screen to play or pause the movie.
```

After adding this text, highlight everything on the page and center it. Figure 15.5 shows what the page should look like in Home Page's editing window.

Figure 15.5.

The Web page in the Home Page editing window.

Finally, you need to change the QuickTime movie so that it plays automatically. Right-click on the movie to open the QuickTime Movie dialog box and click the Both tab, if it isn't already visible. Change the Auto-play option to checked. Also, select the Yes option from the Loop drop-down list so that the movie replays every time it finishes playing.

Save the page with the title Batman Forever and the filename batman.html, making sure you store the page in the Webwork\Quick folder. When you preview the page in a Web browser, it should resemble Figure 15.6.

Figure 15.6.

The batman.html page in Netscape Navigator.

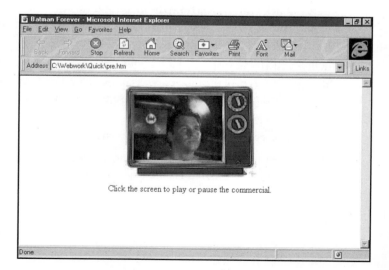

15

When this page is displayed with a Web browser, it looks like the TV and QuickTime movie are all part of the same image. Images run together in this manner if you use line breaks instead of paragraph breaks.

JUST A MINUTE

The movie trailers used during this hour are ™ and © 1997 Warner Bros. and used with their permission. You can visit the Web sites devoted to these films at the following Web page:

`http://www.batmanandrobin.com`

Summary

After using the QuickTime files with this hour's projects, you probably can see why TV stomped radio when it first arrived. Moving pictures are a compelling way to present multimedia information, even if you're presenting every minute of your last vacation.

However, it's important to remember that the QuickTime files shown during this hour didn't have to be downloaded over the World Wide Web. Each of the movies would take more than 15 minutes to download over a 28,800-baud connection with optimal Internet speeds.

QuickTime movies can be a special feature of a home page, but you should consider your audience before using them in place of other less time- and system-intensive graphics.

Q&A

Q Can I display the same QuickTime movie more than once on a Web page?

A You can, but each one will be loaded separately and take up its own share of a user's system resources. It can produce an interesting effect to present more than one copy of a movie side-by-side, but they won't be synchronized with each other if one takes longer to load.

Q Does a QuickTime movie have to include sound?

A No—some QuickTime files have no audio, and other files have no video, which makes calling them *movies* unusual. These audio- or video-only files download more quickly onto a page because they're smaller files.

Q **What's the smallest possible size for QuickTime movies that can be used on a Web page?**

A For extremely short video and audio clips, some Web sites have incorporated QuickTime .MOV files as small as 7K. One of the winner's of the NewMedia QuickTime Web Challenge contest is Mouse Jam, a musical site that uses small QuickTime audio files so that visitors can play instruments in a collaborative musical piece. It's at `http://members.aol.com/mousejam/index.html`.

Q **I would like to display a QuickTime movie at twice its normal size, but it isn't working. What's wrong?**

A Some QuickTime movies can't be resized within a Web page; they can be displayed only at their optimal size. These graphics don't scale very well, in any case, so an enlarged QuickTime movie would look extremely pixilated and grainy.

Quiz

Test your knowledge of this hour by taking this brief three-question test.

Questions

1. Which company developed the QuickTime format?

    (a) Microsoft

    (b) Apple

    (c) Sun

2. What can you use on a Web page to start a new vertical line without taking up a lot of blank space?

    (a) A line break

    (b) A paragraph

    (c) A horizontal rule

3. Which of the following isn't a good choice for a Web page menu of commands?

    (a) Java applet

    (b) QuickTime video

    (c) Animated GIF file

Answers

1. b.

2. a. The paragraph, normally used to start a new section on a Web page, leaves blank space. The line break simply starts on a new line.

3. b. The larger file size of QuickTime videos makes them an unlikely choice for something basic, such as a Web page menu.

15

Activities

The following activities are suggested to expand your knowledge of the subjects covered during this hour:

- ☐ Using one of the QuickTime audio files that's available in an archive on the Web, add some background music to one of the Web pages you have created.

- ☐ Visit http://www.quicktime.apple.com and go to their list of award-winning QuickTime sites. Check out the many examples of QuickTime in use on real pages.

Hour 16

Using Other Page Enhancements

The World Wide Web is constantly being reinvented as developers and publishers devise new ways to present information. To keep up with these changes, Web browsers have to be adaptable.

One way browsers adapt is by using other programs to do some work for them. During this hour, you'll learn about a special type of software called a plug-in, and see how it extends the capabilities of a browser such as Netscape Navigator. The following topics are covered:

- ☐ What plug-in software does
- ☐ Where to find plug-ins
- ☐ How to use plug-ins on Web pages
- ☐ How to use plug-ins with Home Page
- ☐ What the advantages and disadvantages of plug-ins are

Turn On, Tune In, Plug In

At the time of this writing, there are more than 150 types of plug-in software available for Netscape Navigator and other Web browsers. Plug-ins extend the capabilities of a browser by allowing it to handle new types of information, such as 3-D Web pages, live audio broadcasts, spreadsheets, games, and other things.

The name *plug-in* comes from the way the software is easily connected to the Web browser. You install the plug-in after downloading it over the Web, and it configures your browser so that the two programs can work together.

JUST A MINUTE

> The term *plug-in* is commonly used with Netscape Navigator, the browser software that pioneered the concept of using add-ons. However, many plug-ins are offered in slightly different form for use with Microsoft Internet Explorer.

Plug-in software is associated with a specific type of information that the Web browser can't normally handle. The following list represents a sampling of the plug-ins that are offered and the functions they provide:

- ☐ **MicroGrafx QuickSilver:** A way to display vector graphics on the Web—a type of image that's formed by drawing shapes, lines, and polygons. Vector graphics are much smaller than the bitmapped graphics represented by GIF, JPG, and other formats, and can be useful for displaying some images. QuickSilver is available from `http://www.micrografx.com/quicksilver`.

- ☐ **Progressive Networks RealPlayer:** A faster way to experience audio and video presentations over the Web because RealAudio and RealVideo can begin playing while the presentation is being downloaded. RealPlayer is available from `http://www.realaudio.com/products/player/index.html`.

- ☐ **Sony Community Place:** A group of programs using VRML that allows users to meet each other, chat, and work together in 3-D worlds. It features audio chat, a world-construction tool, and its own browser interface. Community Place is available from `http://www.sonypic.com/vs`.

- ☐ **Adobe Acrobat Reader:** A way to read and print Portable Document Format files through a Web browser. These files, which have the filename extension .PDF, contain more formatting information than a Web page. The plug-in is available at `http://www.adobe.com/prodindex/acrobat/readstep.html`.

Setting Up a Plug-In

The project this hour focuses on a useful plug-in you might not have installed on your system yet. PNG Live is a new browser enhancement used to view PNG graphic files. PNG, which stands for *Portable Network Graphics*, is a new image standard introduced as a successor to GIF files.

COFFEE BREAK

PNG was created in response to the announcement in late 1994 that CompuServe would begin charging royalties for some uses of the GIF format. CompuServe made the announcement after a suit was filed by Unisys claiming that GIF violated its file compression patent. PNG is an attempt to offer a free and legally unencumbered public standard for images.

The current versions of Netscape Navigator and Microsoft Internet Explorer aren't equipped to display PNG image files. When you first visit a page containing a PNG file, you will probably be asked if you want to download the plug-in. Figure 16.1 shows the dialog box you would see in Navigator that gives you a chance to download the PNG Live plug-in.

Figure 16.1.

A dialog box in Navigator for the PNG Live plug-in.

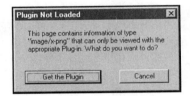

The PNG Live plug-in is available from the following Web page:

`http://codelab.siegelgale.com/solutions/get_it_index.html`

To view PNG files with a browser that doesn't support them, you need to download the PNG Live plug-in. This requires some effort for a visitor to a Web page—in this case, the Windows installation program for PNG Live is 800K.

Installing a plug-in is usually a matter of exiting your Web browser, running the installation program, and restarting your browser. The installation program plugs itself into the browser.

If you install PNG Live to work with your browser, visit the following Web page to see some sample PNG files:

`http://codelab.siegelgale.com/solutions/samples_index.html`

Plug-in software can work completely behind the scenes after it's installed. The PNG image files are then displayed immediately when loaded with a browser that has the PNG Live plug-in.

Using a PNG File on a Web Page

With Claris Home Page 2.0 Lite, you can put information on your pages that requires plug-in software to use. As your project this hour, you'll put two PNG images on the page. One image has 256 colors, just like a GIF file, and the other has 24-bit color, which means it can have thousands of different colors in the image. The GIF standard doesn't support 24-bit color, so in this area, PNG's developers improved on GIF. As a point of comparison, you will also put a GIF file on the page.

To get ready for this project, create a new Webwork\Plugin folder on your system. Go to the Resource folder on the book's CD-ROM and copy the following files into Webwork\Plugin: pulp.png, pulp256.png, and pulp256.gif.

After you're done, start Home Page and create a new document. Plug-in files are inserted on a Web page by choosing the Insert | Plugin menu option. When you choose this option for the first time in Home Page, you'll be warned not to insert the plug-in software itself onto the page, as shown in Figure 16.2.

Figure 16.2.

A warning note box about plug-ins.

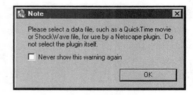

Plug-in software is the program that helps the browser present information, such as PNG Live. What you're inserting on a Web page is the file used by this plug-in—such as a PNG graphic—not the software for the plug-in.

Once you click OK to get past the warning, you can select a plug-in file to insert on the page. Go to the Webwork\Plugin folder and choose pulp.png, which is a 24-bit PNG image. A red square will appear on the page.

Modifying the Plug-In File

You need to set up three things for any plug-in file you include on a page: the file's height, the file's width, and the place where you can download the plug-in software.

16

With your cursor over the red square, right-click to open the Object Editor dialog box. Here you can set up the plug-in file you have just inserted on the page. Click the Both tab so all the fields can be edited.

Although the file in this case is an image, Home Page doesn't know how to deal with new types of information such as the PNG format. The software can't automatically determine the file's height and width, so you have to enter them manually. Enter 214 as the width and 300 as the height.

Also, you need to provide the Web address of the page where you can download a plug-in to view PNG files. Enter the following address:

`http://codelab.siegelgale.com/solutions/get_it_index.html`

It's important not to omit this information because many of the people who visit a Web page don't have all the plug-in software that might be needed. If you supply an address, however, they can go directly to a site where they can download and install the plug-in before continuing on your home page.

To see what this file looks like, you must have installed the PNG Live plug-in to work with your preferred Web browser. If you have, preview the page with that browser. Figure 16.3 shows the result.

Figure 16.3.

A PNG graphic on a Web page, viewed with Netscape Navigator.

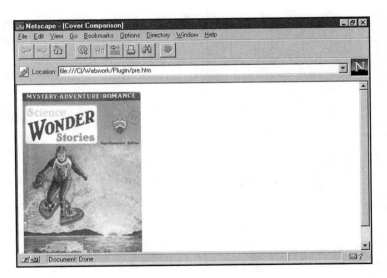

Return to editing the page and make sure that your cursor is to the right of the image you just placed on the page. You might have to scroll down the page to see it. When the cursor's in the right place, press Enter, and it will appear below the red square that represents the PNG image you just added. Use the Insert | Plugin menu option to add another PNG graphic: pulp256.png. Give it the same height, width, and plug-in Web address as the last image.

To see how this image compares visually to a GIF file with 256 colors, insert an image to the right of the pulp265.png plug-in file. Select the graphics file pulp256.gif. Unlike the PNG files, this GIF image is displayed immediately in the Home Page editor.

Preview the page in a Web browser and scroll down so that you see the two side-by-side images. Both of these images will look grainier than the 24-bit PNG file pulp.png because fewer colors have been used to represent the graphics.

Save the page with the title Images and the filename compare.html in the Webwork\Plugin folder.

Trying Other Plug-Ins

There are more than 150 plug-ins currently available, so PNG files are just one of the different types of information you can offer to enhance a Web page. Although Web surfers must download and install a plug-in to use them, PNG graphics are one of the more promising new technologies to be introduced.

Some types of information that become standard on Web browsers start out as plug-ins. Beta versions of Microsoft Internet Explorer 4 include built-in support for PNG, and Netscape has also announced plans to support it.

To see what kind of plug-ins are currently available, visit the following Web page at Netscape's site:

```
http://www.netscape.com/comprod/products/navigator/version_2.0/plugins
```

CAUTION

> Although the Web address for this page includes version_2.0, the plug-in software covers other versions of Navigator and some other Netscape products.

Summary

Like other Web page special effects, such as Java and QuickTime movies, plug-in software requires some thought before use. Some visitors to your Web pages would skip it if they didn't have the necessary plug-in, and others might not be able to run the plug-in software on their computer systems.

Some Web developers reduce the aggravation by offering an alternative that doesn't require a plug-in. Another thing you can do is put the plug-in content on its own pages and invite Web surfers to visit if they've got the plug-in. You have probably visited Web sites that feature Macromedia Shockwave, a plug-in that allows interactive programs to be offered on Web pages. On many sites, there's a Shockwave-only section and a section for everyone else to use.

Plug-ins can offer some advantages, however, to compensate for lost or aggravated Web surfers. For example, if you're offering a collection of photographic images, you might decide that the quality of PNG images will make your page more successful. In other cases, such as live audio and 3-D presentations, using a plug-in is the only way to offer the information.

16

Q&A

Q I tried to offer a PNG file on my Web site and it didn't work. What's the problem?

A Some Web servers must be configured before they can present a new type of information for use with a browser plug-in. For example, America Online isn't equipped to offer PNG files on its member home pages. If you put a PNG image on an AOL home page, it won't be recognized by your browser as a PNG file. When you're ready to put your home page on the Web, you might need to work with your service provider for special types of information, such as plug-in files.

Q Is there any way to know if a Web surfer has a plug-in installed?

A At present, there's no way to determine this in advance. However, if you put all the content that requires a plug-in on a separate part of your home page, you can make it easier for other users to benefit from the rest of your site.

Q When I put my Web site online, does anything special have to be set up to make use of a plug-in?

A In some cases, yes. Many services that host Web pages must be set up to work with specific plug-ins, or they won't work at all with a Web page using the plug-in. When you're ready to put a site on the Web, you should contact the service provider hosting your site if you're using plug-ins. They should be able to tell you if the plug-in will work immediately.

Q How would you put a plug-in file on a page if it doesn't take up any space, such as a RealAudio file?

A If a plug-in doesn't need to take up a specific amount of space on a Web page, you can offer it as a link on a page. The link would connect to the plug-in file itself. You would use the Insert | Link to File menu option instead of Insert | Plugin.

Quiz

Test your knowledge of this hour by taking this brief three-question test.

Questions

1. Which of the following was never used as the meaning of the PNG acronym?

    (a) PNG's Not GIF

    (b) Procter 'N' Gamble

    (c) Portable Network Graphics

2. When you use Insert | Plugin in Home Page, what exactly are you inserting on a page?

    (a) Plug-in software

    (b) A link to download plug-in software

    (c) A file used by plug-in software

3. Which browser popularized the use of plug-in software?

    (a) Microsoft Internet Explorer

    (b) Netscape Navigator

    (c) Chimera

Answers

1. b. PNG's Not GIF was a common answer to the question of what it stood for when the standard was being developed in 1995, and Portable Network Graphics is the established description today.

2. c.

3. b. However, Internet Explorer was quick to adopt its own version of plug-in support.

Activities

The following activities are suggested to expand your knowledge of the subjects covered during this hour:

☐ If you haven't already installed it, go to the PNG Live Web site at `http://codelab.siegelgale.com/solutions/get_it_index.html` and install it for use on your system. Search for PNG at Yahoo! to see some sample PNG images and sites.

☐ Using PNG Live or one of the other plug-ins, create a separate page of your own Web site that showcases the special information.

16

PART
V

Home Page Workshop

Hour

Hour **17**

Planning a Web Site

By now, you have been introduced to the wide variety of features available for Web designers. You have a good idea about what things you can do, and how they're done.

What hasn't been focused on is the big picture: bringing all these skills together to create a Web site. The next four hours are your chance to oversee the creation of a site during all three steps in the process: inspiration ("Whose idea was this anyway?"), perspiration ("Not now, I'm on my break"), and adulation ("You like me! You really like me!").

The following topics are covered during this hour:

- ☐ Deciding on a site idea
- ☐ Scoping out the competition
- ☐ Investigating promotional opportunities
- ☐ Visualizing the site
- ☐ Considering domain names for the site

Site Out of Mind

The first thing you need to do when creating a Web site doesn't involve software, computers, or anything more expensive than a pencil and paper.

You gotta think of something that deserves its own home page.

Although there are now millions of pages on the Web, you still have many services you could offer to the Netsurfing multitudes.

For some people, that service could be a site devoted to your favorite interest or hobby. Because the World Wide Web attracts millions of visitors, many people will be interested in the same things you are, no matter how esoteric, oddball, or fattening it is. Chris Harper turned his interest in the comics cartoonist Jack Kirby into a magazine and World Wide Web site at `http://www.users.dircon.co.uk/~ampcon`.

For others, the service is information related to their careers. Whether you're targeting customers, prospective customers, or people in the same field, you can use the Web as a way to reach them. Dr. John Mangiardi offers information related to his field of medicine at `http://www.brain-surgery.com`.

Many people start off their Web publishing careers by creating their own personal home page, which has several advantages:

☐ Knowledge of the subject matter.

☐ Originality—barring the odd chance that someone has created one for you already. (If so, two words of advice: restraining order.)

☐ The chance to describe someone you've always admired.

Others come to the Web with very specific ideas about what they should offer the wide world, such as the following:

☐ A newspaper composed entirely of fake stories (`http://www.theonion.com`)

☐ A site encouraging people to alienate loved ones, friends, and co-workers (`http://www.aprilfools.com`)

☐ The latest news on the world's most body-confident fat men (`http://www.sumoweb.com`)

The World Wide Web is the only mass medium that's available to anyone. There are no economic or demographic deterrents to prevent you from publishing anything you want. You don't have to conduct market research, you don't have to put up a lot of money, and you don't have to keep your eye on the bottom line.

These possibilities are what makes the Web such an intriguing and eccentric place.

17

CAUTION

> Before you get too caught up in this spirit of freedom, the Web is *not* the digital equivalent of the Summer of Love. If you don't want to be doing the official home page for your cell block next year, you should be aware of any restrictions you might run into regarding obscene or illegal content.

Investigating a Topic

Part of creating a site is defining what it is. You can do this on-the-fly as you build pages, if you're an improvisational sort, or you can document every detail before putting mitt to mouse.

The site you create during the next four hours is a daily question-and-answer feature called Glad You Asked.

JUST A MINUTE

> Glad You Asked isn't just a hypothetical example of a Web site that could be created. It's a working Web site created by the author of the book and offered at `http://www.gladyouasked.com`. You'll be able to work through the process of developing it, visit the finished product, and see behind-the-scenes details about the care and feeding of a Web site. Don't go there yet, though.

17

If you're a regular reader of daily newspapers, you might have seen columns that offer readers a chance to ask questions. Some of them focus on television and movies and can usually be found in the Sunday TV section. Others cover a specific topic, such as gardening, word histories, or consumer fraud.

A few newspaper columns tackle questions of any kind. Perhaps the best-known of these is "The Straight Dope" by Cecil Adams, a syndicated column that runs in alternative newsweeklies and other publications. A Web version is offered at `http://www.straightdope.com` and an America Online version at the keyword STRAIGHTDOPE.

Sizing up the competition is part of the planning process for a site, and The Straight Dope's Web site is probably the first place to go when you're contemplating a like-minded feature. Its home page is shown in Figure 17.1.

To find sites similar to what you have in mind for your site, the best places to start are Web directories, such as Yahoo! (`http://www.yahoo.com`) and Lycos (`http://www.lycos.com`). These two resources are helpful because they organize thousands of sites into specific categories. You should find the categories that fit where your site belongs, and take a look at the sites already there.

Figure 17.1.

*The home page from The
Straight Dope Web site.*

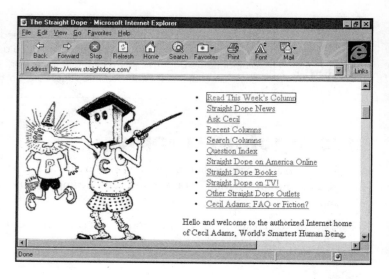

At Yahoo!, instead of searching randomly through the directory, an easy way to find
prospective categories is to search for similar sites. The Straight Dope page is currently being
featured on the following Yahoo! Entertainment page:

`http://www.yahoo.com/Entertainment/Trivia/`

Taking a look at similar sites is a good way to spur your own ideas—or to steal some outright,
if you're the kind of person who roots for the infectious diseases when you watch episodes
of "E.R."

When looking at your prospective site's rivals, you should also take note of something else:
advertisements. Many topics don't lend themselves to much marketing potential—none of
the pages on Yahoo!'s Fungi category, for instance, has taken advantage of obvious tie-ins to
the athlete's foot industry.

A few sites similar to Glad You Asked offer advertising of some kind. The Straight Dope, at
the time of this writing, has a predilection toward liquor ads.

You might not be seeking advertising revenue for your own site, especially when the big ad-
driven Web pages get thousands of visitors every day. However, a growing number of
advertising cooperatives have formed on the Web. These groups organize a bunch of smaller
Web sites together and share advertising efforts.

Some of them are strictly for promoting your site—such as the Internet Link Exchange at
`http://www.linkexchange.com`. By joining that group, you run ads for other members, and
they run ads for your site. Other groups share the revenue of the ads that are sold. eAds at
`http://www.eads.com` and the Commonwealth Network at `http://commonwealth.riddler.com`
are two such services.

17

Visualizing the Site

After sizing up the competition and figuring out your site's place in the world (of the Web, that is), you're ready to define your idea in more specific terms. It could be helpful to answer questions such as the following:

- ☐ What's the title of the site?
- ☐ What's the purpose of the site?
- ☐ How often will new updates be offered?
- ☐ Why should people make this site load automatically when their browser runs?
- ☐ Why should this site be updated regularly when there are any number of prime-time soap operas you could be watching instead?
- ☐ How much time will the site take to maintain?

The correct answers to these questions depend on your goals and the difficulty of putting the site together and keeping it active.

Here's how the questions would be answered for the workshop example:

- ☐ Title: Glad You Asked.
- ☐ Purpose: Answer visitors' questions on topics ranging from trivia to public service.
- ☐ Frequency: Daily.
- ☐ Reason to visit: Curiosity and habit.
- ☐ Reason to update and maintain site: Attract visitors and shamelessly self-promote author's time-based computer tutorials.
- ☐ Maintenance workload: One hour per day.

At this point, you have done a lot of work toward creating a Web site without getting anywhere near your Web page–editing tool. You should have a good idea of what Glad You Asked will be like, based on the description so far, although you haven't made any decisions regarding the site itself—the pages, graphics, text, and other elements.

Considering a Domain

Picking a place to house your Web pages is discussed fully during Hour 21, "Finding a Place for Your Site." However, there's one aspect you might want to consider now because it could change the title you have chosen for the site.

The issue: Do you want a personalized domain name for the site?

Most Web sites are part of a larger site, and their addresses are determined by the company that hosts the larger Web site on the Internet. They have longer Web addresses, such as the following:

```
http://www.city-net.com/~lmann/dps/
http://sctest.cse.ucsc.edu/roth/WebSoup/WebSoup.html
http://www.sjmercury.com/business/gillmor/
```

If you're harboring plans for surpassing Netscape or Yahoo! on the Top 10 most-visited Web sites, you should probably choose a domain name for the site.

 Domain names are the last half of an e-mail address—the part that follows the @ sign. They're a way of finding a site on the Internet without knowing its numeric address—a set of numbers such as `10.20.30.40`.

Having your own domain name for a Web site means you can use a much shorter Web address. Domains can be a way for visitors to remember how to get to your site, a component of a more memorable e-mail address, or the online equivalent of the personalized license plate.

Examples of existing domains are `webmonkey.com`, `startext.net`, and `emmys.org`. There are loosely followed guidelines for what the last part of the domain signifies: `.com` domains are commercial Internet sites, `.net` domains are networks that provide Internet access to others, and `.org` are not-for-profit sites. There are also many others you might come across, such as `.gov` for government sites and `.mil` for military installations.

When you know a domain name, you can usually find the main Web site associated with it very easily. The Web address typically takes the form `http://www.` followed by the domain name. All the sample domains work this way, and their home pages are the following:

```
http://www.webmonkey.com
http://www.startext.net
http://www.emmys.org
```

There are thousands of domains in use today, and most of the ones set up for a specific Web site use the `.com` domain. Many Web surfers have come to expect that the `.com` name is used by big companies and other outfits with well-known names. For example, what's the first place to look for Pepsi's Web site? Many people try `http://www.pepsi.com` to see if it's correct, and it is. The WNBA, the new Women's NBA, is holding court at `http://www.wnba.com`. Dilbert's official site? `http://www.dilbert.com`.

Finding an Available Domain Name

To see if a domain you would like to use is available, you can visit either of the following Web pages:

```
http://rs.internic.net/cgi-bin/itts/whois
http://rs.internic.net
```

17

At the first address, you can type in a domain name and see whether it's available. The second address is the main page of the site, and it has information on how to register the domain and pay for it. Figure 17.2 shows the result of a domain search on gore2000.com. Because this domain was registered when the search was conducted, information is provided on the domain's owner. Figure 17.3 shows the result for a domain that no one has snapped up yet.

Figure 17.2.

Results of an InterNIC search on a registered domain.

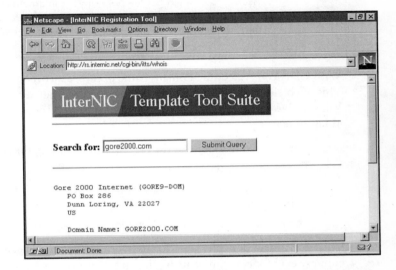

Figure 17.3.

Results of an InterNIC search on an available domain.

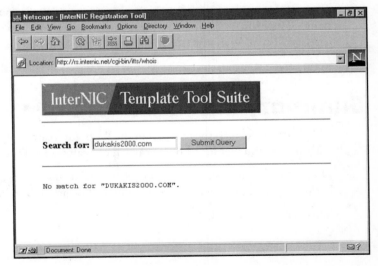

Domain names currently cost $100 to register directly from InterNIC, the group that controls domain name use at the time of this writing.

CAUTION

> Unless you have some experience with Web site hosting and similar issues, you should get the help of your Internet service provider or Web site hosting service. They usually charge a fee to establish a domain, but they can handle everything after you select an available domain name.

With Glad You Asked, the domain name `gladyouasked.com` was available from InterNIC. This Web site will be hosted by Interstice, an Internet service provider based in Incline Village, Nevada. The following information was required to register the domain `gladyouasked.com`:

- [ ] The name and address of the organization running the site
- [ ] The purpose of the site
- [ ] The primary and secondary server names (technical information that was provided by Interstice)
- [ ] The primary and secondary Net addresses (also provided by Interstice)

Choosing a new domain name for use with a Web site is generally done by commercial enterprises or for efforts that are hoping to become commercial. However, neither InterNIC nor your Internet company is going to reject any money you want to spend on a domain name. The primary motivation for using `gladyouasked.com` is to associate the site's name directly with its Web address, which will be the following:

```
http://www.gladyouasked.com
```

Summary

This hour has covered the first part of the Web site creation process: inspiration. Coming up with an idea and planning how to carry it out can take as little or as much time as you want.

Once you have come up with a concept you'd like to set up as a Web site, you're ready to get back to the computer and crank up your authoring tool, Home Page.

What's coming next? Glad You Asked.

17

Q&A

Q Can you register a domain name before you have a place that will host the site?

A No—you need information about the Internet site hosting your Web site when you register the name. InterNIC needs this information to direct Web surfers to your page when they type in your domain name, and the information must be provided immediately.

Q Can you register a domain just for use as an e-mail address?

A Sure—many of the services that register a domain for you and maintain it have an "e-mail only" option. Under this kind of arrangement, you should be able to receive all mail sent to the domain, no matter who it's addressed to on the left of the @ sign. For example, a business could get mail sent to `orders@theirbusiness.com` and also receive mail sent to `complaints@theirbusiness.com`.

Q Why can't I just create the pages and skip all this other stuff?

A If you're doing a personal home page or something that's not too complicated, you might not need to worry about planning or issues like domain-name registration. The next hour is where you'll learn about hands-on issues.

Q None of the domains I would like to use are available as `.com` addresses. What can I do?

A Because thousands of domain names have been registered by now, you have to be extremely creative when selecting a `.com` domain name. Some Web publishers choose an `.org` or `.net` domain if the alternative isn't available under `.com`, but this choice runs against the established guidelines for those domains, unless the site is for a not-for-profit organization or a network.

Quiz

Test your knowledge of this hour by taking this brief three-question test.

Questions

1. Which of the following isn't a good reason to create a Web site?

    (a) Fun

    (b) Communication

    (c) Rapid weight loss

2. What's the first place to look when seeking MTV's Web site?

    (a) `http://mtv.com`

    (b) `http://www.getdown.com`

    (c) `http://www.mtv.com`

3. Which comes first: choosing a domain name or choosing a place to host the Web site?

    (a) The domain name

    (b) The place for the Web site

    (c) The chicken

Answers

1. c.

2. c. a. will work for some domains, but it's not as common as c.

3. b.

Activities

The following activities are suggested to expand your knowledge of the subjects covered during this hour:

☐ Search for a domain name at `http://rs.internic.net/cgi-bin/itts/whois` and try to find a short and memorable one that isn't already taken. Contemplate the amount of money InterNIC must have earned by charging $100 a pop for these things.

☐ If you haven't already tried to create your own full-fledged Web site, use this workshop as a chance to follow along and develop your own. For this hour, answer all the questions about the site that were posed, and search Yahoo! and Lycos for similar sites.

Hour 18

Building the Pages

Once you have a clear idea about the Web site you want to create, it's time to get down to brass tacks, put your nose to the grindstone, wear out the shoe leather, put the pedal to the metal…

Work.

This begins the perspiration step of the process, and a working site will be created during this hour for the project Glad You Asked. You'll be using Claris Home Page 2.0 Lite to develop all the text and text links for the site. The following topics are covered during this hour:

☐ Deciding what to work on first
☐ Describing the pages
☐ Creating the text of each page
☐ Adding links
☐ Testing the site

Getting Started

Web designers often start with the layout of a site and sketch out some possible graphical designs to use. Mapping out the site beforehand keeps you from wasting time on designs that don't work or are rejected.

To develop Glad You Asked, you're going to take the reverse course: The text of the site will be developed first to create a working model and test its functions and features. Because the site is an outgrowth of a newspaper feature—and thus more textual than graphical in nature—this approach should prove to be workable. Designing a site "text first" emphasizes the information being presented and makes any errors in the site's design evident before you've spent time developing graphics and icons.

JUST A MINUTE

A new term is currently being used to describe the person who builds a Web site: *information architect*. This term is one of those perfect job titles for resumes—my own experience selling Atari 2600 video games at Toys 'R' Us has been described as "software distribution consulting" for years. Information architecture sounds like the kind of job that could get you a government grant.

Mapping Out the Pages

First, you need to determine how many pages the site will have when it's launched. Every site must begin with a main page—its home page—and you should store the main page in its own folder on your system with the filename index.html (or index.htm if your system is restricted to three-character filename extensions).

The reason to use index.html as the filename is that it usually shortens the Web address for your site. When you type a Web address into a browser, if you don't include the name of the page itself, most Web servers assume you're looking for index.html.

For example, member Web pages on America Online work this way. The pulp-magazine home page .Pulp uses index.html as its main page, and it uses AOL to host the page. As a result, it can use the following Web address:

```
http://members.aol.com/dotPulp
```

This is the equivalent of typing the following address:

```
http://members.aol.com/dotPulp/index.html
```

18

> **JUST A MINUTE**
>
> Some Internet sites that host Web pages have a different default name, such as default.html. Check with the service provider if you have problems using index.html.

Glad You Asked will have the following pages:

- ☐ **index.html:** The main page, which will display the current question of the day and links to other pages.
- ☐ **archive.html:** Links to all past question pages.
- ☐ **gy072897.html:** This page, and four others like it, will hold questions for five previous days. The filename indicates the question's date, such as July 28, 1997 for gy072897.html.
- ☐ **ask.html:** A page with guidelines on questions and a Mailto link to the publisher.
- ☐ **about.html:** The story behind the site's creation and other promotional information.

To give visitors an immediate means of sending feedback, the site will also make use of a service called LPage, as you'll learn about during Hour 20, "Using Web Resources." LPage hosts guestbooks for other Web sites, allowing visitors to post their comments immediately.

The Home Page

After you have mapped out the filenames and the general purpose of the pages, you're ready to start entering text. If you're going to be building this site as you read along, crank up Home Page and begin a new page.

> **JUST A MINUTE**
>
> If you'd like to create the pages without typing them in, you can cut-and-paste text from the Web pages in the Example\Hour18 directory on the book's CD-ROM.

Enter the text of Listing 18.1 into the editing window.

TYPE **Listing 18.1. The text of index.html.**

```
1: Glad You Asked¶
2: THE QUESTION OF THE DAY FOR AUG. 4, 1997¶
3: Q: Back in the '70s, Bill Cosby slugged one of the Smothers
4: brothers. Do you know what caused the altercation?¶
5: R.M., Fort Worth, Texas¶
```

continues

Listing 18.1. continued

```
 6: A: The battle of the network stars took place in 1976,
 7: according to Ronald L. Smith in the 1985 biography Cosby. At a
 8: time when people were clamoring for more family programming,
 9: Cosby had just premiered Cos, a Sunday prime-time show aimed
10: primarily at children.¶
11: The show, unfortunately, was not well-received. "Bring back
12: Lassie," Smith quoted one critic as saying. "At least that show
13: admitted that it was a dog."¶
14: As Cos was floundering during its eight-week run, Tommy Smothers
15: said something to Cosby at a Playboy Mansion party. They "were
16: not buddies," Smith writes, and after a few words were exchanged
17: Cosby knocked Smothers down with a right to the jaw.¶
18: "Later, the swollen-cheeked comic claimed that he was only
19: trying to complement Bill on his new TV show," Smith writes.
20: "The last words Tommy heard were, 'You've been asking for it.'"¶
21: Previous Questions:¶
22: Friday Aug. 1: Did they charge admission at the Colosseum?¶
23: Thursday July 31: Was Lonesome Dove, Texas, a real place?¶
24: Wednesday July 30: Where did the term honkytonk come from?¶
25: Tuesday July 29: Is there a link between hot dogs and leukemia?¶
26: Monday July 28: Where did Daryl Johnston get the nickname "Moose"?¶
27: HOME ¦ ARCHIVE ¦ ASK A QUESTION ¦ GUESTBOOK ¦ ABOUT THE SITE¶
```

After entering the text, make the following changes to the page:

☐ Line 7: Italicize the text Cosby.

☐ Lines 9 and 14: Italicize the text Cos.

☐ Line 12: Italicize the text Lassie.

☐ Lines 22–26: Turn these lines into an unnumbered list.

☐ Line 22: Make the text Friday Aug. 1 into a link to gy080197.html.

☐ Line 23: Make the text Thursday July 31 into a link to gy073197.html.

☐ Line 24: Make the text Wednesday July 30 into a link to gy073097.html.

☐ Line 25: Make the text Tuesday July 29 into a link to gy072997.html.

☐ Line 26: Make the text Monday July 28 into a link to gy072897.html.

☐ Line 27: Make the text ARCHIVE into a link to archive.html.

☐ Line 27: Make the text ASK A QUESTION into a link to ask.html.

☐ Line 27: Make the text ABOUT THE SITE into a link to about.html.

When you're done, save the page with the title Glad You Asked. Give it the filename index.html, and store it in a new folder called Webwork\Glad. Figure 18.1 shows the page previewed with a browser.

Figure 18.1.

The index.html page viewed in Microsoft Internet Explorer.

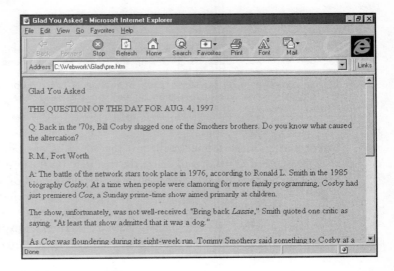

The Question Pages

After you have finished the text version of index.html, you're ready to create the pages for the five previous questions. They will be exactly the same as index.html with three exceptions: a different date, a new question, and fewer previous questions in the unnumbered list.

Instead of creating a new page, use the File | Save As menu option to save a copy of index.html under a new name. Save it as gy080197.html in the Webwork\Glad folder.

For this page, change the date at the top of the page to AUG. 1, 1997. Use the text of Listing 18.2 as the question.

TYPE   **Listing 18.2. The question text of gy080197.html.**

```
 1: Q: I'm curious about something: In the Colosseum, did they
 2: charge admission and have reserved seating?¶
 3: D.C., Fort Worth, Texas¶
 4: A: Aside from the killing, of course, the fan experience at the
 5: Roman Colosseum was similar to today's events. There were 45,000
 6: seats in the amphitheatre, and room for up to 5,000 standing
 7: fans.¶
 8: Tickets, which were heavily in demand, were marked with the
 9: entrance to use as well as the tier and row number of the seat.
10: The emperor rated a luxury box, and senators and other high
11: officials got the best seats.¶
12: Admission was free, because aspiring politicians bankrolled the
13: events. "Whoever sought a political career and the certainty of
```

continues

Listing 18.2. continued

```
14: being elected had only to organize a gladiatorial contest at his
15: own expense," according to The World of Ancient Rome.¶
16: The Colosseum opened in 80 A.D. Most of the biggest attractions
17: involved people fighting each other or animals. Up to 5,000
18: animals were killed on Opening Day of the facility, known
19: officially as the Flavian Amphitheatre.¶
```

After entering this text, italicize the text The World of Ancient Rome on Line 15. The next change you need to make is to delete the first item on the unnumbered list—the reference to the Aug. 1 question—which makes the July 31 question the first in the list. The last change is to the text HOME on the last line of the page itself; it should be used to link to the page index.html. Save this file as gy080197.html, and you're done with that page. Figure 18.2 shows the last half of the page when previewed with Internet Explorer. You can use the figure to verify that you've handled the links to each daily page correctly.

Figure 18.2.

The gy080197.html page viewed in Microsoft Internet Explorer.

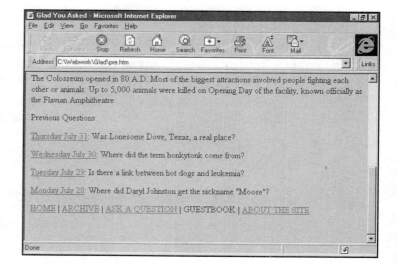

To begin the next question page, save a copy of the current page again under the name gy073197.html. Change the date at the top of the page to the text JULY 31, 1997 and replace the question text with Listing 18.3.

TYPE | **Listing 18.3. The question text of gy073197.html.**

```
1: Q: Was Lonesome Dove, Texas, a real place?¶
2: V.F., Texas¶
3: A: Texas native Larry McMurtry named his fictional Texas border
4: town while visiting Fort Worth, Texas. He saw the church van for
5: Lonesome Dove Baptist Church drive by, and thought it would be a
6: great name.¶
7: Lonesome Dove, located in Southlake, is the oldest church in
8: Tarrant County. It was founded in 1846 and has about 100 members
9: today, according to Pastor Coy Quesenbury.¶
10: Quesenbury said the best guess for the name was that members
11: heard a dove call during the first service. "According to a
12: legend, one of the ladies said, 'Listen to that lonesome dove,'"
13: he said.¶
14: Another theory is that the Baptist church was the "lonesome
15: dove" in the West as of 1846. "There was not another non-Catholic
16: church from here to the Pacific Ocean," Quesenbury said.¶
```

Delete the first item on the unnumbered list of previous questions, which refers to the July 31 question, and you're done with the page. Be sure to save the finished page.

To begin the next question page, save a copy of the current page under the filename gy073097.html in the folder Webwork\Glad. Change the date at the top of the page to JULY 30, 1997, and replace the question with the text of Listing 18.4.

TYPE | **Listing 18.4. The question text of gy073097.html.**

```
1: Q: Where did the term honkytonk come from?¶
2: K.H., Dallas, Texas¶
3: A: Ardmore, Oklahoma. That's probably not the answer you're
4: looking for, but word historians don't know why the term
5: honkytonk was first applied to a "place of low amusement," as
6: Ramon Adams defines it in Western Words.¶
7: The first known reference was in the Feb. 24, 1894, Daily
8: Ardmorite. A newspaper ad promoted a dance hall with gambling
9: and burlesque shows, calling the place a "honk-o-donk."¶
10: The century-old word stuck, though no explanation of its birth
11: has been found. Honkytonk is considered a "reduplication," a new
12: word formed by repeating elements of an existing word.¶
13: Other reduplications are equally nonsensicial, such as
14: boogie-woogie, hocus-pocus, razzle-dazzle and fancy-shmancy.¶
```

After entering the text, make the following changes:

- ☐ Line 1: Italicize the text honkytonk.
- ☐ Line 6: Italicize the text Western Words.
- ☐ Lines 7–8: Italicize the text Daily Ardmorite.

18

Next, delete the first item in the unnumbered list, which refers to the July 30 question, and save the file to finish out this page.

By now, you should know the drill for the next page, gy072997.html. Listing 18.5 shows the text of the question for this day.

TYPE **Listing 18.5. The question text of gy072997.html.**

```
 1: Q: My daughter saw something on television regarding hot dogs
 2: and leukemia. My kids live on hot dogs. Is there any truth to
 3: it?¶
 4: S.H., Fort Worth, Texas¶
 5: A: Concerns were raised by reports in the March 1994 issue of
 6: Cancer Causes and Control, edited by the Harvard School of
 7: Public Health. The publication reported on three studies of hot
 8: dogs and childhood cancers.¶
 9: A study of 440 children in the Denver area suggested a higher
10: incidence of brain tumors and leukemia among children who ate
11: hot dogs once a week or whose mothers did during pregnancy.
12: Another study of 310 children suggested a link between women who
13: ate hot dogs and cured meats while pregnant and brain tumors in
14: their children.¶
15: The third, a look at 232 children with leukemia in the Los
16: Angeles area, found that their only persistent association was
17: hot dogs eaten by the children, or by the father before the
18: child's conception.¶
19: Medical researchers characterize the findings as extremely
20: preliminary, indicating a need for further study rather than a
21: cause for alarm. The American Meat Institute has disputed the
22: research.¶
```

Italicize the text Cancer Causes and Control on Line 6, delete the unnumbered list item for July 29, and save the page.

The last question page is gy072897.html. Listing 18.6 shows the question text.

TYPE **Listing 18.6. The question text of gy072897.html.**

```
 1: Q: Where did Daryl Johnston get the nickname "Moose"?¶
 2: L.M., Fort Worth, Texas¶
 3: A: The Dallas Cowboys fullback was first given the name about
 4: four years ago by quarterback Babe Laufenberg, now a commentator
 5: during game broadcasts for the team. Johnston's road to
 6: "Moosedom" began at a team meeting.¶
 7: "We had all these 5-foot-9 running backs at the time -- all
 8: little guys," Laufenberg said. "Daryl was in the back of the
 9: pack when they came in, and I said something like, "Look at all
10: the deer, and there's a big ol' moose behind them."¶
11: Though Cowboys radio announcer Brad Sham described Johnston as
12: "the magnificent Caribou" during one game, the "Moose" name
13: stuck, and numerous calls for the large antler-bearing mammal
```

18

```
14: can be heard during home and road games.¶
15: The nickname has spawned T-shirts, foam antlers and other
16: Moose-abilia, but Laufenberg said he hasn't received a cut. "My
17: mom did send me a stuffed moose," he said. "I should've gotten a
18: trademark."¶
```

There are no previous questions before this one, so delete the last item in the unnumbered list, and also axe the line Previous Questions:. Save the file and be glad there are only five business days in a week.

COFFEE BREAK

> If you're curious, all these questions and answers are legitimate. They were solicited for the newspaper column "Ask Ed Brice," a feature of the *Fort Worth Star-Telegram*, ghost-written by the author of this book.

The Other Pages

Now that all the similar question pages have been created, the remaining pages are much kinder to the carpal tunnel nerves.

The next page to work on is the page archive.html, a list of past questions. Although this page might become unwieldy at some point and require reorganizing, to start out it will be a short unnumbered list similar to the one on index.html.

Create a new page and enter the text of Listing 18.7. Most of it is a duplicate of some of the text on index.html in Listing 18.1, so you can save time by using cut-and-paste from one page to the other.

TYPE **Listing 18.7. The text of archive.html.**

```
1: Glad You Asked
2: The following questions ran in past editions of Glad You Asked:
3: Friday Aug. 1: Did they charge admission at the Colosseum?
4: Thursday July 31: Was Lonesome Dove, Texas, a real place?
5: Wednesday July 30: Where did the term honkytonk come from?
6: Tuesday July 29: Is there a link between hot dogs and leukemia?
7: Monday July 28: Where did Daryl Johnston get the nickname "Moose"?
8: HOME ¦ ARCHIVE ¦ ASK A QUESTION ¦ GUESTBOOK ¦ ABOUT THE SITE
```

If you didn't cut-and-paste, you'll need to change each date to a question page link, beginning with the text Friday Aug. 1. The text on Line 8 should be used to create links to index.html, ask.html, and about.html, respectively. Don't make the text ARCHIVE link to anything, because that's the current page. If it's already a link, click the Remove Link button of the Link Editor to remove it. Also, make sure the text HOME links to the page index.html.

18

CAUTION

If you did use cut-and-paste, then there's something to watch out for in Home Page: It might change the link and add a reference to a folder on your system. For example, `gy080197.html` could be expanded into `/C:/Webwork/Glad/gy080197.html`. This change causes problems when the Web site is put online because the `/C:/Webwork/Glad/` part of the link refers to your own computer instead of a place on the World Wide Web.

To check for this problem and fix it if needed, highlight each of the links after pasting them onto the page and click the Link Editor button to see what they are linking to. Remove everything in the URL field of the Link dialog box except the filename itself, such as `gy080197.html`.

Save this page as `archive.html` in Webwork\Glad with the title What You Asked.

The next-to-last page (pant! pant!) contains the guidelines for sending questions to Glad You Asked. Create a new page and enter the text of Listing 18.8.

TYPE **Listing 18.8. The text of ask.html.**

```
1: Glad You're Asking¶
2: This Web site depends on a steady diet of good questions. Before
3: you send us a question, you might want to check the archive to
4: see if your mental McNugget has already been answered.¶
5: If it hasn't, send your initials, city, and state by e-mail to
6: socrates@gladyouasked.com.¶
7: One other thing: You also should send the question.¶
8: HOME ¦ ARCHIVE ¦ ASK A QUESTION ¦ GUESTBOOK ¦ ABOUT THE SITE¶
```

After entering the text, make the following changes:

☐ Line 3: Use the text check the archive to link to archive.html.

☐ Line 6: Use the text socrates@gladyouasked.com for a Mailto link to `mailto:socrates@gladyouasked.com`.

☐ Line 8: Use the text on this line for links to index.html, archive.html, and about.html.

Save this page with the title Glad You're Asking and the filename ask.html. Figure 18.3 shows how this page looks when it's previewed with a browser.

The last page you need to create during this hour is about.html, the description of the site. This page gives readers a better understanding of the site when they discover it for the first time.

Figure 18.3.

The ask.html page viewed in Microsoft Internet Explorer.

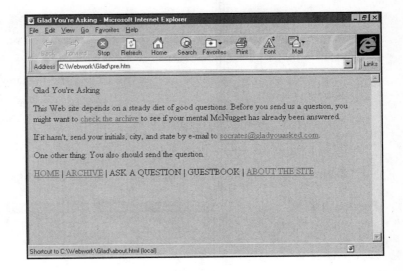

One of the things that's important to establish for any Web site is how often it's updated. Because the Web is a dynamic medium, there's no set expectation for how often people visit a Web site. There are sites that change hourly, daily, weekly, monthly, and hardly ever. If a site has a set maintenance schedule, it should be made clear to people who visit it.

There are dozens of Web sites with "of the day" in their titles, and part of their success has nothing to do with talent, originality, or creativity. It's frequency. If you can make your site a habitual stop for Web surfers, you're one step closer to an Initial Public Offering, millions in investment dollars, and the cover of *Wired*.

On Glad You Asked, the date of each question at the top of the home page indicates its schedule. The about.html is also used to establish the frequency of updates.

Create a new page and enter the text of Listing 18.9.

TYPE   **Listing 18.9. The text of about.html.**

```
1: Who You Asked¶
2: Glad You Asked is updated every weekday (except holidays)
3: with our answer to a visitor's question. The question can
4: come from the world of news, sports, trivia, technology, or
5: anything else within the realm of human experience --
6: especially if the answer's really easy to find.¶
7: This site was created as part of the book Teach Yourself to
8: Create a Home Page in 24 Hours.¶
9: HOME ¦ ARCHIVE ¦ ASK A QUESTION ¦ GUESTBOOK ¦ ABOUT THE SITE¶
```

18

Highlight the text Teach Yourself to Create a Home Page in 24 Hours and use it to link
to http://www.prefect.com/home24, the book's official Web site. On Line 9, use the text to
create links to index.html, archive.html, ask.html, and about.html.

Save this page with the title Who You Asked and the filename about.html in the folder
Webwork\Glad.

This is the last page to be created for the launch of the Web site. Because you have created
all the text links on the pages, you can preview index.html in a browser and navigate to the
other parts of the site.

Figure 18.4 shows one of the pages from the site as it's being previewed in a browser.

Figure 18.4.

*The about.html page seen
in Microsoft Internet
Explorer.*

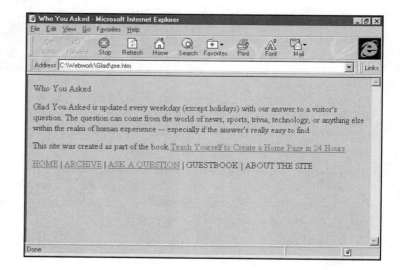

Summary

After all the pages have been created, you have a working Web site, although not a particularly
compelling one. Web surfers who use the text-only browser Lynx or a graphics-off browser
would be right at home, but most other people who point-and-click their way to your site
would expect more.

After you have experienced the joy of text, using all the links to see that everything's in order,
you're ready to start working on the site's graphical design.

18

Q&A

Q **Some Web sites offer a way to write mail on a page instead of a Mailto link. How is this possible?**

A Those pages use a type of Web page called a *form*. You can design one using some Web page editing tools, but not Home Page's Lite version. However, you must also have access to an advanced type of Web server programming called a *CGI program*. Mailto links are the best way to start out before looking into more advanced features.

Q **Should I design a chart indicating how each of the pages on a site link to one another?**

A It hasn't been done with the workshop example Glad You Asked because of the relatively simple organization of the pages. The amount of planning that's done for a Web site largely depends on the size of the project and personal preference.

Q **Is there a way to paste links without having to check them for errors?**

A Apparently not. Because Home Page does a lot of work behind-the-scenes for you, as it does with cutting-and-pasting links, there might be times when the software does something you don't want. Links are the main example of this problem, although you have to be mindful of it when putting images on a Web page, too.

Q **Can I put more than one Web site in the same directory on a Web hosting service?**

A You can, but there are several reasons to put each site into its own directory. First, only one of the sites could use the name index.html for its home page. Second, it would be too easy to confuse which pages, graphics, and other files belong with which site. Having several sites in one directory makes it much tougher to move the site later on or make major changes to its pages.

18

Quiz

Test your knowledge of this hour by taking this brief three-question test.

Questions

1. Which of the following is the least likely filename for a Web site's home page?

    (a) default.html

    (b) index.html

    (c) readme.txt

2. Why should you cut-and-paste between two pages on Home Page?

    (a) Links are copied along with the text.

    (b) Be kind to your carpal tunnel nerves, and they will be kind to you.

    (c) Both of the above.

3. What is a great resume-inflating term for a Web page designer?

    (a) Hypertextual ambassador

    (b) Information architect

    (c) Virtual vicar

Answers

1. c.

2. c.

3. b.

Activities

The following activities are suggested to expand your knowledge of the subjects covered during this hour:

☐ Preview the Glad You Asked Web site within Home Page by using the Preview tool, observing how it can be used to test the links connecting the different parts of a site.

☐ Create your own Web page starting with the text, as you did during this hour for Glad You Asked. Make sure all the links work and the text is what you want it to be before continuing to the next hour.

Hour 19

Creating the Graphics

One of the ways you can hook visitors on a Web site is with memorable graphics. The World Wide Web has become a visual designer's playground, incorporating the best techniques of print, television, and CD-ROM design—along with some new tricks that couldn't exist anywhere else.

Of course, the rest of us get to play there, too, by using the graphics available in Web archives and designing our own with drawing software. During this hour, you'll see how graphics are added to Glad You Asked. The following topics are covered:

- ☐ Adding a background image
- ☐ Adding foreground images
- ☐ Changing fonts and headings
- ☐ Creating an image map
- ☐ Bringing it all together

Ready, Aim, Draw

During this hour you'll see how an all-text Web site develops a visual identity, as graphics are added to the Glad You Asked site. To get ready for the workshop, go to the Resource folder on the book's CD-ROM and copy the files logo.gif, stripe.gif, and menu.gif to the Webwork\Glad folder on your system. These three graphics will be used on each page of Glad You Asked.

JUST A MINUTE

A note for readers who are creating these Web pages as they progress through the workshop: Because all the pages on the site will use the same graphics, the changes made to index.html during this hour will be applied to the other pages, too.

Fonts and Headings

Before adding any graphics, you need to apply some formatting changes to the text. Load the index.html page back into Home Page and highlight all the text on the page.

The font for the Web site will be selected from a list of several fonts, beginning with Verdana. As you learned during Hour 6, "Resizing Text and Using Fonts," when more than one font is specified, the Web browser chooses the first font that's available on a user's system.

With all the text of index.html highlighted, use the Style | Font | Other menu option and enter the following text in the Font Names box to set the font:

```
Verdana,Arial,Helvetica,helvetica
```

The Verdana, Arial, and Helvetica fonts are used so browsers can find a sans serif font that's available on Windows and Macintosh systems. The last choice, helvetica, is a font that's available on some UNIX and Linux windowing systems. If you have one of these fonts on your system, the page's text will immediately change to that font.

Next, make two lines of text centered headings: Set the text THE QUESTION OF THE DAY FOR AUG. 4, 1997 to the Heading 5 size and the text HOME ¦ ARCHIVE ¦ ASK A QUESTION ¦ GUESTBOOK ¦ ABOUT THE SITE to the Heading 6 size.

CAUTION

Take care to use headings instead of font size changes. It's easy to confuse the two, but a font size 5 is much different from a heading 5.

19

Adding Graphics

To begin adding graphics to the Glad You Asked home page, use the Document Options feature to select a background for the page. Select the graphics file stripe.gif from the Webwork\Glad folder, and a vertical yellow stripe will appear along the left-hand side of the page. The graphic—including the yellow stripe and the white background—is 1,500 pixels wide, making it wider than any browser window that's likely to load the page. This width causes the background graphic to tile downward for the length of the page.

Before inserting the next graphic, make sure your cursor is in the upper-left corner of the page and insert the image menu.gif. This pushes the cursor quite a ways down the page, so you have to scroll back to the top of the page to see the image you just added. It's a set of five menu buttons that appear on the page over the yellow stripe. Use the Object Editor tool on this image to make some changes in how it's displayed. Set the border to 0 pixels and choose the Left alignment option.

This graphic includes a large amount of transparent pixels. To see its full size, click your mouse on the graphic and a blue border will appear around it. This border indicates where the edges of the image are, as shown in Figure 19.1.

Figure 19.1.

Finding the edges of a partially transparent graphic.

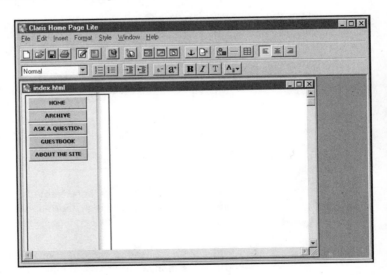

Left alignment causes the remaining text and images on the page to appear to the right of the menu.gif graphic, but this layout isn't displayed correctly, as you can see if you compare the editing window view of the page (shown in Figure 19.1) to the same part of the page in a browser.

The last graphic to add is the logo for Glad You Asked. It should be added immediately to the right of the menu.gif graphic. Scroll down in the editing window until you see the beginning of the page's text, and click your mouse immediately to the left of the text `Glad You Asked`.

Insert the graphics file logo.gif. Use the Object Editor tool to set this graphic to a border of 0 and specify Top alignment. After adding the image, delete the text `Glad You Asked` and change the Alt Label of logo.gif to `Glad You Asked`. This change to the Alt label means that people using non-graphical browsers can see the title of the page.

Save index.html and preview it with your preferred Web browser. It should look like Figure 19.2.

Figure 19.2.

The index.html page viewed in Microsoft Internet Explorer.

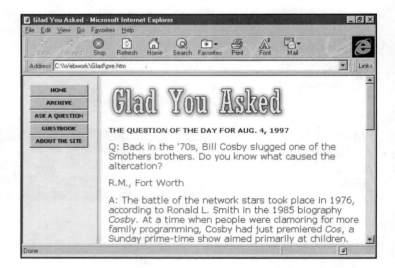

JUST A MINUTE

The Glad You Asked graphics were created using two graphical tools: Micrografx Designer, a drawing program, and Micrografx Picture Publisher, an image-editing tool commonly used to modify photographic images.

Many designers use Adobe Photoshop as their graphics-editing tool because of the many different visual effects that can be created with it. The two Micrografx programs are part of the ABC Graphics Suite.

19

Mapping an Image to Web Pages

To make the menu buttons of menu.gif work, you have to add an image map to the graphic.

 An *image map* is a way to make parts of a graphic link to another Web page. Different regions of an image map can link to different pages, in the same way that different states can be displayed on a road map.

To create an image map in Home Page, right-click your mouse over the image—menu.gif, in this example—and a pop-up menu will appear. Choose the Edit Client Side Image Map menu option.

An Image Map window opens where you can create an image map; you do this by defining a rectangular or circular area on an image and assigning a link to that area. Figure 19.3 shows the window used to create image maps.

Figure 19.3.

The Image Map window.

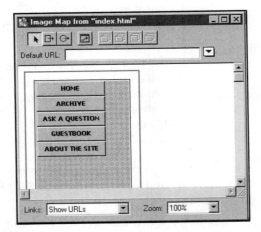

For now, you'll be defining three areas on the menu.gif image: the ARCHIVE button, the ASK A QUESTION button, and the ABOUT THE SITE button. Each of these buttons is rectangular, so you'll be using the Rectangular Link tool of Home Page's Image Map Editor. Figure 19.4 shows this button.

After you click the Rectangular Link button, your cursor changes to a crosshair. Put the center of this crosshair on the upper-left corner of the ARCHIVE button, and then click your mouse and hold down the button. You can create a rectangular area by dragging your mouse. Release the mouse when the area covers the ARCHIVE button, and you can then associate a link with this rectangular area. Make the link archive.html.

Figure 19.4.
Click this button to create a rectangular link.

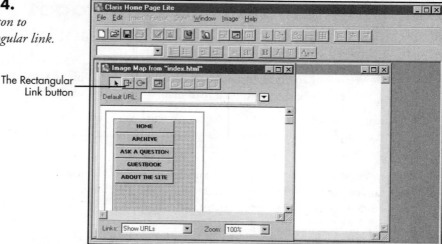

The Rectangular
Link button

JUST A MINUTE

Don't worry if your rectangular area isn't exactly the same size as the button. It's hard to pinpoint the dimensions when the graphic isn't very large. As long as it's reasonably close, it will be functional. You can use the Zoom option on this window to make the graphic larger, and thus easier to put an image map on.

After you add a link to part of an image, the name of the link appears as text above the graphic. This text won't be displayed when the Web page is shown—it's just a reminder as you're working on an image map.

Create another rectangular area over the ASK A QUESTION button and assign it the link `ask.html`. Repeat the process for ABOUT THE SITE and the link `about.html`.

The HOME button doesn't need a link because you're already on the site's home page, index.html. You could create a link to it here, but it would just cause the page to be reloaded.

The last button, GUESTBOOK, will be added during the next hour when you learn how to create a guestbook. Figure 19.5 shows the links you've added in the Image Map window.

Close the Image Map Editor tool to return to the main editing window. Preview the page with your Web browser to see how an image map functions.

19

Figure 19.5.

The Image Map window with links added to the image.

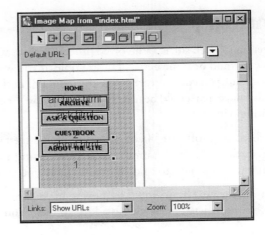

Modifying the Other Pages

The other pages of Glad You Ask have the same three graphics used in the same way, so you'll be repeating almost all the tasks you took with index.html.

Adding graphics to each of the remaining pages involves the following steps:

1. Change the background of the page to white.
2. Change the font of all the text to `Verdana,Arial,Helvetica,helvetica`.
3. Add the background image stripe.gif.
4. Add the image menu.gif with a border of 0 pixels and Left alignment.
5. Add the logo image logo.gif with a 0-pixel border, Top alignment, and an Alt Label of `Glad You Asked`.
6. On the page ask.html, delete the text `Glad You Asked` at the top of the page after replacing it with the logo graphic.
7. On the other pages, make the first line of text a Heading 5 size, as you did with index.html, and center the text.
8. Make the text and links at the bottom of the page a Heading 6 size, and center it.
9. Create an image map on menu.gif for every button except the GUESTBOOK button and the current page's button.

When these changes have been made, Glad You Asked will be a functional Web site with one exception: the guestbook. It will be added in the next hour.

Summary

Creating a Web site is an involved process, but it's worth going through as an exercise to see how it could be done better. For example, if you wanted to put the same image map on an entire site, you could create a page that contains nothing but the image map with all its links. This image map could be used to start off a new Web page, instead of starting with an empty editing window.

Web-editing software like Home Page makes the task of page building easier, but any site bigger than a certain number of pages is going to be time-consuming to create and to maintain. You have to find shortcuts where you can.

During the next hour, you'll see how to make use of resources that are publicly available for Web sites, when a guestbook is added to Glad You Asked.

Q&A

Q What's the default URL field in the Image Map Editor tool?

A This field defines the page that should be a link when someone clicks a part of the image that isn't mapped to anything. It wasn't used with the menu buttons of menu.gif because it wouldn't make sense to go to a different page if the user clicked on the area outside the buttons.

Q Why do some pages of the Glad You Asked site scroll below the last line of text?

A This issue happens because of the many transparent pixels used in the menu.gif image. For all the text to appear to the right of the vertical yellow stripe, menu.gif extends 800 pixels downward on the page. Most of these pixels are transparent, so their only purpose is to keep text from appearing at the lefthand margin of the page. This technique is similar to using a spacer graphic.

Q What's the difference between Top and Bottom alignment when used with images?

A These two alignments affect how an image is displayed alongside other images that are to the right or left of it. With Top alignment, the top edge of each image will be equal, and with Bottom alignment, the bottom edge of each image will be the same.

19

Q Should Alt Labels be used with all images on a site?

A Ideally, you should include them with any images when there's no alternative offered in the text. The logo graphic logo.gif had an Alt Label because it's the only place at the top of the page where the site's title appears. If a Web surfer came to the page with a text-only or graphics-off browser, he or she wouldn't see any title at all without the Alt Label. The menu.gif image wasn't given an Alt Label because all those buttons are duplicated at the bottom of the page. It's good practice to supply an Alt Label or a text alternative for any image if it serves a purpose other than decoration.

Quiz

Test your knowledge of this hour by taking this brief three-question test.

Questions

1. What's it called when an image is subdivided into different areas, each one used with a different Web link?

    (a) Hyperlinks

    (b) An image map

    (c) A can of worms

2. What's one of the most popular image-editing tools for Web page designers?

    (a) Crayola crayons 64-crayon box

    (b) Adobe Photoshop

    (c) Home Page Lite

3. Which two shapes can be used as regions of an image map?

    (a) Rectangles and squares

    (b) Parallelograms and polyhedrons

    (c) Circles and rectangles

Answers

1. b. A hyperlink is just another term for a link.

2. b.

3. c. A dodecahedron is a 20-sided shape, and if you didn't know that, you probably had a more active social life than I did in high school.

Activities

The following activities are suggested to expand your knowledge of the subjects covered during this hour:

☐ Now that you know how to create and use image maps, you can add them to images of people. If you use this new skill to review different sections of a person's body, make sure they're either peace-loving or living in a distant city.

☐ During the last hour an activity compelled you to create a home page as an all-text site, so this hour completes the prodding by urging you to add graphics to it. You're running out of time in which to impress Sams.net Publishing with your industrious behavior. If this was a college course, you'd be calculating your grade with all the possible extra credit, just to see if there was still hope. (Maybe it's just me.)

Hour 20

Using Web Resources

After following along with the steps needed to produce a working Web site, you might be ready to retitle the workshop "Glad It's Almost Over." The last step toward completing Glad You Asked is an important step in the creation of any site: making use of Web resources.

You might be disappointed to discover this, but you're not the first person who fell off the turnip truck with dreams of Web page creation on his or her mind. There are thousands of people like you out there, and many are putting together sites with a lot more toil than money.

Some Web sites have been created to offer a resource to home page publishers, and you'll see how to make use of them during this hour. The Glad You Asked site will be adding a guestbook from the Lpage Web service company. The following topics are covered:

☐ Finding resources for developers

☐ Taking note of other site offerings

☐ Creating a guestbook quickly

☐ Adding it to a site

☐ Testing it out

☐ Publishing the site

Be My Guest

During this hour, you'll be investigating how to add a guestbook to the workshop project Glad You Asked. A guestbook is a popular feature of many Web sites, and the Lpage service makes it easy to use one with your own pages.

 A *guestbook* is a part of a Web site where visitors can make public comments about the site. With many guestbooks, including the one offered by Lpage, comments are published immediately in the guestbook.

Like other resources for Web pages, Lpage offers its service for free because it's selling ads at the top of its users' guestbooks. The company claims more than 4 million visitors have logged entries in Lpage guestbooks, so the idea appears to be successful.

The following are some examples of Web resources you might be able to draw upon:

- ☐ Ad-sharing programs with other Web sites
- ☐ Shared links between sites covering similar subjects
- ☐ Gateways that enable e-mail delivery from a Web page
- ☐ Counters that keep track of visits
- ☐ Programs to split revenue from advertising

To find these services, you can search Yahoo! or similar indexing databases. However, an easier and more productive way to hunt out valuable services is to watch the surf.

While you're surfing the Web, take note of what's offered on a site. If you start seeing the same feature on many different sites, it might be worth considering for your own. Many Web page developers found the Internet Link Exchange this way because so many other pages had featured its ads.

The Internet Link Exchange, available from `http://www.linkexchange.com`, is an ad-swapping service for Web publishers. Members of the Link Exchange run each other's banner ads under a system set up by the exchange, and the more your site is visited, the more often it's promoted on other sites. See Figure 20.1 for an example of a banner ad.

 Banner ads are advertisements that appear at the top or bottom of Web pages. The ads are usually rectangular and run most of the width of a page; some feature animated sequences.

20

Figure 20.1.

*A page with a banner
advertisement.*

Getting Ready to Add a Guestbook

The Lpage guestbook service has also quickly become popular on Web sites. To use an Lpage guestbook, you need to create a page containing the links needed to add entries to the book and view the entries left by others.

Instead of creating a page from scratch, load the page ask.html from the Webwork\Glad folder into Home Page. Before making any changes, save a copy of this page as guest.html.

This step saves you the effort of re-creating graphics, and it requires only some minor tweaking to make the menu buttons work.

Make the following changes to this page:

1. Change the title of the page to Glad You Stopped By, and also replace the text at the top of the page from GLAD YOU'RE ASKING with GLAD YOU STOPPED BY.

2. Edit the image map to make the ASK A QUESTION button a link to ask.html. To open the Image Map editing window, right-click over the image and choose the Edit Client Side Image Map option.

3. Turn the text ASK A QUESTION at the bottom of the page into a link to ask.html, using the Link Editor tool.

20

Also, delete the main text of the page, which begins with `This Web site` and ends with `send a question`. Replace that text with the following text:

```
If you'd like to make a comment about the site or the questions
and answers you've seen here, feel free to use the guestbook
provided by the Lpage service. We will be gladder if you send
questions directly to us, though. It will prevent any of this
site's visitors from proving they're smarter than we are.¶
View our guestbook¶
Sign our guestbook¶
```

Change the last two lines of this text into an unnumbered list. They will be used for links after you have established a guestbook for this Web site.

Setting Up a Guestbook

Information on setting up a guestbook through Lpage is available from the following Web address:

```
http://www.lpage.com
```

The first step in setting up a guestbook is to choose a name for your book—something that corresponds with the name of your site. The name must contain only letters or numbers, so for Glad You Asked the name `gladyouasked` was selected.

CAUTION

> Because the guestbook for Glad You Asked has already been created at Lpage, you won't need to visit Lpage to create one for this workshop. The next hands-on experience you can get is adding links to the guestbook on the Glad You Asked site itself. Keep in mind that when creating a guestbook for your own Web site through Lpage, you have to select a name that isn't being used by another site.

The next thing to choose is a category for your guestbook to be added to Lpage's directory. The categories are similar to those for Web indexing services, such as Yahoo!, and you can change the category later, if you like. The category News | Daily was chosen for the workshop project.

To finish creating a guestbook on Lpage's Web server, you must identify the Web site you're going to use it with, the title of your site, and its Web address. You must also supply your own e-mail address.

20

Next, you must select a password to be used later when you want to maintain your guestbook. This password is essential for you to have some control over what goes in the book. If you lose it, you can't delete entries, read private messages, or handle other upkeep-related functions.

As one of the final steps before the guestbook is ready to use, you need to supply some keywords that identify your site and its purpose. These keywords should be as descriptive as possible because you want people to find you when they search through Lpage's database or any other list of Web pages.

For Glad You Asked, the following keywords were used:

`Glad You Asked trivia questions answers daily Home Page Teach Yourself 24 Hours`

The last information to provide is your city, state, and country, which will also be included in Lpage's searchable database.

Adding Links to the Guestbook

When you have finished the setup process, the guestbook will be created on Lpage's server and you can make use of it right away. You will be sent some HTML tags to paste on your page that give visitors access to the guestbook.

To do the same thing yourself, you can create two links on the guest.html page. First, change the text `View our guestbook` into a link to the following:

`http://www.lpage.com/wgb/wgbview.dbm?owner=gladyouasked`

Change the text `Sign our guestbook` into a link to this page:

`http://www.lpage.com/wgb/wgbsign.dbm?owner=gladyouasked`

These links might change if Lpage revises its procedures, but at the time of this writing, you can use links such as the preceding ones for any guestbook established for Lpage. The only thing that would change is the name of the owner, which was selected when the guestbook was being created.

After adding these links, make the text `directly to us` into a Mailto link to `mailto:socrates@gladyouasked.com`, and you're done.

Save guest.html and preview the page in a Web browser to see the Lpage guestbook in action. With Lpage, some aspects of the guestbook can be configured by the page developer, so you can emulate your site's visual look. For example, if you'd like the guestbook to have the same

20

background color, background graphic, text colors, and link colors, you can set them up when your guestbook is created. Figure 20.2 shows a sample entry for the Glad You Asked guestbook.

Figure 20.2.

A guestbook entry for Glad You Asked.

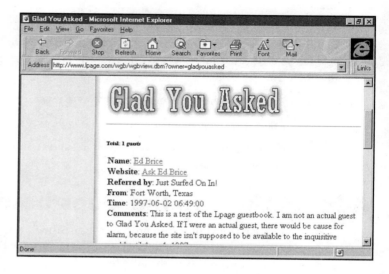

If you're working along with this project, you have one last task to finish before the project is done. You need to change all the pages so that the GUESTBOOK button and GUESTBOOK heading both link to guest.html.

There's no quick way to do this, so you have to load each page individually and make the changes.

TIME SAVER

If you'd like to skip this last part of finishing off the site, the full site of Glad You Asked can be examined at its Web address:

http://www.gladyouasked.com.

The Glad You Asked Web site is available at the following Web address:

http://www.gladyouasked.com

The site is offered as an ongoing example of Web site development. If you see something there you'd like to know about, related to the subject of the site or Web development, send an e-mail or make a comment through the guestbook.

20

Summary

When part of the Web site development process was described as perspiration, you might not have realized that some of the hard work was being done by other people. You can make use of many free resources to improve your own sites.

The Glad You Asked workshop is done. When you bring a site like that onto the Web for the first time, you'll feel a sense of accomplishment and an eagerness as you await the third phase of Web development: adulation.

Unfortunately, to get the love of the Web surfing masses, you have to continue toiling on your site. It takes a lot of effort to maintain a successful home page. During the next four hours, you'll learn how sites are published and promoted.

Q&A

Q Can the Lpage guestbook run on the same server that provides my Web hosting services?

A Lpage hosts all guestbooks it offers on its own machines. The company isn't releasing its programs for use on other Web sites. However, if you customize your guestbook to look like other pages on your site, you can disguise the fact that the guestbook isn't hosted in the same place as your site.

Q Can an Lpage guestbook be used instead of making an e-mail address available?

A You *could* do this with Lpage's private-message option, but you run the risk of missing out on mail because of system outages or other unexpected circumstances. Most guestbooks are being used as a complement to e-mail rather than a replacement.

Q Why should a guestbook be used instead of a Mailto link to a site's publisher?

A It's a personal preference, but the main advantage to using a guestbook is that it gives visitors a way to communicate with each other, in addition to communicating with you. This feature could create some administrative hassles if visitors post profanity or other comments you find objectionable, but if you're willing to spend the time overseeing the guestbook, it's a popular feature for a site.

20

Quiz

Test your knowledge of this hour by taking this brief three-question test.

Questions

1. What Web advertising service was mentioned during this hour?

    (a) Internet Link Exchange

    (b) Commonwealth Network

    (c) Doubleclick

2. Which of the following can be used as a valid name for an Lpage guestbook?

    (a) Dennis Rodman Fashion Tips Guestbook

    (b) dennisbebad

    (c) I.B.Bad.

3. What aspects of a guestbook's display can't be modified?

    (a) The background

    (b) The text color

    (c) The font

Answers

1. a., but all three are advertising services. Visit `http://commonwealth.riddler.com` for details on the Commonwealth Network and `http://www.doubleclick.com` for information on that service.

2. b. Names are restricted to letters or numbers.

3. c.

Activities

The following activities are suggested to expand your knowledge of the subjects covered during this hour:

☐ If you have a Web site and you'd like to exchange banner ads with other services, visit the Internet Link Exchange at `http://www.linkexchange.com` to find out more about its free ad-swap service.

☐ Add an Lpage guestbook to one of your own Web sites.

20

PART VI

Home Page Publishing

Hour

Hour 21

Finding a Place for Your Site

From this point on in the book, you won't learn any other way to enhance the look or quality of your Web pages. Your bag of Web design tricks is full, and you're ready to venture forth into the world, Home Page in hand.

However, your new skills won't be much use if you can't show them off on the World Wide Web. This hour and the following three cover how to put your home page on the Web and make sure the world knows about it. During this hour, the following topics are covered:

☐ Finding a site to host your home page

☐ Choosing between AOL, Internet providers, and other services

☐ Publishing Web pages for free with GeoCities

☐ Using AOL to publish your home page

☐ Selecting your own domain name for your home page

Finding a Home

When you're ready to put a Web site on the World Wide Web, you have to find a place for it to call home. Fortunately, shopping for space to store a Web site is the ultimate buyer's market—you can pick any host in the world, and some even offer their services for free.

Before you start looking for a provider, you should find out whether you already have free Web space available to you that's going unused. The following services offer free hosting to their subscribers:

- ☐ America Online: `http://www.aol.com`
- ☐ Concentric: `http://www.concentric.net`
- ☐ Netcom: `http://www.netcom.com`
- ☐ Sprynet: `http://www.sprynet.com`

This list isn't an attempt to be comprehensive—these are just a few of the larger services that should be available to most readers, and many others also offer free Web hosting. If you're using an Internet service provider, a free Web site might be part of your subscription benefits, so be sure to check before seeking any other service.

If you don't turn up a free Web page that's already available to you, the GeoCities service at `http://www.geocities.com` hosts Web sites for anyone who has an Internet e-mail address.

What You'll Need

Generally, these services provide from 1M to 2M of disk space for storing your Web pages, graphics files, and anything else you're offering. There are usually terms you must agree to about the content of your home page—as a hedge against obscene, illegal, or abusive material—but additional fees aren't required.

JUST A MINUTE

Some Internet service providers do charge an extra fee to subscribers for hosting Web pages, and this might make sense when you're looking for a permanent place to keep pages. If you're just fooling around while you go through this book, both America Online and GeoCities are good choices.

When you're zeroing in on the place you'll be putting pages, you need to get some extra information to use it. First, you need to know what Internet server you'll be connecting to in order to transmit your pages. For a page to be offered on the World Wide Web, it must be stored on a computer that's permanently connected to the Web and ready to accept visitors.

21

Internet sites establish this permanent connection by installing a Web server. The server knows how to receive visits from people using Web browsers and send those people any documents that are requested.

When you direct your Web browser to a page, the browser makes a connection with a specific Web server somewhere on the Internet. That server then figures out which page you want and sends you the page and all the graphics and other elements included on it.

For example, if you go to the Web page `http://www.mcp.com/sams/index.html`, a Web server at Macmillan Computer Publishing receives your request. The Macmillan server fetches the document index.html in the sams directory and sends it out. The main page of the Sams.net Developers' Resource Center then shows up on your browser.

In addition to a Web server, an Internet site has another server that's equipped to receive your pages and anything else you send it. This server is called an *FTP server* because it uses File Transfer Protocol to send and receive files.

Often, the Internet server you use to publish a Web site has *ftp* in its name because it uses FTP. For example, when you upload a page to GeoCities, you use the server `ftp.geocities.com`.

After you know the server, you need to know the user name and password to use when connecting to it. If you have ever downloaded a file from an FTP server, you probably didn't have to use a user name and a password to get it. Many of these servers offer anonymous downloading, which means they don't ask who you are before letting you connect to the site.

This isn't true of Web site publishing, however, because sites need to protect themselves against abuse. To send files to an FTP server, you usually must have a valid user name and password for that server.

CAUTION

Unless you're using your own Internet service provider to host your pages, this user name and password will be different from the ones you're using to connect to the Net.

In addition to a user name and a password, you need to know the name of the directory where you should put your files when you send them. Some FTP servers automatically put you in the right directory when you make a connection, but if the directory isn't handled automatically, you need to find out the correct directory from your service provider.

The following sections describe some of the places that offer free Web pages, either as part of a subscription or to anyone with Internet access. Some of the specifics might change after this book goes to press, but each of the services has been offering Web space for more than a year, so their policies have had time to become established.

21

GeoCities

Many people choose GeoCities for Web site hosting; it has supplied free home pages to thousands of people. You can sign up for a page immediately while visiting the GeoCities Web site at `http://www.geocities.com`.

The service is divided into 34 sections called *neighborhoods*. Each neighborhood is loosely tied to a specific theme, such as television, computing, or education, and they have evocative names, such as BourbonStreet, EnchantedForest, and SunsetStrip. When you visit a specific neighborhood, you see rows of home pages displayed as houses on a street, each with its own address number.

The neighborhood and address number are used as part of the Web address of each GeoCities home page. For example, the following is a GeoCities address:

`http://www.geocities.com/RainForest/2701/`

This page is in the RainForest neighborhood at address number 2701, and it was the home of the World Wildlife Federation of Malaysia when this book was written. Figure 21.1 shows the site.

Figure 21.1.

A Web site hosted by GeoCities in the RainForest neighborhood.

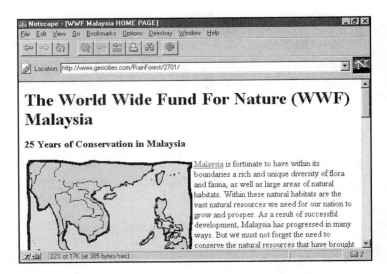

Before you can request your own free home page, you must surf through GeoCities and find a neighborhood that fits the theme of your page. When you decide on one, you must pick an unused address number for your page. This can be difficult in some of the areas with popular themes, such as the entertainment- and television-related neighborhoods, so you might have to look at more than one neighborhood before finding a place to call home.

After you have done that, you'll get a chance to register for a user name, and a password will be sent to you.

CAUTION

> The content guidelines for GeoCities prohibit vulgar, obscene, or illegal material. Also, there are restrictions against using these pages for commercial purposes, multilevel marketing schemes, or other for-profit enterprises.

Another benefit of GeoCities is the ability to get mail by using your user name with the service. If your GeoCities account is greenlama, mail sent to greenlama@geocities.com will be forwarded to your main e-mail address.

To transmit your home page to GeoCities, you can use FTP software, which will be described during Hour 23, "Sending Your Site Through FTP Software." GeoCities also offers utilities to make it easier to send your pages, graphics, and other files.

America Online

Although you might not know it from using the service, America Online offers free space for home pages to its subscribers. You can use up to 2M of disk space for pages, graphics, and other files, and an additional 2M is available for any other screen names under the same account. The content restrictions are similar to those of GeoCities.

To find out about this feature, visit the keyword MY PLACE on AOL. America Online offers two ways to put your home page on its system. In the My Place area, you can directly upload files to the site. This feature is supported with Claris Home Page 2.0 Lite, as described in the next hour, "Publishing Your Site."

You also can use special AOL software to create and modify your home pages. Visit the keyword PERSONAL PUBLISHER for the details.

Used with Home Page, AOL is probably the easiest service for a novice to use when transmitting documents to put on the World Wide Web. All you have to know is your screen name and password, and your work will be published on the Web.

When you publish your home page, the Web address is based on your screen name. The following is the home page address of an AOL user named dotPulp:

```
http://members.aol.com/dotPulp/index.html
```

Figure 21.2 shows the Web site, a directory of links related to pulp magazines.

21

Figure 21.2.

A Web site hosted by AOL.

Your Internet Provider

There's no typical way in which an Internet service provider makes Web space available for users. Some charge for the service, others don't, and the procedures for transmitting your pages vary, too.

For most Internet service providers, you need some kind of FTP software to transmit your home page to the site that will host it. This procedure is explained in Hour 23.

As stated previously, you need to know four things to send your home page: your user name, your password, the Internet server to connect to when sending pages, and the remote directory where the pages should be stored.

Factors to Consider

When selecting a permanent host for a Web site, you have many choices available to you—especially if you're willing to pay for the service. Before making a final decision, however, you should monitor the performance of a host after your pages are on it. All Internet Web servers are *not* created equal; some have more Internet capacity and better hardware to speed up delivering information to Web surfers. Also, some Internet sites become overtaxed by offering too much Web space or getting too many hits to the pages that are there, which can slow down transmitting your home page.

The only ways to determine a host's Internet capacity are to see how the pages load when you use them and pay attention to any feedback you get from visitors to your page. If you're using the same Internet provider and Web space provider, your page is more likely to load quickly when you use it because the machines are probably in the same network. This might not be the case when people in distant places visit your home page.

If you're using an Internet service provider as a host instead of AOL or GeoCities, you might be able to get a personalized domain name for your home page. Doing so can give Web surfers an easier way to find your site because an address such as `http://www.hindenburg.com` is easier to remember—and type in—than something such as `http://www.interstice.com/usr/pub/~hindenburg`.

Registering a domain name currently costs $100 from InterNIC, the service that registers names and keeps track of where they're located on the Internet. This fee covers the first two years of registration, and there's a $50 renewal fee after that.

If you want to find out whether a domain is still available, visit the following Web address:

`http://rs.internic.net/cgi-bin/itts/whois`

This Web page is a searchable index of all registered domains. To register the domain you want to use, you'll have to work with the company that's going to host your Web pages. They will probably handle the actual process of registering the domain, but there might be an additional fee of $25 or $50.

Summary

Now that you know how to choose a site to host your home page, you need to select one before beginning the next hour, "Publishing Your Site." Although only a few service providers were mentioned by name in this hour, there are many more than can offer Web space hosting and information on how to handle the process.

Before worrying about any of that, though, you should see how the Publish feature of Home Page works. It's a tool that makes it possible to put Web sites online without learning how to use different software to transmit the pages and other documents that make up the site.

Q&A

Q How much of a barrier will a 2M limit be when I'm hosting my Web page?

A If you're just starting out, and creating some relatively simple home pages, you probably won't come close to the 2M limit of many hosting services. What makes it harder to fit everything in is graphics files, which take up a lot more disk space than Web pages.

21

Q Is there a way to wait for a space to open up in a popular GeoCities neighbor-hood, such as Silicon Valley?

A Finding an open address in a popular GeoCities neighborhood is largely hit-or-miss. Some neighborhoods such as Silicon Valley can become completely filled with home pages, so you have to look for an open address several times before chancing on one that has become available again.

Q Is there an advantage to paying for a Web site hosting service over GeoCities and AOL's free offers?

A In most cases, the primary advantages of a Web site hosting service are page-loading speed, customer service, and additional capabilities such as CGI Gateway programming. GeoCities and AOL have supplied Web space to thousands of people, and they can't take the same kind of personal approach that a small Internet service provider could offer.

Q A domain I want is taken with the .com suffix, but it's available with the .net and .org suffixes. Can I use one of them instead?

A The .net suffix is for Internet sites that function as networks, and the .org suffix is aimed at not-for-profit organizations and charities. However, both .net and .org are used sometimes by companies that couldn't register the .com domain they were hoping for, and they have been supported by InterNIC.

Quiz

Test your knowledge of this hour by taking this brief three-question test.

Questions

1. Which of the following is a GeoCities neighborhood?

   (a) BourbonStreet

   (b) VodkaBoulevard

   (c) LoveCanal

2. Which service requires you to use a specific remote directory when publishing your home page?

   (a) America Online

   (b) None do

   (c) Internet service providers

21

3. True or False: You can publish your home page by using a special area of AOL.

    (a) True

    (b) False

    (c) Define "special."

Answers

1. a.

2. c. Usually, although some Internet providers set it up so that the default directory is the correct one.

3. a. The AOL keywords MY PLACE and PERSONAL PUBLISHER have the details.

Activities

The following activities are suggested to expand your knowledge of the subjects covered during this hour:

☐ Join GeoCities and pick a spot for a Web site, traveling through the different neighborhoods until you find one that suits the topic of your prospective site. You can request a page and explore the service before finishing your own Web site.

☐ Visit InterNIC and search for a good domain name, either for use with your own home page or just out of curiosity about what's available. You'll quickly understand how hard it has become to find a good unused domain name because thousands of people now own their own domains.

21

Hour 22

Publishing Your Site

If this book were the senior prom, the past 21 hours covered the process of finding a date, acquiring the tuxedo or dress, renting the limo, and ordering an industrial supply of breath mints and hair care products. This hour is the Big Night. Hop in the car, pick up the date, and pay homage to the deities of hedonism and dance funk.

During this hour, you'll be experiencing the pageantry of putting your home page on the World Wide Web. You'll be able to use Claris Home Page 2.0 Lite to transmit your files to a service such as America Online or a Web space provider, and those pages can be seen by the entire world. The following topics are covered over the next hour:

- [ ] Getting your site ready to publish
- [ ] Setting up Home Page to publish the site
- [ ] Using America Online or Internet services
- [ ] Choosing how to publish the site
- [ ] Handling errors that occur
- [ ] Maintaining your site

Getting Ready

When you're ready to put a site onto the World Wide Web, your first choice will probably be to use Home Page's built-in Publish feature. Publishing a Web site means copying all its pages and other files from your computer to a computer that's permanently connected to the World Wide Web.

To use the Publish feature of Home Page, you must have an account set up with your Web site provider—America Online, your Internet service provider, or some other service, such as a Web page hosting company.

You need to have a few things handy to get started:

- [ ] Your user name
- [ ] Your password
- [ ] The remote directory to place files in (unless you're using America Online)

To give you some experience publishing a home page, during this hour you should upload either the Edward George Bulwer-Lytton home page created previously or one of your own creations, if you've been doing the after-hour activities recommended in the book.

CAUTION

> Keep in mind that you're going to be putting these pages onto the World Wide Web, where it's entirely possible for anyone to see them—including your parents, parole officer, and priest. You might want to use Edward George's site if your own work is embarrassing, illegal, or morally deficient. However, if the pages you create do suffer from those three faults, be prepared to handle a lot of visitors to your site.

Once you've decided which site to publish for this hour's tutorial, you need to make sure that all of the site's files are in the same folder and that the folder contains no files that are unrelated to the site. Home Page publishes every file it finds in that folder and all its subfolders, so you have to be careful to include nothing but pertinent files.

There's one exception to this rule: Any graphics files that you've imported from a library, such as the "Made by Claris Home Page" button from the Bulwer-Lytton site, don't have to be put in the folder. Home Page grabs them from the library folder when the site is published.

Using the Publish Feature

If you're using America Online as your site host, you have to be connected to that service before running Home Page. If you're not presently online, close down Home Page now, connect to AOL, and restart Home Page.

AOL users have a separate area to store Web pages for each screen name under their account. The screen name is used as part of the Web site's address. To use Home Page to publish a site on AOL, you have to log onto the service using the screen name the pages should be stored under.

Also, if you have never published the pages using AOL before, you need to go to the keyword MY PLACE and click the Go to My Place button. This causes AOL to allocate the space where your pages will be stored.

If you're using a service other than AOL, you must be connected to your Internet service provider before publishing the site. However, you don't have to exit Home Page, so you can connect now or wait until you've configured the software with the information needed to publish the pages.

JUST A MINUTE

If you're not using America Online, connect to the Internet the way you normally would. Even if your Web space provider is different from your Internet service provider, you'll log onto your normal Internet service with Home Page.

To begin the process of publishing a site, click the Publish button on the toolbar, which is shown in Figure 22.1.

Figure 22.1.

Click this button to use the Publish feature.

The Publish button

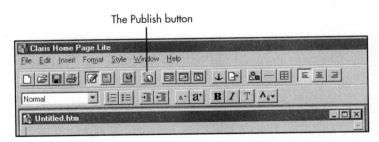

After clicking the Publish button, the first thing you'll see is a window asking whether you want to create a site definition file or use an existing one. A *site definition file* tells Home Page how to connect to the site that's providing Web space to you, and it also determines some aspects of how your home page will be organized when it's published.

For this example, choose to create a site definition file and click OK. You are then told that your site definition file needs to be saved in the same folder as the site itself. For the Bulwer-Lytton site, that means your site definition file should be saved in the folder Webwork\Stormy. Give the definition file the name Stormy.wst and save the file.

After you save your site definition file in the right folder, you'll see a dialog box with three tabs to pick from: FTP Settings, Image Policy, and Statistics. The FTP Settings tab should be visible on top because that's where you'll start out. Click the FTP Settings tab if it isn't visible. Figure 22.2 shows this dialog box.

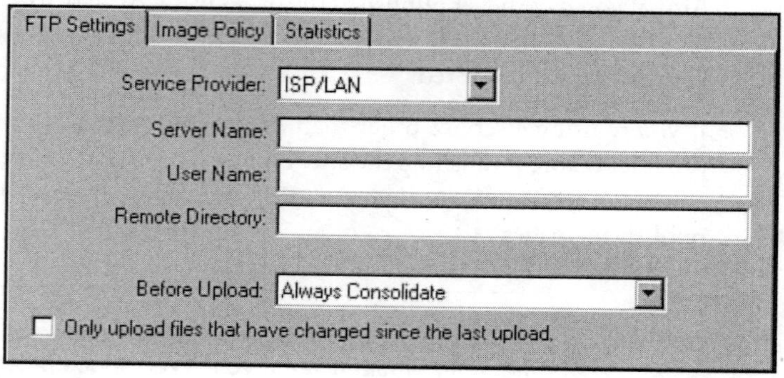

Figure 22.2.

The FTP Settings tab.

| FTP Settings | Image Policy | Statistics |

Service Provider: ISP/LAN ▼

Server Name: [   ]

User Name: [   ]

Remote Directory: [   ]

Before Upload: Always Consolidate ▼

☐ Only upload files that have changed since the last upload.

File Transfer Settings

The next step in the site-publishing process is to establish the FTP settings you'll be using. *FTP* is short for *File Transfer Protocol*, and it's the way your computer knows how to communicate with the computer that will store your home page.

Choose the service provider you're using as the host for your site: ISP/Lan, if you're using an Internet service provider, or America Online, if you're using that service.

America Online users need to enter their screen names in one field but don't have to change anything else in the FTP Settings dialog box. Screen names aren't case sensitive, so you don't have to worry about capitalizing them in a specific way for them to work.

If you're an ISP/LAN user, you must enter your server name, your user name, and the remote directory on the server where the home page should be stored. Other than the user name, you might not know what to put in the other fields. The service providing Web space to you should be able to tell you the server name and remote directory to use. This information is often available in the help files on the service's Web site.

The server name is the Internet site you have access to for storing files. If your service provider has designated ftp.prefect.com as the server name, then enter that in the Server Name field. The user name is the name you use to log onto the service—usually from 3 to 8 alphanumeric characters. The remote directory is the place where you should be putting your files, and it's something you need to find out about from your Web space provider.

For both America Online and ISP/LAN users, there are two options that you should leave unchanged for this project. First, the selections in the Before Upload drop-down list determine whether Home Page should retrieve all images related to the site before it's

22

published, which streamlines the process a bit. You can choose from three options: Always consolidate, Never consolidate, and Ask me each time. Leave the Before Upload set to the Always consolidate option—it's one less thing to worry about.

Second, the last field in the FTP Settings tab is a checkbox labeled "Only upload files changed since the last upload." The box should be unchecked, which causes all the site's files to be transmitted every time you publish the site. For now, leave that box unchecked to make sure all the files are sent. When you're using Home Page later to maintain your own Web site, you might want to check this option to speed up the time it takes to publish your work.

JUST A MINUTE

> *Upload* might be an unfamiliar term, but if you've ever downloaded a file, you have a good idea what it means. Uploading a Web site is the same thing as publishing it—all the files that make up the site are sent to the computer that will be storing it for presentation on the World Wide Web.

Handling Images

The next thing you have to determine is how images on your site should be handled when it's published. You establish that in the Image Policy tab, so click it to bring it to the front. Figure 22.3 shows this tab.

Figure 22.3.

The Image Policy tab.

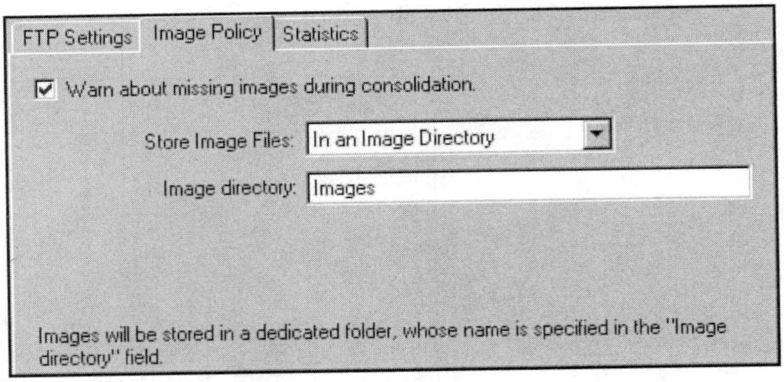

FTP Settings	Image Policy	Statistics

☑ Warn about missing images during consolidation.

Store Image Files: `In an Image Directory` ▼

Image directory: `Images`

Images will be stored in a dedicated folder, whose name is specified in the "Image directory" field.

The Image Policy tab should already be set up as follows:

☐ There should be a check next to the box "Warn about missing images during consolidation."

☐ The choice for Store Image Files should be set to the "In an Image Directory" option.

☐ The Image directory field should have the value Images.

Change any of these settings that aren't correctly set. This configuration is the easiest one to deal with when publishing a site. It puts all graphics files in a directory called Images, which will be a subdirectory of the remote directory you specified in the FTP Settings tab, if you're using an ISP to host your Web site. If you're using AOL, a subdirectory called Images will be created from the directory where your screen name's Web pages are stored. Any graphics files that aren't found cause a warning to be generated, and you get a chance to hunt for the files on your system.

If you change the Store Image Files option to "With the HTML File," you won't have to specify an Images directory because the graphics files will be stored in the same directory as all the Web documents that make up your site. It has become more common for Web publishers to put all graphics files into their own subdirectory, with a name such as Image or Images, because it's a little easier to deal with directories that contain a smaller number of similar files. However, it's more a matter of personal preference than anything else, so you can pick either method for storing images.

Site Statistics

The last tab in the dialog box is Statistics, and it's just an abbreviated version of the Document Statistics feature discussed during Hour 4, "Putting Images on Your Page." The Statistics tab shows the name of the directory that will be published on the Web, the number of pages that are going to be published, and their total file size. Click the Refresh Now button to make sure these statistics are current, and you'll get an idea of how big the site is in terms of file size and page count. Figure 22.4 shows the Statistics tab for the Bulwer-Lytton Web site.

Figure 22.4.

The Statistics tab.

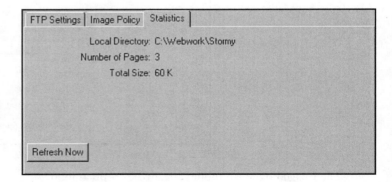

CAUTION

22

If the local directory in the Statistics dialog box isn't correct, that means your site definitions file was saved to the wrong directory. You can either close the Publish window and start again, or close the Publish window, move the site definitions file to the correct directory, and reclick the Publish button. With the latter course, you get a chance to load an existing site definitions file, and you can select the file you just moved to its proper directory.

Uploading the Site

Once all these settings have been selected, if you're connected to America Online or the Internet, then you're ready to publish the site. Click the Upload Site button. It's at the bottom of the Publish dialog box, and you might have to scroll down to see it. If you have selected the ISP/Lan option instead of America Online, you'll have to enter your password before you can upload the site.

When the file transfer begins, you can press the Escape key at any time to cancel the publishing process—if something looks amiss, feel free to hit Escape and check the settings.

If the transfer is proceeding correctly, you'll see several small message boxes informing you of what's taking place. The main boxes that are displayed show which file is being uploaded and how many files have been uploaded so far. Figure 22.5 shows an example of the message box you'll see as a site is being published in Home Page.

Figure 22.5.

Home Page tracking the progress of your site uploading.

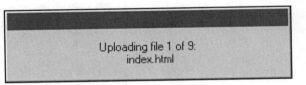

Uploading file 1 of 9:
index.html

After the transfer, your pages should be accessible on the World Wide Web. Some Web space providers institute a delay between the time a page is uploaded and the time it's available, but most, including America Online, make the pages available immediately.

If you used America Online, your site is now available at a Web address based on your screen name. If your screen name is greenlama, the following Web address would contain your site:

http://members.aol.com/greenlama

If you used your Internet service provider, many of these providers follow the same addressing scheme for their users' home pages—the service's Internet domain followed by /~ and your user name. For example, if your user name is greenlama and Interstice is your Internet provider, your page would be at the following address:

http://www.interstice.com/~greenlama

Unless you're using America Online, you might need to find out from your service provider where your home page ends up after you publish it. This information is often available in the help section of your provider's Web site.

Troubleshooting

Although the Publish feature usually runs smoothly if the settings are correct and your computer can make a connection over the Internet to your Web space provider, you might run into some problems when trying to publish a site.

The easiest error to diagnose is when you're using an ISP/Lan and the password you entered is incorrect. A dialog box pops up to let you know about the error, and you can click the Upload Site button again to reenter your password.

If Home Page runs into any other difficulties, you'll see a message box with a red × mark and some extremely cryptic text. Figure 22.6 shows an example of one of these error message boxes.

Figure 22.6.

The error message from an unsuccessful Publish attempt.

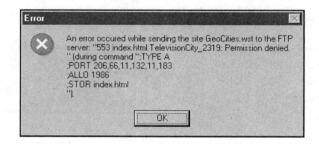

This message isn't going to give you enough information about what's causing the problem, so you should just fix the likely culprits and try it again.

If you're using America Online, you need to make sure you're still connected to the service. As stated earlier, to use Publish you must be connected to AOL before running Home Page, and you must still be connected when you click the Upload Site button.

If you're using any other service, you need to make sure your remote directory is correct. Problems with your user name or password should have triggered the "wrong password" error described previously, but you might want to double-check those settings also.

These potential errors are the only things to go over if you're having problems. America Online usually runs seamlessly with the Publish feature, although you might not be able to see the pages on the World Wide Web immediately if the service has its home page area down for maintenance.

If you're not using America Online, your Internet service provider or Web site provider should be able to help with problems you're having.

COFFEE BREAK

America Online has provided one free diskette containing their software for every man, woman, and child on the planet and a couple of thousand disguised extraterrestrials living among us. If you're having trouble getting a Web space provider to work with the Publish tool, you ought to consider joining AOL to try out Web publishing during the free trial period. It's also an excellent chance to visit one of AOL's online bookstores and buy extra copies of this book. They make great stocking stuffers and can be hollowed out easily to hide valuables.

Another way to make your pages available on the Web is to use FTP software to publish your site, which is covered during the next hour, "Sending Your Site Through FTP Software."

Home Page's Publish feature is extremely convenient for publishing a new site and making changes to existing pages. Once any difficulties are ironed out, you should be able to use it right away to maintain your site.

One thing you won't be able to do, however, is delete any pages or other files that you publish. Deleting pages requires using FTP software, which is described in the next hour. If you just want to make a page's contents unavailable on the Web, you can replace an existing page with a blank document of the same filename.

Summary

Now that you have put a Web site on the World Wide Web, you're more qualified to judge whether it's as exciting as the senior prom. It certainly surpasses the thrill of mine back in 1985, but that's a story for *Teach Yourself Not to Run Wearing Tight Pants in 24 Hours*.

During the next hour, you'll learn how to use FTP software to publish your site.

Q&A

Q Can I use the Publish feature with the free home page space offered by GeoCities?

A Apparently, you can't use Home Page to directly upload your site to GeoCities because it generates an error when the transfer is attempted. However, it's possible to use FTP software to do this, as you'll see in the next hour.

Q How can I publish more than one Web site on America Online, if each has its own file called index.html?

A You can publish more than one Web site by putting each of your sites in a subfolder of the same folder and treating them as part of the same large site. You should put your site definition file in the main folder and select the option to upload only the modified files.

Q **What can I do if some files aren't showing up on AOL when I upload them by using the Publish feature?**

A If you visit the Web site and some pages, image files, or other files are missing, you can check to make sure they were transmitted correctly by using AOL. Go to the keyword MY PLACE and click the Go to My Place button. You'll see a directory of all the pages uploaded to that screen name's Web site storage area, and you can go to the Images subdirectory if you chose to create one in the Publish dialog box.

Q **Do I have only one directory at my disposal on my Internet provider's Web space, or can I put multiple sites there?**

A Handling multiple sites is easier with an Internet service provider or Web space provider than it is with America Online. Create a different site definition file for each site, and add a subdirectory to your remote directory setting. For instance, if your remote directory should be /usr/public_html, you could make it /usr/public_html/habanero for a Web site about Habanero peppers. If the habanero directory doesn't exist when you first publish the site, Home Page will create it.

Quiz

Test your knowledge of this hour by taking this brief three-question test.

Questions

1. What's another term for uploading?
    (a) Publishing
    (b) Downloading
    (c) Freeloading

2. What troubling situation do you not have to worry about when publishing your own site?
    (a) Anyone on earth can read it.
    (b) The Publish feature sometimes requires a little tinkering to work successfully.
    (c) It might be selected as Mirsky's Worst of the Web.

3. What does FTP stand for?
    (a) Faster Than Pumas
    (b) File Transfer Protocol
    (c) Files To Publish

22

Answers

1. a. Downloading is the opposite of uploading.

2. c. Mirsky retired in late 1996 after becoming discouraged that he had been publishing his work for a year and wasn't rich yet.

3. b.

Activities

The following activities are suggested to expand your knowledge of the subjects covered during this hour:

☐ If you're using AOL, follow the instructions provided at the keyword MY PLACE and upload a site to one of your screen names. It's more difficult than Home Page's Publish feature, but you can delete files and handle other administrative tasks more easily.

☐ If you didn't publish your own personal home page this hour, consider yourself shamed. Get it ready and put the whole shebang online through the Publish feature. The world needs to know more about you, your loved ones, and your strange hobbies.

Hour 23

Sending Your Site Through FTP Software

Hour 22, "Publishing Your Site," was described as "Prom Night" because it was your first chance to publish a home page on the World Wide Web using Claris Home Page 2.0 Lite software.

However, some people skip the prom, and you, too, can skip using Home Page to publish your Web pages. With the FTP software you get from this book's CD-ROM or some other source, you can transmit your files to a service such as a Web space provider or GeoCities, and those pages can be viewed by the entire world. The following topics are covered during this hour:

☐ Getting your site ready to publish
☐ Getting and installing FTP software
☐ Using your Web hosting services
☐ Setting up FTP software to publish the site
☐ Handling errors
☐ Maintaining your site

Getting Ready

During the past hour, you learned how to use Home Page's Publish feature to automate the process of publishing your home page. If you run into problems using this feature with your Web hosting provider, or you would prefer having more direct control of the process, you can use FTP software to handle the task.

The acronym *FTP* stands for *File Transfer Protocol*. As discussed in previous hours, it's the common way for two computers on the Internet to exchange files with each other. FTP software is available for all operating systems that can access Internet services such as the World Wide Web and e-mail, and it's not any more complicated than copying a file from one directory to another. You might have used FTP software in the past to download files from a site on the Internet.

COFFEE BREAK

> Many Web browsers, including the current versions of Netscape Navigator and Microsoft Internet Explorer, have some built-in functions of FTP software. If you have ever gone to a Web page that began with `ftp://` instead of `http://`, as in `ftp://www.microsoft.com`, you were using FTP software without knowing it. Unlike standard FTP software, however, these browsers can only receive files.

Getting and Installing FTP Software

Using FTP software to publish a Web site is discussed fully during this hour. The primary software that will be used is FTP2000, a Windows 95 product that's available on the CD-ROM that accompanies this book. You can install it by following the directions in Appendix C, "This Book's CD-ROM."

If you don't have FTP software for your operating system, or you're a Windows 95 user who would prefer to try something other than FTP2000, there are several products available from the World Wide Web to try out.

To find these products, visit a file repository Web site, such as www.shareware.com. *Shareware* is software that's available to try out for free for a brief period, after which you're asked to pay if you continue using the software. FTP2000 is an example of a program that's available as shareware—you can try it for 30 days before some of the advanced features are disabled, and you can use the basic features indefinitely while you decide whether to register the software by ponying up $39.95.

23

JUST A MINUTE

More information on FTP2000 is available from its developer, Quintessential Objects, at http://www.qoi.com.

Setting Up the Software

The requirements for using FTP software are similar to those for using the Publish feature of Home Page. You must have an account with your Web site provider, such as your Internet service provider, GeoCities, or something else. Also, you need the following information to publish your site:

- ☐ Your user name
- ☐ Your password
- ☐ The remote directory where files should be placed

JUST A MINUTE

America Online users can't use FTP software to publish their sites because they don't have direct access to the directory where files must be placed. Both Home Page and AOL have built-in features for publishing Web sites on AOL.

For this hour's work with FTP software, you should publish the Edward George Bulwer-Lytton home page on the Web, even if it's the site you worked with in the previous hour. Some elements of this project are more complicated than those in Home Page, and they might make more sense with specific references to the Bulwer-Lytton home page.

Once you have selected a site as your FTP guinea pig, you must put a few things in order. First, check to see that all the Web pages, images, and other files that make up the site are in the same folder (or subfolders of the same folder) on your system. A common method of organization is to put all the Web pages in one folder, all graphics files in an images subfolder, and all other files in the main folder.

If your home page uses any files from a Home Page library, such as the "Made by Claris Home Page" button on the Bulwer-Lytton main page, you need to make a copy of these files and put them in the site's main folder or a subfolder before you can use FTP software.

For example, the file chpmade.gif is the "Made by Claris Home Page" button graphic. It's stored in a subfolder of the Claris Clip Art folder on your system. Before you can publish the Bulwer-Lytton home page with FTP software, you need to store a copy of the chpmade.gif file in the Webwork\Stormy\images folder on your system.

After doing that, you must make a change to the page within Home Page so that the chpmade.gif image is coming from the right place on your system—the images folder. To make a change, right-click your mouse over the image and choose the Set Src command from the menu that pops up. You should see a long, confusing folder reference, such as the one shown in Figure 23.1.

Figure 23.1.

Identifying the location of an image.

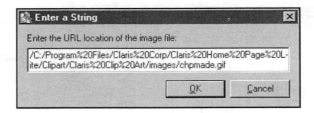

The reference in Figure 23.1 indicates the folder on your system where the library graphics file is stored. It's in the Program Files/Home Page Lite/Clipart/Claris Clip Art/images folder in the figure.

You won't be using a reference like this when the page is on the World Wide Web because the folder won't exist on the Web server offering your site. Instead, you want to change the reference so that it pulls the graphics file from the images subfolder. Change the text field of the Enter a String dialog box to the following:

```
images/chpmade.gif
```

This value causes the chpmade.gif graphics file to be pulled from the images subfolder.

Beginning the Transfer

Once your site is ready to publish and you have FTP software installed on your system, you're ready to get things rolling. The first step is to connect to the Internet the way you normally do. FTP software relies on an active Internet connection to reach your Web site host and transfer files to it.

Once you're online, run your FTP software. Most FTP software looks similar to file-management software, such as Windows 95 Explorer—files and folders are displayed in different windows, allowing you to drag one or more items from one window to another. Figure 23.2 shows the first screen you see once FTP2000 has been loaded.

In FTP2000, there's a window on the left-hand side of the screen that displays the files in the currently selected folder. In Figure 23.2, the current folder is C:\Webwork\Stormy, the main folder of the Bulwer-Lytton home page. The window on the right-hand side of FTP2000 displays a folder on the host Web server where you'll be publishing your site.

Figure 23.2.

Getting started with FTP2000.

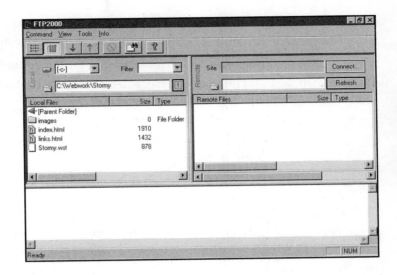

Using your FTP software, make sure the current folder you're looking at on your system is Webwork\Stormy, if you're publishing the Bulwer-Lytton site, or the main folder of another site you're transferring instead.

Next, you need to set up your FTP software to make a connection to the Web server hosting your site. In FTP2000, this is done by clicking the Connect button, which opens the Site Manager dialog box, shown in Figure 23.3.

Figure 23.3.

The Site Manager dialog box.

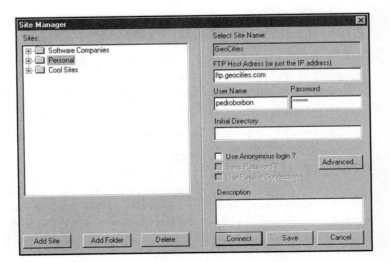

In this box, highlight the Personal folder title and click the Add Site button. The New Site dialog box opens, and you should enter the following information in it:

☐ In the Site Name field, enter the name of the service hosting your Web site.

☐ In the FTP Host Address field, enter the name of the Internet site where you have access to upload files, such as `ftp.prefect.com`.

☐ In the UserName field, enter the name you use to log onto this service.

☐ In the Password field, enter your password for this service, which will be obscured by * marks when you type it.

☐ Make sure the Anonymous box isn't checked.

After entering these fields and clicking OK, you return to the previous dialog box. Highlight the name of the site you just created settings for and, in the Initial Directory field, enter the name of the remote directory on the server where the site should be stored. This field should be empty if the server stipulates that the default directory should be used.

If you're unsure of any of these settings, you need to check with your Web host service.

TIME SAVER

Most services that offer Web page hosting can give you help on how to use FTP software to put files on their own Web sites, so you might be able to save time by checking the help files there before contacting the company by e-mail or phone.

Publishing Your Home Page

Everything is now ready for the transfer to begin. Click the Connect button and FTP2000 will attempt to make a connection to the site that's hosting your Web pages. If it's successful, you will return to the window that displays a folder on your system. It shows a folder on the remote system, also—the one where your Web site's files should be transferred.

Figure 23.4 shows both windows open in an attempt to transfer files to GeoCities.

Transferring files using FTP2000 or other types of FTP software is similar to copying or moving files on your own system. You highlight the files in question and drag them to their new location, or use Cut, Copy, and Paste commands as needed. In FTP2000, highlight the following items in your Webwork\Stormy folder: the index.html file, the links.html file, and the images folder. Drag them to the Remote Files window and drop them there. A dialog box then opens, asking you to confirm the request; if everything looks normal, click Yes.

If the images subfolder doesn't exist on the Web server, you'll be asked whether to create it. Click Yes.

Figure 23.4.

Transferring files through FTP2000 to GeoCities.

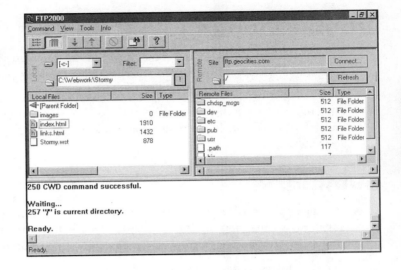

Once all the files have been copied into the correct remote directory, in most cases you can see them right away by using a Web browser and going to the address that contains your newly published home page. You might need to check with your Web hosting service to find out the address of your new site. Some Internet service providers use a similar scheme for addressing: The service's domain, followed by the text /~ and your user name, such as the following:

```
http://www.interstice.com/~greenlama
```

This address would be for a user of the interstice.com service with the user name of greenlama.

Advanced FTP Features

FTP software can be a little harder to use than Home Page's Publish feature, but it does offer some additional features you can use to maintain your Web site. For example, you can delete Web pages and other files.

In FTP2000, you can delete files by highlighting them and choosing the Command | Remote File Options | Delete Selected Folder(s) or Files(s) menu option. (You can also right-click over the highlighted items and choose the Delete menu option that appears.) You'll be asked to confirm your decision to delete the highlighted items—make sure you really want to take this action. Although Windows 95 puts deleted files into the Recycle Bin, where they can be retrieved immediately if you have a change of heart, the same isn't true of FTP software. Once you choose to delete a file on a Web server, it's gone.

Using FTP software, you can also create new folders and files, using different options of the Command | Remote File Options menu.

Troubleshooting

Troubleshooting FTP software comes down to the same tasks as troubleshooting Home Page's Publish feature. You must double-check to make sure your user name, password, Web hosting server name, and remote directory are correct.

Once those settings have been established correctly, and you've gone through a successful file transfer, FTP software is easy to use when maintaining your home page and any other sites you publish.

Summary

Although many novice users might prefer to use the Publish feature of Home Page, FTP software is worth trying out. It can be used to transfer files without loading Home Page, and some FTP software offers features that aren't currently part of the Home Page Lite version.

FTP2000 is an example of this type of FTP software because one of its advanced features is the ability to edit a file directly that's located on a Web server. If you have a small typo to fix or some other small correction, you can use FTP 2000 to load the page into an editor on your system and make the quick change.

Q&A

Q Is there a way to create subfolders within GeoCities?

A Because that service offers Web pages to thousands of people, its FTP site operates in a slightly different manner than most others you might use. You don't see the files you have transferred when they arrive, and you can't create subfolders. If you're developing a site for publication on GeoCities, put all the files that make up the site in the same folder.

Q Can I use FTP software to publish different home pages in different places on the Web?

A It's possible with most—if not all—versions of FTP software. With FTP2000, you can establish as many different FTP sites as you need, and each can be customized with a different server, user name, password, and remote directory.

Q Does it matter which FTP software is used to send files to a Web site?

A As long as the software works, no. There are several FTP programs available for Windows, Macintosh, and UNIX systems. Visit a file archive, such as http://www.shareware.com, and search for FTP to find some for your system.

23

Q Can I use the anonymous FTP feature to publish a site without a user name and a password?

A Probably not in any case, because Web server administrators require a user name and password for security reasons. When you're publishing a home page, you're creating files on a remote computer system. Password authentication limits abuse, and it prevents people from overwriting your site with their own documents later on.

Quiz

Test your knowledge of this hour by taking this brief three-question test.

Questions

1. Where's a good place to go to find FTP software to try out?

    (a) File repositories, such as www.shareware.com

    (b) This book's CD-ROM

    (c) Online services, such as America Online

2. What's one thing FTP software can do that the Home Page Publish feature can't?

    (a) Make julienne fries

    (b) Create new folders on the Web hosting system

    (c) Replace existing files with a newer version of the same document

3. What word means "a set of rules through which two entities can communicate with each other"?

    (a) publication

    (b) protocol

    (c) pet peeves

Answers

1. a., b., and c. Make sure you're getting programs from a trusted source, because anything you run that was received over the Internet might be infected with a virus or could be intentionally damaging to your system.

2. b. Both FTP software and Home Page allow you to replace an existing Web page or other file with a newer version of the same document.

3. b.

Activities

The following activities are suggested to expand your knowledge of the subjects covered during this hour:

- ☐ If you have created one of your own home pages, use FTP software to put it online, if it's ready for worldwide exposure.

- ☐ Even if you're not ready to put a Web site online for any other reason, put together a list of your favorite sites and publish it on GeoCities or AOL. You'll get some confidence using FTP software and join the millions who already have done the same thing on their Web pages.

Hour 24

Telling the World

One of the more astounding things about the World Wide Web is inherent in its name: It really is worldwide. As you have probably read a half-dozen times by this point, a Web page you put on the Internet can be viewed by anyone on the planet who has its address, a Web-ready computer, and time to kill.

However, the world isn't likely to visit your page unless you find a way to let them know about it. This book's final hour focuses on this element of Web page creation, on the assumption that you're interested in having visitors drop by your virtual homestead. The following topics are covered:

- [ ] Announcing your site
- [ ] Using search engines and directories
- [ ] Making a Usenet Web announcement
- [ ] Trying other promotional strategies

Hello World

The suggestions in this hour assume that you have put a Web site on the Net and want the world to stop by. If you're not interested in having anyone see your page, or any part of a site, putting it on the Web is a bad idea. Even if you do nothing to promote your home page, it could show up in places like AltaVista and WebCrawler, if just a single person puts a link to your page on his or her page. These search engines send out Web robots that travel from link to link, putting each page they hit into the database.

Once you have created your Web site and you're happy with how it turned out, you're ready to proclaim its existence. There are two basic types of services that offer listings of Web sites: directories and search engines.

Directories, best epitomized by Yahoo!, organize Web sites into a hierarchy based on the purpose of the sites. This structure is beneficial to directory users because the sites can be found more easily, but directories require a lot of employee effort to maintain and can be slow to catch up to new sites. Figure 24.1 shows an example of a Yahoo! directory for the MUMPS programming language. Several sites are listed, along with headings linking to pages related to MUMPS programming companies, organizations, and user groups.

Figure 24.1.

A listing of related Web sites compiled by Yahoo!.

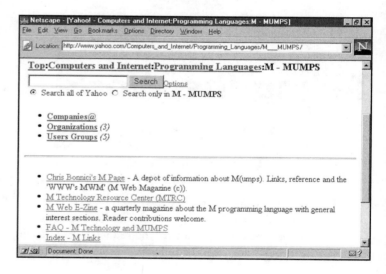

Search engines, such as AltaVista and WebCrawler, provide large databases of Web pages. No effort is made to organize the material, however, so users must try to find what they're looking for by entering search text and special search commands. These search engines are quick to display new information, but it can be difficult, if not impossible, to find some sites if you don't try the right search text. Figure 24.2 shows a sample search conducted for pages referring to the actor Sam Whipple.

Figure 24.2.
An AltaVista listing of sites containing specific text.

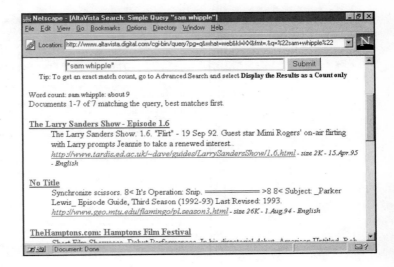

Making Announcements to a Group of Sites

The best place to start announcing your new Web site is probably Submit It!, at `http://www.submit-it.com`. Submit It! allows you to make an announcement to more than a dozen different Web directories or search engines at the same time. You enter information about your site and yourself, including the best e-mail address to use when contacting you. Submit It! then makes it as easy as possible to submit your site to different services that list Web pages, so you don't need to type the same information all over again on each service you go to.

There are free and pay versions of Submit It! The free version offers 17 different services, including InfoSeek, WebCrawler, and AltaVista. The pay version gives you 100 different services, and the cost ranges from $60 to $300, depending on the number of pages submitted.

Some of the services you use Submit It! to reach require a little more information to include your site in their databases. This requirement is usually true of directories, where you must choose a subject area that matches your site, but search engines such as AltaVista don't require any information other than your page's address.

Submit It! lets you choose which services to submit your site to and which ones to disregard. When starting out, you will probably choose to send it to all 20 of the free services. A few of them might be inappropriate for your site because of content restrictions on the service. The rest, however, will take the submission and consider it for inclusion. Figure 24.3 shows the checklist of sites that Submit It!'s free service can be used with.

Figure 24.3.

Beginning a Submit It! submission.

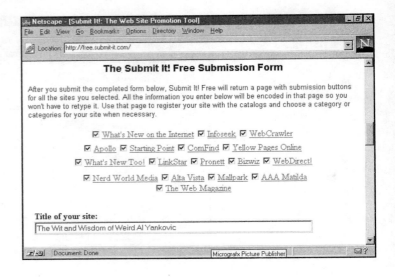

JUST A MINUTE

With the exception of search engines, you're not guaranteed a listing in any of the services that your Web pages are submitted to. Some services reject pages based on their content or their description, and others might take a long time to consider your submission before adding it to their database.

When composing your Submit It! information, be sure to take some time to make the title and description of your site interesting. The title doesn't have to match the title on your Web site's index.html page, so you can pick anything you like. The description is the text that people see when your page comes up in a directory, so you need to make it sound compelling to stand out amid many competing pages. The description should be 25 words or less because some directories reject submissions that are longer.

The description of a site is the first exposure many Web surfers have to the pages it represents. It could also be the last exposure, because there's always somewhere else to go on the Web. The following recommendations will help you create a more compelling description:

☐ Don't restate the site's title in the description—both are displayed in directories promoting your site.

☐ Get to the point, describing exactly what the site contains.

☐ Sell the site—use the description as a promotional tool.

24

Yahoo!

One service that isn't included in Submit It! is definitely worth contacting on its own. Yahoo! was the first popular World Wide Web directory back in 1994–1995, and it remains the most popular directory today. To add your home page to this directory, you need to go to the page on Yahoo! that most fits your page's subject area.

For example, if you've created a page about flags, it probably should be included in the Reference/Flags section of Yahoo! You could recommend that it be added to that page by going to the References/Flags page and clicking the Add URL graphic at the top of the page.

When you click the Add URL graphic, you're taken to a page where you can enter the same kind of information requested by Submit It!, with a few Yahoo!-specific requests included, such as additional pages on Yahoo! where your site could be listed.

This might seem a bit redundant, given that you're reaching only one service instead of 20, but Yahoo! is worth the effort. Being listed in Yahoo! is a sure-fire way for a new Web site to attract many first-time visitors because of the large amount of traffic that goes through Yahoo!

CAUTION

> Because listings are added to Yahoo! manually, the service can be extremely slow at adding Web pages to its directory. It's also the most selective of the directories, declining to include many pages submitted by Web publishers. If your site isn't added to Yahoo!, try again after a few months or after a major revision to your pages.

Usenet Web Announcements

One of the ways many people keep up with developments on the World Wide Web is to use the Usenet discussion group `comp.infosystems.www.announce`. This group has a moderator who distributes non-commercial announcements of new Web sites and posts changes in the status of existing Web sites. Figure 24.4 shows a listing of Web site announcements from the discussion group as they appear through AOL's Usenet reader.

An announcement published on `comp.infosystems.www.announce` is sent to Usenet servers around the world, where it can be seen by thousands of readers for a week or longer before the message is replaced by newer announcements.

To see how to write your announcement and read some guidelines for what's acceptable and what isn't, visit the official Web page for the group at the following Web page:

`http://vader.boutell.com/~grant/charter.html`

If you write an interesting announcement for your site and follow the rules for posting, it should be included on `comp.infosystems.www.announce` within a few days of submission.

Figure 24.4.
Scanning titles on a Usenet discussion group.

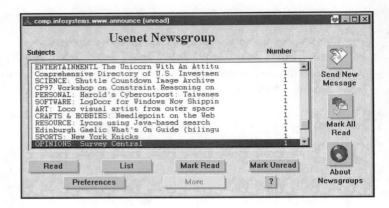

CAUTION

Although you might be tempted to promote your Web page on other Usenet discussion groups, you should do that only when you know it's acceptable to the participants of that specific group. In most cases it isn't, and posting a promotional message on those groups is a quick way to get e-mail hot enough to burn the eyebrows off the next three generations of your family.

Attracting Visitors

There are many other ways to make people aware of your Web site, such as winning an award like Cool Site of the Day at `http://cool.infi.net` (shown in Figure 24.5) or Cool.Com at `http://www.cool.com`.

Figure 24.5.
The Cool Site of the Day's home page.

24

If you'd like to get a quick rundown of sites that give awards and how recently they were updated, you can visit the Web Soup page at the following address:

```
http://sctest.cse.ucsc.edu/roth/WebSoup/WebSoup.html
```

This site is an all-text page that extracts the latest award winners from some of the better known award sites on the Web. It isn't going to be easy to win some of these awards, especially the more established ones, such as Cool Site of the Day. However, it's a great way to cause a surge in the number of visitors to your page, if you do win.

Summary

The main way to attract visitors to a page you've created doesn't involve any kind of PR effort. If you update the page often and on a regular basis, the number of visitors will increase over time as people who like the site put a link to it on their pages, and other people find your site through those links.

However, that isn't always the case if the content isn't compelling—as I have learned with my rarely browsed homage to the cast of the TV sitcom *Empty Nest*. However, if you have the endurance to maintain a regularly updated Web page and you enjoy what you're doing, it's a rewarding avocation.

For some folks, it's an obscenely rewarding vocation. The creators of Yahoo! started that service as a hobby when they were still at Stanford, and at the time you could attempt to list all the interesting Web sites in the world without being thought a lunatic. The founders are now multimillionaires who have endowed their own chair at the school.

Although there aren't any 24-hour tutorials on how to replicate their success—at least not any we're sharing with the public—the World Wide Web remains a medium in a state of constant invention. It's like having a mellifluous voice at the dawning of radio drama in the '30s, being a crazy redheaded comedienne with a Cuban bandleader spouse during the Golden Age of television, or being the first technical author to think, "Hey—maybe I ought to set aside my interactive TV tutorial and write a book about this new Java thing."

There's no telling what's coming up on the World Wide Web, because it's still too young to be predictable. The only thing you can reasonably assume is this: No matter what happens, someone at Sams.net will be there to help you learn it in a set time period.

Your completion of *Teach Yourself to Create a Home Page in 24 Hours* makes you a pioneer. Whether you use this opportunity to change the world—or celebrate long-running situation comedies—is entirely up to you.

As for me, remember the *Empty Nest* episode where Morgan Fairchild visits her childhood friend Dinah Manoff and falls for Richard Mulligan even though he's Dinah's dad? If that event doesn't have "very special Web site" written all over it, I don't know what does.

—Rogers Cadenhead

Q&A

Q Why would you want to be listed in 100 different directories and search engines?

A For a commercial home page, the answer is probably that the cost of using Submit It! is negligible compared to the possible benefit if the site becomes a popular one. For everyone else, it's largely a matter of what your expectations are for the site. Many people are probably content to use the free listing service of Submit It! instead of spending money for more listings.

Q Why does Yahoo! sometimes require more than one submission to have a site listed?

A There's no way to determine why a specific site isn't listed in Yahoo!, since the service doesn't send e-mail letting a Web developer know that a submission has been rejected. The only contact from Yahoo! is when a site has been accepted. The most likely cause for being left out is getting lost among all the other submissions Yahoo! must get in a given day.

Q Why can't commercial sites be announced on `comp.infosystems.www.announce`?

A Because the group is moderated by a volunteer, that person's discretion is what determines its content. The volunteers involved in `comp.infosystems.www.announce` decided to promote only non-commercial sites through their Usenet group, and one of their concerns was not spending their free time to promote a for-profit business.

Q How long does it take to be added to the AltaVista search engine?

A Usually, when you submit the address of a Web page to AltaVista, it pulls the data off that page quickly and adds it to the database within a week.

Quiz

Test your knowledge of this hour by taking this brief three-question test.

Questions

1. Which service is not a part of Submit It!?

    (a) AltaVista

    (b) Yahoo!

    (c) Infoseek

24

2. True or False: It's OK to post an announcement advertising your Web site on Usenet discussion groups, as long as you limit it to 25 groups or less.

   (a) True

   (b) False

   (c) Truth and falsehood are outdated concepts

3. Which former *Family* star played Dinah Manoff's sister on *Empty Nest*?

   (a) Park Overall

   (b) Kristy McNichol

   (c) Marsha Warfield

Answers

1. b.

2. b. Usenet etiquette dictates that advertisements not be posted on specific groups without knowing whether it's acceptable, and it's definitely inappropriate to post to large numbers of groups at the same time.

3. b.

Activities

The following activities are suggested to expand your knowledge of the subjects covered during this hour:

☐ If you'd like to continue learning about related topics through the *24 Hours* line of books, be sure to check out Sams.net Publishing's *Teach Yourself HTML 3.2 in 24 Hours* by Dick Oliver and *Teach Yourself Java 1.1 Programming in 24 Hours* by Rogers Cadenhead, the author of this book.

☐ If you don't want to learn about related topics, buy the books anyway in case you change your mind later.

PART
VII

Appendixes

Hour

Appendix A

Upgrading to Claris Home Page 2.0

After you have used the Lite version of Claris Home Page for 24 one-hour tutorials, you are probably curious about the "heavy" version. Claris Home Page 2.0, which retails for $99, has a Web page at the following address:

`http://www.claris.com/support/products/clarispage/`

Home Page was chosen for this book because of the features it offers and its ease of use. It's one of the more affordable, fully featured Web page creation tools currently available. Also, Home Page was designed to be easy for novices to use—no knowledge of HTML is assumed, and, as you have seen while reading this book, you don't need HTML knowledge to create interesting home pages.

The full version of Home Page 2.0 offers the following enhancements:

- [ ] The ability to create and edit Web pages with frames
- [ ] A way to integrate forms into your pages
- [ ] Expanded clip art libraries

☐ The ability to edit a Web page directly from the Web server offering the page

☐ HTML source code editing, with colored text for the different syntax

☐ A spelling checker

☐ The ability to click on a GIF image to make part of it transparent or to make it an interlaced image

☐ The ability to hide HTML programming tags if you don't know how to use them or to reveal them if you do

☐ Support for displaying images aligned to the left or right of text

☐ The ability to change the size of cells in a table

☐ Web page uploading by using FTP

☐ The ability to preview the look of a background image while in edit mode

☐ QuickTime movie support

☐ Plug-in support

Appendix B

Sample Web Page Templates

by s. d. meyers

If you made it this far, you have probably mastered the basics of creating a home page, unless, of course, you're reading this book backward. Assuming you did read the book in the proper direction, and you understood it, you might be wondering what's going on here somewhere beyond the end of the promised 24 hours. Let me tell you…

I once took a painting class with a rather renowned, yet eccentric art instructor, and he bestowed this wisdom upon me. He said that "staring at a blank canvas is extremely intimidating, and as long as the canvas is blank, you'll never get anything done at all. To overcome this obstacle," he continued, "take a brush with a goodly amount of paint and quickly paint anything on the canvas, or if you're at a total loss, just put a big *X* on it. Once you've done that, you'll no longer be afraid of the canvas."

He rambled on some more about never using black paint because black is neither a color nor does it exist in nature, but that's a different story. However, starting with a "tainted" canvas not only made sense in some strange way, but it worked rather well. And that's what this appendix is all about: tainted canvases, or in this case, tainted Web pages (better known as *templates*).

I've given you three templates you can use for whatever you want: inspiration, to rip off icons, whatever—you paid for it. You can find them in the \Tmplts directory on the CD-ROM that came with this book. This appendix shows you what you can do with these templates, and although the first one is quite simple (it's even called "simple"), the other two are examples of complex layouts with tables and frames.

The "Simple" Template

The simple template represents a fairly simple Web page: a couple of graphics and something to say. Just because it's simple, however, doesn't mean it should be ignored. Often, complex layout overshadows good content, and excellent content is much more valuable than a few bells and whistles.

Simple.html, shown in Figure B.1, is located on the accompanying CD-ROM in the Simple directory, which is found at D:\Tmplts\Simple\simple.html on most systems.

JUST A MINUTE

> The directory paths I'm listing here are for Windows 95 and NT 4.0. If you're using a Macintosh, the directory structure is the same; just keep in mind that *D:* is what Microsoft calls a CD-ROM drive. You should be able to figure out the rest.

The only really interesting feature of this Web page's layout is the way the text wraps around the graphics. To wrap your text, just set the alignment of your image to either Right or Left. After you do that, seemingly little happens in Home Page; that's because Home Page doesn't currently display Right and Left alignments properly. (See Figure B.2.)

If you look at the second image in Home Page, you can see that three elements aren't displayed correctly. Can you guess what they are? (The first two are really easy.)

- [ ] First of all, the image does not even show up! This is because the image file is a JPEG file, which works great in most Web browsers; Home Page, however, can't display them.
- [ ] Second, as I mentioned for the first image, the text isn't properly wrapped.
- [ ] Finally, the image is on the left side of the page when it's set to appear on the right! This is just something Home Page does. As you can see in Figure B.1, everything turns out OK in the browser, and that's what's important.

B

Figure B.1.

Simple.html seen within a Web browser.

S. Kribble Jr.'s Home Page

Hi! Welcome to my home page. My name is S. Really that's it... just one letter and a period! I was named after mt Dad. His name is also S., but he dosn't have a Jr. stuck to the end. All the kids at school used to make fun of me, and my teacher usally just don't get it at first either, but I think everyone is o.k. with it now.

I'm in 5th grade if you are wondering. I'm in Mr. Jones class. I hate him! He's a really bad teacher. The other day I was playing around on one of the computers at school. I had got on to the internet and like got into some government computer with lists of like everybody, most of the stuff was boring, like how much money they have and stuff, but some of the stuff was cool, like if people were arrested or if the government was watching them, it was all there... really cool! Anyway, I was supposed to be doing other stuff, like trying to find something out about this stupid painting in France, and like it's on the internet, and that's supposed to be cool... Well it's not. It's really super NOT cool. But Mr. Jones sent me to the principals office, and they called my dad ands stuff. I think I'm smarter then Mr. Jones and the Principal, that's why they're so mean. I bet the Principal can't even use a computer. Really, I think he's retarded or something.

My dad is pretty cool, but sometimes he get wierd and stuff. He's like this electronic person that people pay lot's of money to. He designs computer chips for some really super big computer company. He say's that one day his company will rule the world. I don't know about that, but it could be cool. I know my Dad has a really super cool computer! He get's a new one like all the time. Sometimes I get to use his older ones, but he never lets me touch the ones he uses for work, because once I like goofed something up and somthing didn't work right, like when you did division it could give you like a really wrong answer. Well I don't know if I really did it, but my Dad isn't taking any chances.

The really wierd thing about my dad is he and a bunch of other people are really wierd about toast. I mean toast is cool, but I mean these people like think it's the greatest thing in the world. I hope that's not something that like Kids inherit from there Fathers because I don't ever want to be that strange.

I have a cat named Grapefruit. Grapfruit is a really cool cat so I put her picture here. I had a goldfish once too but it died. Cat's live longer then goldfish, you can also play with them and stuff, so I think that cat's are much better pets. The picture of Grapefruit is when she was just a kitten. She's gotten alot bigger since this picture was taken.

Anyway, I don't have anything else to say right now so I'll leave you with a few helpful links.

- If you ever need to find out about some stupid art in France it's probably here!
- If you want to e-mail me my e-mail address is username@host.com.
- If you want to learn about toast visit this page.

Figure B.2.

What simple.html looks like in Home Page.

The Tabled Template

As I mentioned, content is the most important element of a Web page, but suppose you have absolutely nothing valuable to say? Well, then you have to rely on pure design and layout alone. Luckily for you, Home Page creates complex tables in a wonderfully easy way, and tables are currently the best way to create interesting, enticing layouts.

The tabled template, found on the CD-ROM in the \Tabled directory, uses tables to create a unique layout and design. (See Figure B.3.)

Figure B.3.

Table.html (seen here in Netscape Navigator) uses tables to create an interesting layout.

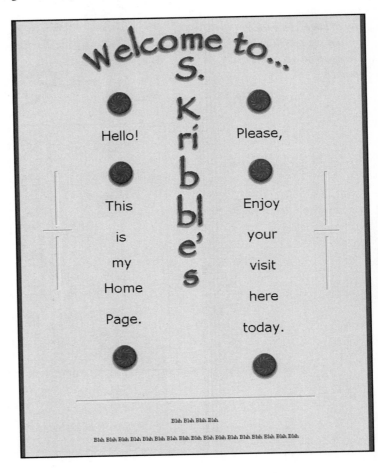

How did I do this? Well...

☐ First, I created a single image that contained the `Welcome to...` `S.` `Kribbles` text as I wanted it to appear on my Web page.

☐ Next, I broke the figure up into two separate figures: one containing `Welcome to...` `S.` and the other containing `Kribbles`. (You can see how these figures fit together in Figure B.4.)

Figure B.4.

Table.html as seen in Home Page; the border around the table's cells doesn't show up in the browser.

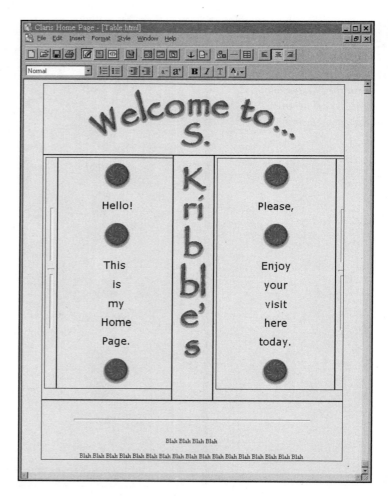

☐ Then I created a table with three rows and three columns.

☐ I selected the top-left cell and then used the Object Editor to set this cell to span all three columns. I repeated this with the bottom-left cell as well.

☐ I dropped the Welcome to... S. graphic (saved as `top.gif` in \Tabled\gifs\) into the top frame and centered it. Then, I dropped the Kribble's graphic (saved as `middle.gif`) in the center cell of the table and centered it.

☐ Next, I selected the whole table and used the Object Editor to set the border, cell spacing, and cell padding all to `0`.

☐ Finally, since I'm after an exact layout here, I set the table's width to an absolute 540 pixels and the center cell to an absolute width slightly larger than my `middle.gif` (in this case, the image is 64 pixels wide, so I made the table 72 pixels wide). Also, I set the remaining two cells in the middle row to 234 pixels each ($234 \times 2 + 72 = 540$).

JUST A MINUTE

> The reason I set the initial table width to 540 pixels is because 540 pixels is just about the right width to fit nicely on a television screen. Why is that important? Well, now that we have such things as WebTV, you must adjust your designs accordingly if you want everyone to be able to properly view your pages.

Now that I have my basic table layout, I can add my content in the left and right cells of the middle column, as well as some extraneous content in the bottom row.

TIME SAVER

> To add the design on the left and the right of the page, I actually created separate tables within the left and right cells of the main table. Then I simply added standard horizontal lines. However, by changing the height to something really large (Home Page allows you to enter horizontal line heights only up to 100 pixels, but larger sizes are possible if you actually want to edit the HTML code) and the width to something small (5 pixels in this template), you get vertical lines instead of horizontal lines! The advantage of this is that you get effective graphics without having the user download any extra graphics.

Remember that more information on using tables can be found back in Hours 10, "Building Your First Table," and 11, "Creating More Sophisticated Tables."

The Framed Template

The first two templates are OK, but nothing you couldn't have figured out yourself with the skills you have already learned from this book. This final template, however, is going to help you do something that couldn't be done easily with the version of Home Page on the CD-ROM—and that's to create a Web page with frames.

B

The retail version of Claris Home Page does have its own Frame Wizard that allows you to create your own frame layouts. Or you could just pick up any recent book on HTML (such as *Teach Yourself HTML in 24 Hours*, Sams.net Publishing) and learn to create your own frames the old-fashioned way.

Before you get ahead of yourself, though, first take a look at what a framed Web page really is and how it works. A sample is shown in Figure B.5.

Figure B.5.

Frame.html in Netscape Navigator.

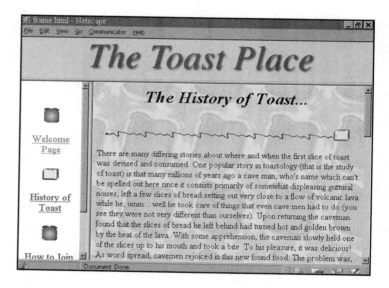

What you're actually seeing in Figure B.5 is three different Web pages placed together in frames as defined by the frameset document—in this case, frame.html.

In the framed template, you might notice that there are six HTML files; frame.html is the frameset, and the other five are just normal HTML files.

A framed Web page is really two or more normal Web pages, organized by a special type of Web page called a *frameset*. The purpose of the frameset is to tell the browser how each frame is laid out, and which HTML document should be displayed in each frame.

In the framed template, there are three frames. The top frame loads the document called header.html, which consists of a single graphic. (See Figure B.6.) This frame has been set with a designated height of 80 pixels, meaning that any graphic placed in header.html up to 72 pixels (the equivalent of one inch) will fit nicely at the top of the page. This particular frameset is also set up not to display a scrollbar.

B

Figure B.6.

*Header.html seen in
Home Page.*

The frame on the left, below the header, loads the document contents.html, which is basically
an index containing links to the remaining three HTML documents (Page1.html, Page2.html,
and Page3.html). (See Figure B.7.) The only thing out of the ordinary about this Web page
is a simple tag lurking behind the scenes; it tells the browser that any link accessed from this
frame will open up in another frame named "Main" (the name of the frame right next to
contents.html).

Figure B.7.

*Contents.html viewed in
Home Page.*

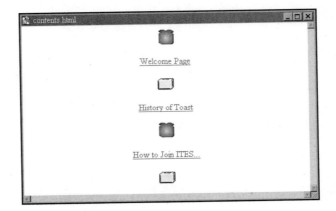

The third and final frame is the big one—the frame providing the Web page's main content.
Again, like the other frames, it's a standard HTML document, such as the ones you created
in Home Page. For this template, I have created three pages (because it would be kind of
boring and useless to demonstrate frames without giving them a purpose). By default,
Page1.html is displayed when frame.html is loaded, but when you click on one of the other
links in contents.html, this frame changes to display the appropriate document, as shown in
Figure B.8.

If you ever want to create your own frames, you can do one of two things:

☐ Learn enough HTML to hand-code them.

☐ Buy an editor that can create them for you (such as the full version of Claris Home
Page, which is shown opening frame.html in Figure B.9).

Figure B.8.

Page2.html in Home Page; like the other documents, it, too, is just an ordinary Web page.

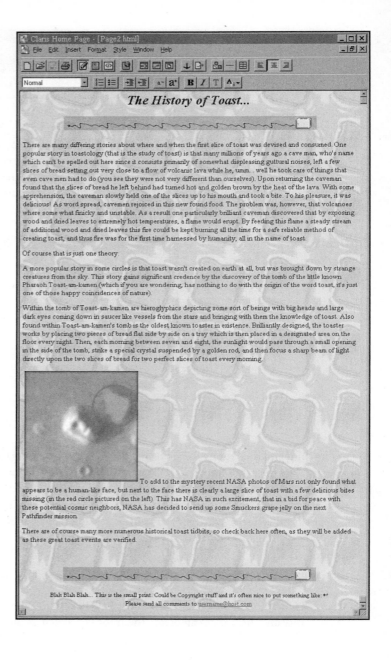

B

Figure B.9.

Although the Lite version of Home Page on the CD-ROM won't open frame.html, the full version, as shown here, can.

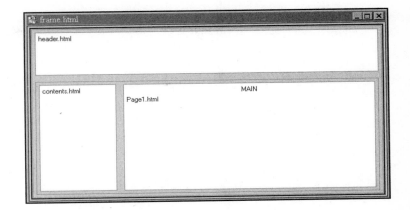

Summary

Well, that concludes the discussion of the templates I've included here. I hope they're helpful in, if nothing else, giving you a dirty canvas to paint over. Before I leave you with just the few remaining appendixes, let me say (or write, actually) that these templates are for your use with no strings attached. You can use them just as they are (why you would want to, I can't say), borrow bits and pieces of them, or even trade them with your friends if you'd like! Usually, however, borrowing the content of other people's Web sites *without* their permission is a very bad thing and can even be illegal. Always ask first! Oh, by the way, if these templates do help you in any way, let me know by e-mailing me at smee@iquest.net (don't send me e-mail trying to sell me anything, though—I don't want it!).

B

Appendix C

This Book's CD-ROM

The CD-ROM included in the back of *Teach Yourself to Create a Home Page in 24 Hours* contains the trial version of Claris Home Page 2.0 Lite that's used throughout the book. It also contains all the Web pages and other files created during the one-hour lessons in the book, so you can check them against your own work (or cheat and use cut-and-paste functions to avoid typing anything in).

In addition to these book-related materials, the CD-ROM has some applications and utilities that you might find useful.

JUST A MINUTE

> Please refer to the file readme.wri on the CD-ROM (Windows) or the Guide to the CD-ROM (Macintosh) for the most current listing of the software. You can find instructions for installing the CD-ROM on the "Install" page at the back of the book.

Windows Software

The following programs are available as shareware, which let you try a program for a certain amount of time before deciding whether to buy it; demo versions, which run for a set amount of time before being disabled; or freeware, which is free for use now and forevermore.

JUST A MINUTE

> Claris Home Page 2.0 Lite is not supported by Claris Corporation. Please contact the publisher for any technical support.

HTML Tools

- [ ] Claris Home Page 2.0 Lite
- [ ] Hot Dog 32-bit HTML editor
- [ ] HoTMetaL HTML editor
- [ ] HTMLed HTML editor

Graphics, Video, and Sound Applications

- [ ] Paint Shop Pro 3.12 graphics editor and graphics file format converter for Windows
- [ ] SnagIt screen capture utility
- [ ] ThumbsPlus image viewer and browser

Utilities

- [ ] Adobe Acrobat viewer
- [ ] WinZip for Windows 95
- [ ] WinZip self-extractor

Macintosh Software

The following programs are available as shareware, which let you try a program for a certain amount of time before deciding whether to buy it; demo versions, which run for a set amount of time before being disabled; or freeware, which is free for use now and forevermore.

C

HTML Tools

- ☐ Claris Home Page 2.0 Lite
- ☐ BBEdit Lite 4
- ☐ BBEdit 4 demo

Graphics, Video, and Sound Applications

- ☐ Graphic Conveter v2.1.4
- ☐ GIFConverter v2.3.7
- ☐ Fast Player v1.1
- ☐ Sparkle 2.4.5
- ☐ SoundApp v1.5.1

Utilities

- ☐ ZipIt for Macintosh
- ☐ ScrapIt Pro
- ☐ Adobe Acrobat

About Third-Party Software

Please read all documentation that's included with a third-party product, usually in a file named readme.txt, license.txt, or something similar, and follow the guidelines for use.

C

Appendix D

This Book's Web Site

One of the goals of this book was to teach a complete beginner to create Web pages. The crack team of scientists at Sams.net Publishing determined that the average reader, spending an average of 24 hours, could create above-average home pages with this book and Claris Home Page 2.0 Lite.

However, some of our scientists unfortunately took the words "crack team" to mean something other than "really skilled dudes." Consequently, rampant drug abuse among our researchers puts their results in doubt.

Because of this, it's entirely possible that you have questions about the book. You might even have spotted a possible error or something that needs more clarification. Our copy editros keep a close eye on things, but it's entirely possible that an eror or too was missed.

To account for this possibility, an official Web site has been created to support readers of *Teach Yourself to Create a Home Page in 24 Hours*. It's at the following address:

```
http://www.prefect.com/home24
```

This Web site, which is updated by the author, Rogers Cadenhead, will feature several different types of offerings:

- Error corrections and clarifications, with corrected text and other material that will help

- Answers to readers' questions, when they aren't already answered somewhere in the book

- Links to other Sams.net book pages, which give you a quick way to see what else is available from Sams, including the other books of the *24 Hours* series

- All the Web pages developed during the past 24 hours, giving you a chance to see them, along with the supporting graphics and other necessary files

- Updated links to the sites mentioned in this book, so that you don't have to scramble through Yahoo! and search engines when an address in this book has changed

- Links to the sites of readers who have created interesting home pages based on their use of this book

The *24 Hours* books represent a new line from Sams.net, and your suggestions, comments, and questions are strongly encouraged. In addition to visiting the site, you can contact author Rogers Cadenhead at the following e-mail address:

`home24@prefect.com`

You also can visit the official Sams.net Web site—the Developers' Resource Center—at the following address:

`http://www.mcp.com/sams`

Please feel free to voice all opinions, whether you want to name your next child after me or you're arranging to have your third cousin Bruno rearrange my bicuspids. If you've created a Web page with this book and put it on the Internet, be sure to send the address in an e-mail because I'd like to see it.

—Rogers Cadenhead

D

Appendix E

Glossary

ActiveX   A Microsoft technology that allows interactive programs to be offered on Web pages. ActiveX is similar to Java in function, but it uses a different method of security, and ActiveX programs can be designed with several different computer programming languages.

Alt Label   A line of text describing an image, Java applet, or other page element. This label is displayed on Web browsers that can't handle the information or are configured not to handle it.

America Online   An online service that offers its subscribers free space for their own Web pages. Home Page's Publish feature can be used to transfer a Web site's pages, graphics, and other files to AOL's Web hosting service.

anchor   A spot on a Web page that's given a name so you can jump directly to it with a link.

Animated GIF   A series of GIF files that have been combined into a single file that's displayed as an animated sequence.

applet   A program written with the Java programming language that's presented on a Web page and runs automatically when the page loads.

browse   One of the verbs used to describe the process of visiting Web pages with a browser. It's also called surfing.

browser   Software used to view Web pages.

cache   A temporary storage area for pages that a Web browser has recently viewed. These pages can be reloaded from the cache quickly if the page is visited again.

client-side image map   A way to link different parts of an image to different Web pages.

Common Gateway Interface (CGI)   A method of sending information to programs running on the Web server. CGI programs are often used to send mail directly from a Web page, to order products, and to perform other interactive features.

domain   The address of a computer on the Internet, including Web servers, FTP archives, and many other types of sites. A user's Internet address is made up of a user name or other identifier followed by an @ sign and a domain name.

domain name system (DNS)   An Internet addressing system that associates a domain name (such as noplace.com) with a numeric address (such as 10.20.30.40). The domain name is easier for people to remember, and the numeric address specifies where the Web site can be found.

downloading   Receiving a file from another site and storing it on your system.

e-mail (electronic mail)   A way to exchange text and other information privately from one person to another.

encryption   The process of encoding information so that it remains private. Most Web pages aren't encoded, but many ordering systems and other situations involving confidential information use an encoding system to preserve privacy.

form   A Web page with text fields and other areas that should be filled out by the viewer. Forms use CGI programs to send information back to the Web page developer.

frame   A rectangular region of a Web page that separates the region from other parts of the page. All other parts of the page are frames as well, and each can function as though it were a Web page running in its own window. Frames aren't supported by Claris Home Page 2.0 Lite.

FTP (File Transfer Protocol)   The common method for sending a file from one system to another on the Internet. An FTP site is an archive of files that can be downloaded.

GeoCities   A Web service based at http://www.geocities.com that offers free home pages to Internet users. The pages are organized into individual communities around common topics, such as science fiction, philosophy, and technology.

guestbook   A section of a Web site that's devoted to comments from visitors. Many guestbooks, such as the one offered to Web page publishers by LPage at http://www.lpage.com, put visitor comments online immediately after they're submitted.

E

home page   The main page of a Web site, which is used as a starting point by Web surfers visiting the site, the main page linking to other parts of the site, or a combination of both.

HTML (HyperText Markup Language)   The formatting language used to create Web pages. Claris Home Page 2.0 Lite and other HTML editors create HTML programs behind the scenes as pages are created.

HTTP (HyperText Transfer Protocol)   The established method for sending a Web page or other information from a Web server to a Web user.

hypertext   A document that includes links to other documents, allowing readers to jump from one document to another. The World Wide Web is a gigantic hypertext system.

Internet   A large network of commercial, academic, and private computer systems connected to share files, e-mail, the World Wide Web, and other services.

Internet Explorer   An advanced Web browser created by Microsoft Corporation that's available for free download from the Web site `http://www.microsoft.com/ie`.

Internet service provider (ISP)   An enterprise that offers accounts for individuals or companies to access Internet services, such as e-mail, Web pages, and FTP archives.

InterNIC   The Internet service based at `http://rs1.internic.net` that maintains the files needed to run the domain name system, which associates domain names with IP addresses.

intranet   A network that functions like the Internet but is available only within a private enterprise, such as a company's offices. Intranets allow information exchange without the security risks inherent in being available on the entire Internet.

Java   A programming language that allows interactive software to be included on Web pages. Web-based Java programs are called *applets*.

link   An icon, a picture, or a highlighted string of text that can be clicked to go from the current Web page to another one.

Mailto link   A link on a Web page that contains an Internet e-mail address instead of a reference to a page or other file on the Web. When the link is clicked, an e-mail application is launched so that a letter can be sent to the address, if the browser is configured to handle the link.

multimedia   A type of information that combines several types of media: text, images, sound, video, and animation.

Netscape Navigator   A popular World Wide Web browser developed by Netscape Communications Corporation that includes many of the advanced features that have been created for use on Web pages.

network   A set of computers connected to each other so they can share information.

pixel   An individual dot in a computer graphics image. The size of pixels vary depending on the monitor being used.

Plug-in   A program that can handle types of information a Web browser can't normally handle, such as the RealPlayer software that plays RealAudio files.

resolution   The number of pixels that make up an image, which is represented by listing its width and height dimensions, as in "640×456."

search engine   A World Wide Web site that offers a way to search for information on other pages.

server   A program that serves a specific type of information over a network, such as a Web server that transmits Web pages.

source   The text and HTML programming commands that make up a Web page. It can't be viewed within Claris Home Page 2.0 Lite, but can be seen by using a browser such as Internet Explorer or Netscape Navigator.

table   Elements of a Web page that have been organized into rectangular rows and columns.

tag   An HTML programming command that indicates how to display part of a Web page.

text editor   Any word processing software you use to edit text.

text-only browser   A Web browser, such as Lynx, that doesn't support graphics, fonts, or other graphical features. These browsers load pages much more quickly but often don't support things such as tables, frames, and other HTML features.

URL (uniform resource locator)   An address that indicates the location of a Web page or other file that can be viewed over the World Wide Web.

World Wide Web (also the Web, W3, or WWW)   A group of documents on the Internet that are created with HTML and connected to each other through hypertext links.

E

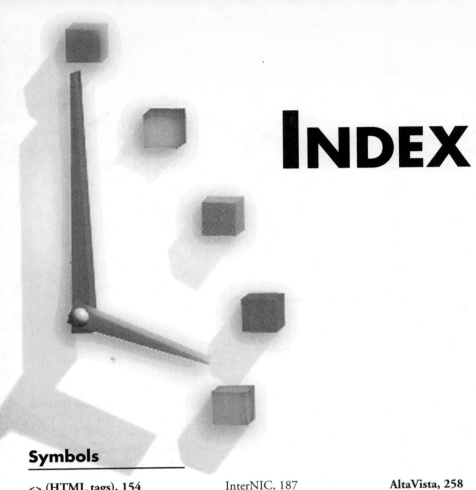

INDEX

A V I A C O M   S E R V I C E

The Information SuperLibrary ™

Bookstore

Search

What's New

Reference

Software

Newsletter

Company Overviews

Yellow Pages

Internet Starter Kit

HTML Workshop

Win a Free T-Shirt!

Macmillan Computer Publishing

Site Map

Talk to Us

CHECK OUT THE BOOKS IN THIS LIBRARY.

You'll find thousands of shareware files and over 1600 computer books designed for both technowizards and technophobes. You can browse through 700 sample chapters, get the latest news on the Net, and find just about anything using our massive search directories.

All Macmillan Computer Publishing books are available at your local bookstore.

We're open 24-hours a day, 365 days a year.

You don't need a card.

We don't charge fines.

And you can be as LOUD as you want.

The Information SuperLibrary

http://www.mcp.com/mcp/   ftp.mcp.com

MACMILLAN COMPUTER PUBLISHING USA

A VIACOM COMPANY

Technical ---- Support:

If you need assistance with the information in this book or with a CD/disk accompanying the book, please access the Knowledge Base on our Web site at **http://www.superlibrary.com/general/support**. Our most Frequently Asked Questions are answered there. If you do not find the answer to your questions on our Web site, you may contact Macmillan Technical Support at **(317) 581-3833** or e-mail us at **support@mcp.com**.

Teach Yourself Active Web Database Programming in 21 Days

Dina Fleet et al.

Based on the best-selling *Teach Yourself* series, this must-have tutorial uses a day-by-day approach and real-world examples to teach readers the ins and outs of Visual Basic programming with databases for the Web.

Shows how to use Visual Basic to create powerful content on the Web. Explores data-aware controls, database connectivity with Visual Basic, and HTML scripting. Covers Visual Basic 5.

$39.99 USA; $56.95 CAN;   1-57521-139-4   700 pp.
Internet-Programming   *New—Casual*

Laura Lemay's Web Workshop: Advanced Graphics and Web Page Design

Jon Duff and James Mohler

With the number of Web pages increasing daily, only well-designed pages will stand out and grab the attention of Web browsers. This book illustrates, in classic Laura Lemay style, how to design attractive Web pages that visitors wil return to. The CD-ROM contains HTML editors, graphics software, and royalty-free graphics and sound files and follows the book's examples to create graphically pleasing Web pages.

Teaches beginning and advanced design principles. Covers emerging topics such as Shockwave, Java, VRML, and vector graphics on the Web.

$49.99 USA; $70.95 CAN;   1-57521-317-6   408 pp.
Internet-Online/Communications   *Accomplished*

Teach Yourself Visual C++ 5 in 21 Days, Fourth Edition

Nathan Gurewich and Ori Gurewich

This book merges the power of the best-selling *Teach Yourself* series with the expert code knowledge of Nathan Gurewich and Ori Gurewich to create the most efficient way to learn Visual C++. In just 21 days, its hands-on approach provides all the training needed to transform a novice into a knowledgeable programmer. Question and Answer sections shed light on common programming problems. CD-ROM includes sample applications, source code, and more!

$35.00 USA; $49.95 CAN;   0-672-31014-7;   832 pp.
Programming   *New—Casual*

The Big Guide to Netscape Communicator 4

Brad Harris and Bill Vernon

This book is an easy, complete, and fun guide to Netscape Communicator 4 for beginners and causal users. It is organized into more than 60 bite-sized chapters that make it easy for readers to find exactly what they need to know. *The Big Guide to Netscape Communicator 4* includes a "Yellow Pages" section created by Infoseek that profiles more than 3,000 of the best, most interesting sites on the World Wide Web.

Covers Navigator, Messenger, Collabra, Conference, Composer, and Netcaster. CD-ROM includes a fully licensed version of Netscape Communicator 4 for Windows 3.1, Windows 95/NT, and Macintosh, and an extensive collection of Netscape plug-ins and helper applications.

$29.99 USA; $42.95 CAN   1-57521-301-X   850 pp.
Internet-General   *New—Casual*

Add to Your Sams.net Library Today
with the Best Books for Internet Technologies

ISBN	Quantity	Description of Item	Unit Cost	Total Cost
1-57521-139-4		Teach Yourself Active Web Database Programming in 21 Days (Book/CD-ROM)	$39.99	
1-57521-317-6		Laura Lemay's Web Workshop: Advanced Graphics and Web Page Design (Book/CD-ROM)	$49.99	
0-672-31014-7		Teach Yourself Visual C++5 in 21 Days, Fourth Edition (Book/CD-ROM)	$35.00	
1-57521-301-X		The Big Guide to Netscape Communicator 4 (Book/CD-ROM)	$29.99	
		Shipping and Handling: See information below.		
		TOTAL		

Shipping and Handling: $4.00 for the first book and $1.75 for each additional book. If you need to have it NOW, we can ship product to you in 24 hours for an additional charge of approximately $18.00, and you will receive your item overnight or in two days. Overseas shipping and handling add $2.00. Prices subject to change. Call between 9:00 a.m. and 5:00 p.m. EST for availability and pricing information on latest editions.

201 W. 103rd Street, Indianapolis, Indiana 46290

1-800-428-5331 — Orders   1-800-835-3202 — FAX   1-800-858-7674 — Customer Service

Book ISBN 1-57521-325-7

Installing the CD-ROM

To install the CD-ROM, please follow these steps:

Windows 95/NT 4 Installation Instructions

1. Insert the CD-ROM into your CD-ROM drive.
2. From the Windows 95 or NT 4 desktop, double-click on the My Computer icon.
3. Double-click on the icon representing your CD-ROM drive.
4. Double-click on the icon called "setup.exe" to run the CD-ROM installation program.

Windows 3.x/NT 3.51 Installation Instructions

1. Insert the CD-ROM into your CD-ROM drive.
2. From File Manager or Program Manager, choose Run from the File menu.
3. Type <drive>\setup and press Enter;' <drive> corresponds to the drive letter of your CD-ROM. For example, if your CD-ROM is drive D:, type D:\SETUP and press Enter.
4. Follow the onscreen instructions.

Macintosh Installation Instructions

1. Insert the CD-ROM into your CD-ROM drive.
2. When an icon for the CD-ROM appears on your desktop, open the disc by double-clicking on its icon.
3. Double-click on the icon named "Guide to the CD-ROM," and follow the directions.